Object-Oriented Programming Under Windows

Stephen Morris

BUTTERWORTH
HEINEMANN

An Imprint of Butterworth-Heinemann Ltd
Linacre House, Jordan Hill, Oxford OX2 8DP

ℛ   A member of the Reed Elsevier group

OXFORD   LONDON   BOSTON
MUNICH   NEW DELHI   SINGAPORE   SYDNEY
TOKYO   TORONTO   WELLINGTON

First published 1994

British Library Cataloguing in Publication Data
A CIP catalogue record for this book is available from the British Library

ISBN 0 7506 1792 6

Typeset by Butford Technical Publishing, Bodenham, Hereford
Printed and bound in Great Britain

Contents

3   The Windows Environment   49

4   Creating an Application   57

Preface

The increasing popularity of Windows has transformed the way programs are used and written. Traditionally, programs were developed as self-contained applications, which took complete responsibility for every aspect of the PC and its operation: creating displays, accessing the disk and sending results to the printer. When a program was run, it took full control of the PC and no other program could be run until the first program had completed its tasks. Programs were written using a structured approach, with a line of logic that started at the top of the program and worked straight down to the bottom. The order in which users could access different aspects of the program was under the control of the programmer.

With the advent of Windows and other new 'environments', all this has changed. Windows can run more than one application at a time, and offers standard features such as display windows, icons, mouse control and drop-down menus. The traditional programming methods have become redundant.

Windows requires programmers to use object-oriented programming (OOP) methods. Here, the user is presented with a screen offering many different 'objects': buttons, windows, icons, menus, lists, etc. Any of these objects responds to a number of 'events': the mouse button being clicked, the object being dragged and so on. The user has full control over the order in which tasks are carried out and the programmer must provide code to account for all the possible events that can occur. The user may also jump from one application to another without warning.

Using OOP methods, the programmer creates the display and determines the initial screen design but then allows the user to take control. With the new programming methods has come a whole new set of 'buzzwords': polymorphism, inheritance and encapsulation, for example. These rather daunting words actually describe fairly simple concepts but, like most aspects of computing, a mystique has built up around object-oriented programming that makes it seem inaccessible to the uninitiated. However, once these basic concepts have been mastered, programming under Windows and similar environments becomes a rewarding occupation.

The term 'object' applies to theoretical data structures, as well as the intuitively obvious objects seen on a screen, but the principles remain the same. This book aims to show how OOP techniques can be applied, with particular emphasis on programming under Windows, which is where most OOP programs will be written. However, the theory is covered to the extent that the principles can be applied to any other environment.

The book uses a variety of languages to demonstrate that the principles can be transported from one language to another with relative ease. In order to give a broad view of OOP principles and their application in different languages, three languages are considered: C++ (both Microsoft and Borland versions), Borland Pascal With Objects, and Microsoft's Visual Basic. Each of these comes in the form of a substantial package and, therefore, it is impossible to cover any of them in detail. Instead, they are used to illustrate the main points that are described. Comparisons between the languages show their similarities and highlight their principal differences.

This book should appeal to anyone who is intending to write programs for Windows or other, similar environments. It should also be useful for experienced programmers who are planning to move over to OOP methods. While the book is not a user guide for any of the languages described, it should provide enough information for anyone to set up simple applications and to decide which of the languages suits them best. Knowledge of Windows is assumed but no previous programming experience is necessary.

Object-oriented methods provide a fascinating new approach to the creation of computer software and, when applied to the Windows environment, enable programmers to design and build sophisticated applications with comparative ease.

Acknowledgments

I would like to thank Microsoft Corporation for providing me with copies of Visual C++ and Visual Basic, and Borland Ltd. for C++ and Pascal With Objects. Thanks also to Emily for her help in the preparation of this book and Hugh for the clipboard illustration.

1 | Introduction to Object-Oriented Programming

There has been a great deal of discussion on the merits of object-oriented programming (OOP) methods in recent years, in magazine articles and books. Sadly, much of the debate has revolved around an increasing vocabulary of jargon words and phrases. The main concentration has been on the theory of OOP methods, with little investigation of the practicalities of object-oriented programming and how it is applied to the real world.

This is extremely off-putting to anyone new to the topic and has resulted in the myth that OOP is a highly-complex discipline, to be avoided by the majority of humble programmers. It is true that the theory of OOP is complex but this very complexity has meant that most OOP languages have developed frameworks which, when applied to practical problems, result in easier, more bug-free programming.

The majority of the book looks at the practical aspects of object-oriented programming and shows how quite complex applications can be built up in a very short time, with particular reference to the Windows environment. This first chapter explains the principles of OOP and shows that, when looked at dispassionately, there is not a lot of substance behind the jargon and the hype. OOP can, and should be, fun, profitable, effective and, above all, open to *all* programmers, whatever their backgrounds.

LANGUAGE DEVELOPMENT

The rapid increase in popularity of Windows over the last few years has resulted in a revolution in the way many people work. In the past, personal computers were capable of running only one program at a time; switching to a new application meant closing down one program and starting up another. (The exceptions were a few background programs, or TSRs, that sat in memory waiting to be activated by a 'hot-key'; usually these were minor applications, such as screen-dump programs and calculators.)

Now, running under Windows or similar environments, it is possible to have many applications active simultaneously and to switch with ease from one to another. This requires a new way of thinking for users: not only how to operate the applications but also how to organise their work. It also demands a new approach from the programmer; rather than a structured sequence of actions from top to bottom, the program must allow for the user jumping in and out of the application and selecting options in any order.

The result is that traditional programming methods – and the languages that they used – are no longer viable in the Windows environment. Object-oriented programming methods provide the framework for writing efficient Windows applications.

Programming methods for the early computers were cumbersome, slow and extremely limited. These computers were programmed by setting rows of switches either on or off, each switch representing one binary digit (or *bit*), taking the value 0 or 1. This was time consuming and severely restricting.

The next stage was the development of the *stored program*. The principle was the same – with the same binary machine code – but the information was held in the computer's magnetic core memory. From there it was a small step to entering code in more manageable numbers: *hexadecimal* (base 16) for example, with each digit representing four bits.

This type of programming was still prone to mistakes, so matters were improved by the arrival of the *assembler*. An assembler allows programs to be written using mnemonics, abbreviations that represent the instructions in a more memorable way: for instance, ADD to represent the code to add two number together. The assembler takes the mnemonics and converts them, more or less on a one-to-one basis, to the binary code. The advantage of assembly-language programming is that, theoretically at least, it results in the fastest, most efficient programs possible, since there is a direct relationship between the program code and the final machine code. Assembly-language programming is still used for applications where timing is critical, and modern assemblers even allow object-oriented constructions.

The real leap in programming progress came with the first *high-level languages*: Algol, Fortran and, later, COBOL. These languages allow instructions to be written in English-like text. A *compiler* takes each instruction and coverts it to the necessary machine code. But it also allows you to use names (variables) to represent items of data, so that the same program can be used with any input. Programs written in high-level languages are more compact, easier to understand and less likely to have bugs.

The disadvantage is that the compilation is likely to result in redundant code and unnecessarily complicated routines being included in the final executable program. This also reduces the speed of operation of the program.

The early high-level languages were rather specialised: Fortran ('FORmula TRANslation') for scientific use, COBOL ('COmmon Business Orientated Language') for use in the business world. The advent of BASIC ('Beginners All-purpose Symbolic Instruction Code') in the 1950s resulted in a high-level language that bridged the gap between scientific and business use, being equally suited to either task, but at the same time simple enough for anyone to learn.

However, the simplicity of early BASIC was also its downfall; the first versions of BASIC were very rudimentary, and characterised by the necessity of numbering each line. The instruction set was very limited, the mainstays being LET, GOTO and IF. Variable names were restricted to two characters: a number and a letter. The result was a single, long, rambling program, with unintelligible variable names and control of program flow achieved with the iniquitous IF...GOTO combination. This led to 'spaghetti' programming – with the program branching forwards and backwards, in tangled lines of logic.

In addition, the language was limited in its file-handling and input/output capabilities. All of this gave BASIC a bad reputation among 'serious' programmers; BASIC was fine for anyone starting out in programming but not suited to applications in the outside world. This is a reputation that BASIC has never really shaken off, even though it has now evolved beyond recognition.

Meanwhile, new programming methods were being devised by the theoreticians, resulting in a new wave of high-level languages. Among these, one that has stood the test of time is Pascal. This is firmly based in *structured* programming methods, in which the action of any program is expected to start at the top and work steadily down to the bottom, with no backwards or forwards leaps. Sections of code are omitted or selected by IF...THEN...ELSE constructions. Routines are repeated by the use of REPEAT...UNTIL, WHILE...DO, FOR...DO and CASE constructions. These principles were later incorporated into BASIC. Of course, structured programming is, like all methods, very much an illusion; when the compiler produces the executable code, this will be riddled with JMP instructions, taking program execution in every direction. The important thing is that the *source code* (the code produced by the programmer) should be clear, logical and easily followed. This makes it easier to trace and remove bugs but at the cost of the efficiency of the end product.

The next stage was the advent of *procedural* programming. Here, the tasks to be performed by a program are separated out into individual named routines that are called from within the main program or by other procedures. This has many advantages:

- The main program may be very short, consisting of some initialisation code and calls to a few procedures, perhaps with the order of execution being determined by a CASE statement.

- The same procedure can be re-used many times within a program. Thus, once a procedure is known to be bug-free, the program will be secure wherever the procedure is called; there is no danger that a change made in one part of the program is forgotten for a repeat of the code elsewhere.

- Procedures can be re-used in other programs, ensuring that all programs work in a similar way, follow the same rules and provide the user with a consistent 'interface'.

- A change in approach can be rapidly – and safely – introduced in all applications. For example, a change in menu colours can be introduced by amending the relevant procedure and then recompiling all the applications that use it.

- Procedures can use *local* variables, variables whose data exists only as long as the procedure is executing, or which store data that can be used only by that procedure.

The result is that procedure-based programs, whatever language they are written in, end up as a jumble of independent procedures, many with built-in data structures, held together by a series of calls. Within each procedure the code should be structured.

This approach was ideally suited to C, a programming language that aims to reduce the language itself to a minimum, the main functionality being provided by libraries of procedures (termed 'functions'). C programs also bear a close relationship to the final machine code, making them extremely efficient, and they should be portable across operating systems. C++ is the OOP extension to C.

The latest advances came with the arrival of object-oriented programming. OOP methods have been advertised as a totally new approach to programming, and indeed object-oriented programming does require some re-thinking on the part of programmers. In fact, OOP methods are a surprisingly small step away from procedural programming.

PRINCIPLES OF OOP METHODS

From a theoretical viewpoint, objects are difficult to describe and comprehend, and it is better therefore to begin with a practical view, where objects are more intuitive. Many books describe OOP by reference to analogies such as apples and oranges, or waiters and customers in restaurants. However, this can be confusing and it seems better to stick to the 'real' world that we find in the computer. The obvious place to start is Windows; it is here that object-oriented programming is really essential.

An *object* can be thought of as an independent procedure that contains both the instructions and data to perform some task, and the code necessary to handle various messages that it may receive. Physically, under Windows at least, most objects will have some visual appearance.

For example, a dialogue box is an object. On screen, it is physically distinct from any other object and, within certain pre-defined bounds, can be handled independently of any other object. The code for the dialogue box includes all the instructions necessary to draw the box on the screen, display a text string in the title bar and include a control-menu box in the top left-hand corner. The dialogue box object includes all the data needed to build the box: for example, the data that determines the colour of the box and the thickness of the lines. Finally, the object contains all the procedures needed to

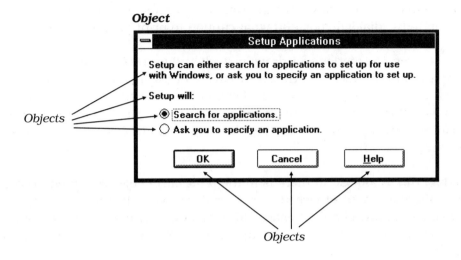

Figure 1.1 Examples of objects

react to the events that might occur: for instance, dragging the dialogue box to another part of the screen.

When you call up a dialogue box, other objects will also be displayed: for example, a message string and OK and Cancel buttons (Figure 1.1).

Most of the data and code is not available to the program outside the object. The only way of achieving anything is to send messages to the object; the object may respond by sending a message back. For instance, if the user places the mouse pointer on the dialogue box title bar and then drags it to some other part of the screen, Windows generates a message to indicate that this has happened. As part of the message, Windows passes information to tell the object where it is being dragged to. The object responds to this message by invoking its internal procedure to redraw the dialogue box in its new position.

There are also special functions, called *constructors* and *destructors*, for doing the work of creating and deleting the dialogue box. When the dialogue box is to be created, the constructor is invoked. This has passed to it such information as the text to be displayed in the title bar and the size of the box. The constructor then generates the new object. The destructor destroys the object when it is no longer needed, along with all of its code and data.

Of course, when a dialogue box pops up on the screen you are not looking at just a single object. Contained within it are other objects: a text object for the main message and an object for each of the buttons. Each of these is an entirely separate and independent object. When the dialogue box object is being constructed, it in turn calls the constructor function for a button object, passing it the information it needs to tell it where to put the button in relation to the dialogue box and what caption to print on it (e.g. 'OK').

The button has its own instructions for drawing itself and for responding to events. For instance, there is a button procedure that is invoked when Windows passes a message to say that the button has been clicked; the click procedure for the OK button does the fancy graphics work for imitating a button press, carries out any other requirements specifically required for this particular dialogue box (e.g. saving a file), and then calls the dialogue box's destructor function.

Broadly speaking, this is almost all there is to the *principle* of object-oriented programming. However, there are a lot of jargon words for describing all this, and a bit more detail. The remainder of this chapter delves a little more deeply into the theory of OOP; the rest of the book then addresses the application of the theory in a Windows environment.

Finally, it should perhaps be noted that if you were to take apart the executable code that makes Windows run you would find a structured program. Object-oriented programming is only a convenience for software developers; behind it is a set of CASE statements and other structures that provide a simplified front-end for the programmer. Ultimately, all executable code exists within computer memory in the tangle of JMP statements that are the only things the chip at the core of the PC can understand.

ENCAPSULATION

Perhaps the most important distinction to make between object-oriented programming and traditional procedural programming is that an object is an independent program segment that, in a sense, has a life of its own, separate from other objects in the program; procedures, on the other hand, are merely sets of instructions, possibly with their own local data, that have been created for convenience. Whether you combine procedures or split them up is a matter of personal preference. Objects, on the other hand, will usually represent some real concept: a dialogue box, a button or a list for example. The boundaries of the object are usually much more intuitively defined. (Because of this link between programming objects and real concepts, object-oriented programs are sometimes referred to as *simulations*.)

An object contains all that is needed to make a particular aspect of the program carry out its tasks:

- The procedures that are needed to respond to incoming instructions

- The data that is needed by these procedures

Object

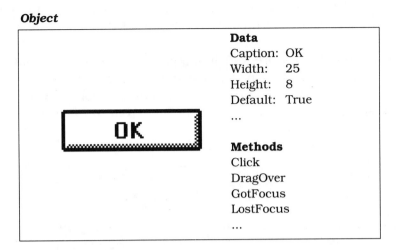

Figure 1.2 Data and procedures for command button object

Figure 1.2 shows a simple object – a command button – with some of its data and procedures. This process of bundling together procedures and data is referred to as *encapsulation* and is central to object-oriented programming. In this way, each object is insulated from the rest of the application. Since the object is using data contained within it, or passed to it, and executes only internal procedures, it is much easier to track down bugs and less likely that a bug in one object will affect some other part of the system in an apparently unconnected way.

The data in objects will not change between one use of the object and the next, unless you decide otherwise; variables are not initialised automatically, so objects can remember data values. An object can be said to have a *state*, which consists of the current values of its variables. For instance, a radio button or check box can be either checked or unchecked, and will remain in the same state until changed. The state of the button exists within the object as an item of data.

An object's internal variables are often referred to as *properties, attributes* or *instance variables*.

METHODS

The terminology of OOP is different to that of other programming systems. This arose initially from the fact that the original designers wanted to make the connection between the programming techniques and the outside world. Thus the procedures within an object are usually referred to as *methods*. To confuse matters further, they are also known as *member functions* when programming in C++. (There is some logic in this, since each method is, in fact, a C++ function and is a member of the set of the object's functions.) The terms 'method' and 'member function' can be regarded as interchangeable.

The distinction between procedure and function is very blurred in many languages. Theoretically, a *procedure* is called in a standalone statement and may have arguments passed to it, then carries out some task. A *function* usually forms part of a statement, may have arguments passed to it, and returns a value that replaces it in the statement. For example:

```
MsgBox "OK?", 33, "Check"              'Procedure to display message box
Answer = MsgBox("OK?", 33, "Check")    'Function returns code to indicate
                                       'key pressed
```

However, in C terms, procedures are usually called functions. Thus procedures, functions, methods and member functions may be taken as synonymous.

Windows itself has about 600 functions. These functions carry out all the usual Windows operations, and Windows objects are built up and operated by calling the functions.

Methods fall into two groups: public and private. *Public methods* are those procedures that respond to instructions coming in from outside the object; *private methods* are internal procedures that are called by the public methods in order to perform some sort of processing. For example, the OK button in a Save File dialogue box will have a public method to respond to the button being clicked; this may call a private method that does the actual work of saving away the data.

CLASSES AND OBJECTS

A dialogue box, a radio button and an OK button are all clearly objects, but where do they come from? It would be possible to write a program where each and every object was individually defined and existed when the program was first run but this is not always practical. Many applications – such as Excel or Word – allow the user to create a series of windows; each of these is a separate object but these intangible objects cannot exist in the code. The solution is to use classes.

A *class* is a template for an object. A class defines what an object will look like and how it will behave. An object is an *instance* of class.

For example, there will be a class that defines a dialogue box, determining the size, shape, colour, initial position and so on. Each time the dialogue box pops up on screen the application is creating an object, an instance of the class, perhaps with a different set of text labels. These are different objects from the same class. Similarly, two command buttons may be objects from the same class (Figure 1.3). (In practice, the buttons will be from different classes, as they will need different methods.)

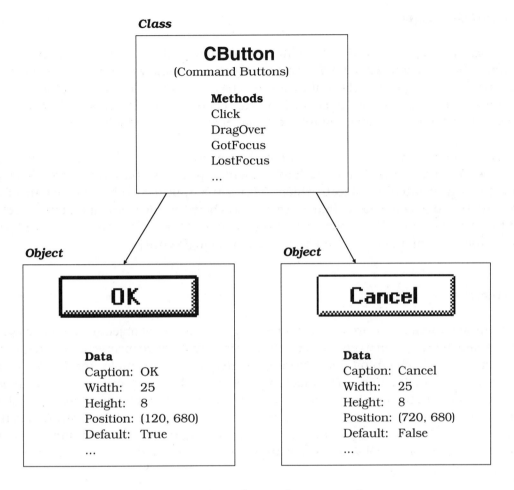

Figure 1.3 Two objects from same class

Within a program, the code for a class (and its private data) is defined and then specific instances of the class are declared, creating objects. (This is analogous to the definition of a user-defined type in C or a record type in Pascal or BASIC, with variables being subsequently declared for the user-defined type.) When an object is created, space is set aside for copies of the private variables (sometimes called *instance variables*); the methods only exist within the class definition of course. If two objects need different methods, then they must be instances of different classes.

Perhaps the most important point is that all object must be created when the program is run, and should be destroyed when no longer needed.

User-interface objects

Any program will end up with a large number of classes, from which are derived many different objects. There will be different types of object. Some will be rather hypothetical in nature, for example objects that define record layouts for a database; others will be visually obvious, for instance dialogue boxes and controls. The objects that are actually displayed on screen are generally referred to as *user-interface objects*.

The actual items that are visible to the end user are sometimes referred to as *visual interface elements*. Each visual interface element appears on the screen and associated with it is a user-interface object, which defines the appearance and behaviour of the element. Although some books make a distinction between the element and its object, in fact the element is merely the physical representation of the object; from a practical point of view the element and object can be treated as a single entity.

Abstraction

The term 'abstraction' features quite frequently in discussion of object-oriented programming. Again, it is a jargon word for a simple process: *abstraction* means using a high-level representation of something and ignoring the details. For example, the BASIC PRINT statement is an abstraction of the machine code needed to carry out the display action; by using a PRINT statement you remove the need to write the machine code to display a value. Similarly, procedure and function names are abstractions of the instructions they represent; instead of writing the code to perform the task, the procedure or function name will do the same job. Finally, a class is an abstraction of the data and procedures that combine to define it.

MESSAGES AND EVENTS

Objects get instructions to act and receive data using messages. A *message* is, in traditional terms, a call to a procedure. For example, a message might tell a dialogue box that the mouse has been moved while the button is down (i.e. it has been dragged), and will include the new co-ordinates as data in the message. This is the same as a call to the Drag method of the box. The data that is passed is the argument to the call. The object may respond by passing data back (the return values).

In a similar way, objects call methods in other objects by sending messages to them. There is a message associated with each public method.

In addition, Windows can send a large number of messages to your application (about 200 of them). For instance, Windows will send messages to an object each time the mouse button is clicked, the mouse is moved or a key is pressed. You must decide how to handle the many Windows messages with which your objects are being constantly bombarded. For instance, an OK button may respond to a mouse click or the ENTER key being pressed, but ignore everything else.

There is a direct connection between messages and events. An *event* is some occurrence within the system that triggers a message. For example, every movement of the mouse, button press, key press or tick of the system clock is an event; each of these events results in a Windows message being passed to the relevant object. Either there will be methods defined for the object to handle the messages or the messages will be ignored.

INHERITANCE

Most objects are related in one way or another to other objects. A File Open box is just a special type of dialogue box, a check box is a special kind of button. Therefore, you can usually define a new type of object by amending the definition of some other object. This is *inheritance.*

Object-oriented programming always starts with a *base class*. This is the template for a basic object. The next stage is to define a new class, called a *derived class*, which is an extension of the base class. The derived class may include additional methods that did not exist in the base class; it may also redefine methods (or even scrap them altogether). This is illustrated in Figure 1.4.

To make life simpler, a derived class does not have to redefine all the methods in the base class. Instead, when you declare that a new object is to inherit the properties of a base class you need only define those methods that are new or changed. All other methods from the base class are assumed to be part of the derived class as well. This has the great advantage that when a method is altered in a base class, the same change will automatically apply to all derived classes (unless the method is redefined in a derived class).

This process of inheritance can (and usually will) continue over a series of classes. A class that is derived from a base class can itself become the base class for other derived classes. In this way, object-oriented programs build up a *class hierarchy.*

In some situations, a class is never intended to have objects of its own. The class is just there to provide the base for a collection of derived classes. The base class may declare a set of methods without defining them to do anything useful; the actual definitions will be made in the derived classes. In this way the derived classes respond to a common set of calls but in different ways.

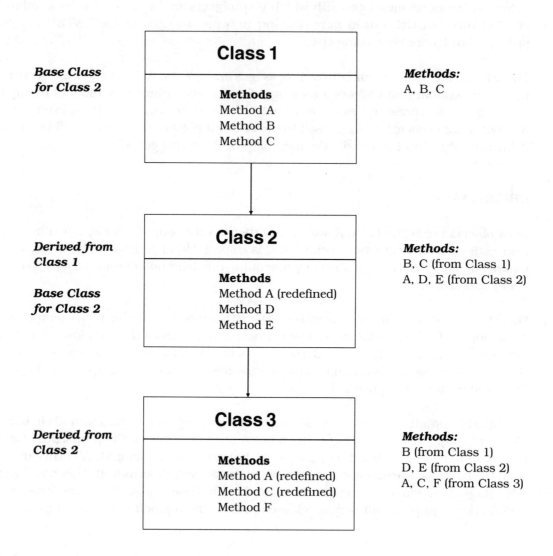

Base Class
for Class 2

Class 1

Methods
Method A
Method B
Method C

Methods:
A, B, C

Derived from
Class 1

Base Class
for Class 2

Class 2

Methods
Method A (redefined)
Method D
Method E

Methods:
B, C (from Class 1)
A, D, E (from Class 2)

Derived from
Class 2

Class 3

Methods
Method A (redefined)
Method C (redefined)
Method F

Methods:
B (from Class 1)
D, E (from Class 2)
A, C, F (from Class 3)

Figure 1.4 Principles of inheritance

Composition

In some cases, one class *contains* another and the private data list will include a declaration of an object. This is called *composition* and should not be confused with inheritance. The first class is not derived from the second; instead, it requires the second in its definition.

The container classes are referred to as *composite* classes or *aggregate* classes.

Inheritance in ObjectWindows

This is how frameworks such as Borland's ObjectWindows work. In this case, all on-screen objects are created from classes that are derived from a single base class, TWindowsObject (which, in turn, is derived from two other classes). Part of the hierarchy for the C++ version is illustrated in Figure 1.5. (The Pascal version of the hierarchy does

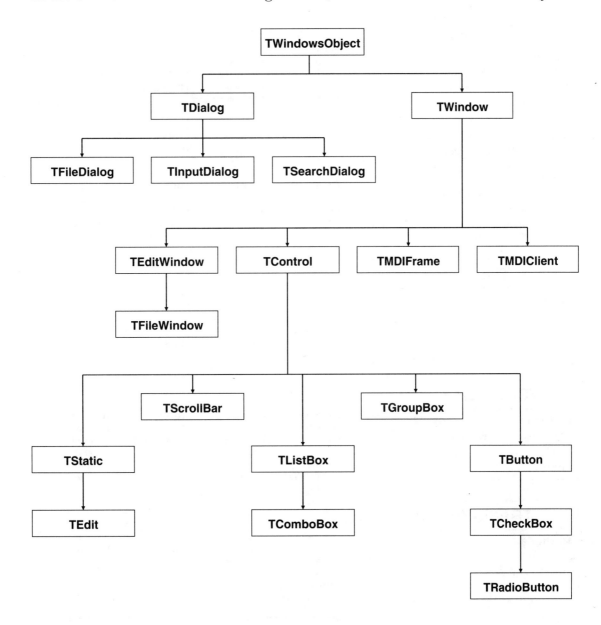

Figure 1.5 Part of the ObjectWindows class hierarchy (C++)

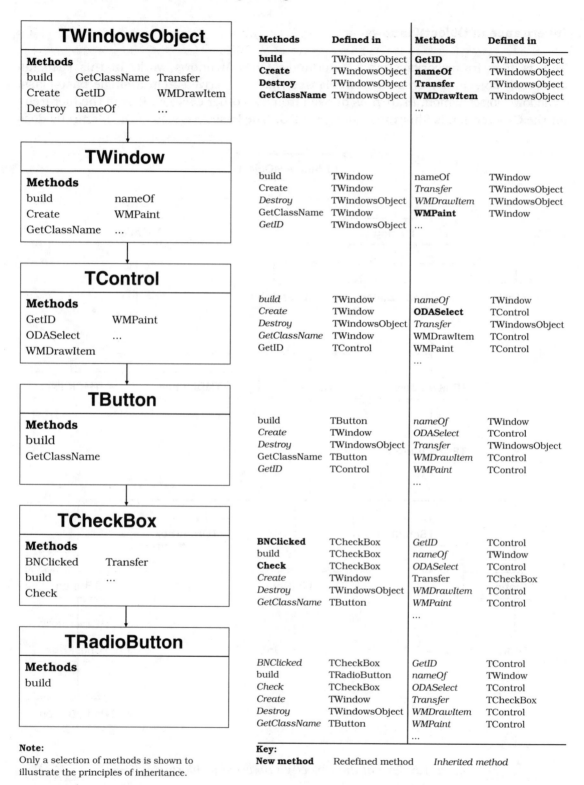

Note:
Only a selection of methods is shown to
illustrate the principles of inheritance.

Key:
New method   Redefined method   *Inherited method*

Figure 1.6 Inheritance for TRadioButton in ObjectWindows

not have a TSearchDialog class – though there are other classes not shown here – and its MDI frame class is called TMDIWindow instead of TMDIFrame.) Two classes are derived from TWindowsObject: one that defines a dialogue box, the other a window. The dialogue box is used in turn as the basis for file selection, input and search boxes. Everything else is derived from TWindow. One of the most important classes is TControl, a generic 'control' that is not used for generating objects but is used as the base class for scroll bars, list boxes and buttons, for example. The TButton class is adapted to form the check box class, which in turn is the base for the radio buttons class. This same hierarchy is used for both the C++ and Pascal implementations of ObjectWindows.

In this way one object evolves from another and, at the end of the chain, may show little trace of its origins. Figure 1.6 illustrates this process for a part of the hierarchy, showing how the class for a radio button is derived from TWindowsObject. These libraries are described in more detail in Chapter 2.

Remember that any class at the end of the chain will not include definitions of all the methods it uses. The full definition of a radio button, for example, is built up from methods from all the classes in its evolutionary history.

Within your C++ program you can declare instances of any of these classes to create objects; or you can derive new classes from the ObjectWindows classes, modifying their appearance and behaviour as required.

Inheritance in Visual Basic

With ObjectWindows, you will have to write a C++ program in order to use the framework. However, you can then modify the classes as required. For Visual Basic, life is made simpler – and consequently less flexible.

Visual Basic, as supplied, provides you with a standard set of classes: windows, buttons, list boxes, etc. Window objects are defined by creating a new *form*, using drop-down menu options. The features of the window (minimise and maximise buttons, title, etc.) are defined by selecting values for a series of *properties*. In a similar way, other objects are added to the form by selecting the object from the toolbox and then defining its properties, in the same way as for the window. In the background, Visual Basic is using the values of the properties as the parameters for creating objects.

This approach gives you a number of advantages:

- The objects for the application are created without the necessity to write any code at all.

- You can see instantly what the objects will look like and how the application will appear to the user.

- Setting up the user interface takes very little time and the application is easily modified.

There are, of course, disadvantages as well:

- The appearance of the application and its behaviour are dependent on the classes supplied with Visual Basic.

- You cannot create new classes directly, so the class hierarchy cannot be extended (but you can create *custom controls*, which are derivatives of existing classes).

Despite these disadvantages, it may be thought that Visual Basic provides a rather more foolproof, if somewhat less exciting, programming method than its ObjectWindows rivals.

Inheritance in Visual C++

Microsoft's Visual C++ combines both approaches to form its framework. At the heart of Visual C++ is the Microsoft Foundation Class Library. This is very similar to the ObjectWindows framework and has many equivalent classes. However, it is a more extensive class framework; the main part of the framework is illustrated in Figure 1.7.

To make life easier, Visual C++ comes with an *integrated development environment* (IDE). This consists of a number of tools that will let you create objects on-screen, in the same way as for Visual Basic, generating the code for you. The final C++ code is available to be amended so you can see the classes that have been created and make changes directly in the code should it become necessary.

For this reason, Visual C++ will be used for most of the examples in this book. Its simple approach to the creation of applications is used to demonstrate the principles of OOP methods, while the code that is generated shows how a C++ program can be built up.

Direct and Indirect Base Classes

Some texts make a distinction between 'direct' and 'indirect' base classes:

- The *direct* base class is the one from which a class is derived.

- The *indirect* base class is any class higher up the hierarchy which features in the derived class's inheritance.

For example, in the ObjectWindows hierarchy, TControl is the direct base class for TListBox while TWindow and TWindowsObject are indirect base classes. The TWindowsObject class

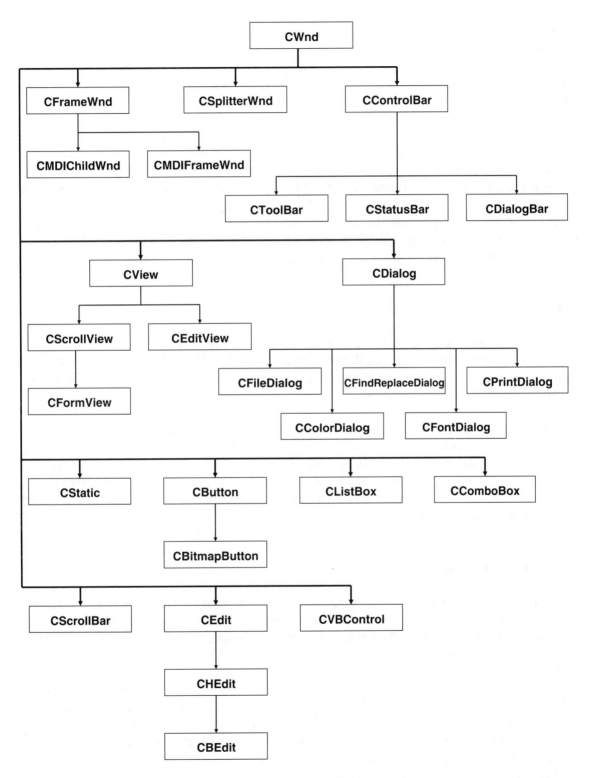

Figure 1.7 Part of the MFCL hierarchy

is a direct base class for TDialog and TWindow, and an indirect base class for all other classes in the hierarchy.

Multiple Inheritance

So far we have considered only classes that are derived from a single class. It is also possible for a class to be derived from more than one base class. In such a case, the derived class inherits all the member functions and data members of *all* its base classes. This is called *multiple inheritance*. Essentially, it just means that two or more classes are being combined.

This is demonstrated by the ObjectWindows hierarchy, where TWindowsObject is derived from two classes, Object and TStreamable.

POLYMORPHISM

Two or more classes that are derived from the same base class are said to be *polymorphic*. The word 'polymorphism' means, literally, 'many forms' and is simply a rather grand term for expressing the fact that two objects may share many characteristics but have unique features of their own.

Dialogue boxes and text windows are polymorphic: they have a similar appearance, both have control-menu boxes and a title bar, and can be dragged to a new position. But there are differences as well: dialogue boxes cannot be minimised or maximised but windows may be; the user cannot change the appearance of a dialogue box but a window may be resized. Polymorphism is a way of describing the ways in which objects are the same and the ways in which they differ.

Overriding Methods

When new classes are derived from a base class they may redefine some of the base methods. For instance, a general TControl class will have a method to respond to a mouse-click message; the TButton and TListBox classes that are derived from this base class will have redefinitions of the mouse-click method.

These new methods *override* the base method. When the user clicks on the button or the list box, it is the method for that object that is invoked rather than the method for the base class. The mouse-click methods for the button and list box will have the same name (which is the name of a method in the TControl class) but will behave in different ways. This is an example of polymorphism; both objects can respond to a mouse click but will do so in different ways.

The principle has far reaching effects. It means that you can send a message to an object without knowing what type of object it is or how it will respond. When the mouse button is clicked, Windows sends a message to the affected object without having any idea of what the result will be. The code that determines the response is encapsulated in the object.

In this way, there is no need to have a complex CASE statement to decide the reaction for every conceivable object or position on the screen. It doesn't matter that you don't know where the user has moved things on the screen. All you need to do is call the mouse-click procedure for the object that is currently occupying the position on the screen indicated by the pointer. The method with the name matching the message will be invoked. The program will have a pointer to an unknown object and only when the program is run will the object be identified and the relevant method executed.

Polymorphism is therefore a vitally important concept but there is no need to worry too much about the theory. A few practical examples will soon show that, when applied to a real situation, polymorphism is intuitively obvious. By the time you have produced a few object-oriented programs you should be starting to wonder what all the fuss was about.

SUMMARY

The main principles of object-oriented programming can be summarised as follows:

- Each visual element, data structure or other entity in an application is an *object*. An *application* consists of many separate, independent objects.

- An object *encapsulates* all the *methods* (procedures and functions) and data needed for it to operate correctly. The data is usually accessible only through the class's *public methods*. The values of the object's variables determines its *state*.

- The behaviour of an object is determined by its *class*. A class is a template for objects, each new object being an *instance* of the class.

- New classes are derived from *base classes*. Each *derived class* can be the base class for other classes. The result is a *class hierarchy*.

- A class *inherits* the methods of its base class (and all classes above it in the hierarchy). A class can add new methods or *override* those of the base class by redefining them.

- Objects from different classes may have methods with the same names, but these methods will respond in different ways. This is *polymorphism*.

2 | Programming Languages

Object-oriented programming is a discipline; as such it is not tied to any particular programming language. Theoretically at least, almost any language can be used for object-oriented programming. In practice, no one in their right minds would attempt to produce an object-oriented program in anything other than a language that has been extended specifically for that purpose.

There are a number of such languages currently available, and these are being enhanced all the time. This chapter chronicles the events leading up to the creation of OOP languages and describes the three languages that illustrate this book.

The following products are used as the basis of the examples in this book:

- Microsoft Visual C++

- Borland C++

- Borland Pascal With Objects

- Microsoft Visual Basic

These languages are the ones most commonly used by Windows developers, and OOP implementations by other software producers will closely follow the guidelines set down by Microsoft and Borland.

APPLICATION SIZE

Anyone who has used a computer for some time cannot fail to have noticed the worrying trend in the physical size of software packages. In the first few years of the IBM PC, an application program, such as a word processor or spreadsheet program, would typically be supplied on a single 360K disk. This disk contained all that was needed to run the program, save data and produce output on the screen or printer. Programs could even be run from floppy disk (and frequently were!) Documentation was a single, brief manual. Programs were only difficult to use when badly programmed.

Since those halcyon days, software packages have expanded at an alarming rate. It is now not uncommon for even the most basic of applications to be provided on ten or twenty high-density 1.44 Mb disks, with documentation of similar magnitude. There have been great leaps in the facilities provided by the programs, of course, and we are all capable of producing results that ten years ago were unimaginable. Even so, software producers have become so keen to outpace their rivals that most of us never use the vast majority of the features provided.

However, much of the increase in application size has arisen from the diversity of the hardware; each new piece of hardware needs special instructions for the software to be able to use it. For instance, for any new printer, the program must know the codes needed to change fonts, spacing or typestyle; for any display, the program must know the number of pixels on the screen and the colours they can show. These special instructions are held in *drivers*, special files that are supplied for each device. Therefore, a large number of the extra disks supplied with software packages are packed with drivers for dozens – sometimes hundreds – of different hardware devices.

This is where Windows is supposed to come to the rescue. Windows takes over all communication between the application program and the hardware: the printers, screen and serial ports. Windows includes drivers for all these devices and the application programmer can concentrate on producing code to solve a problem.

This should result in simplified applications and smaller packages but be warned: this simplification has not yet filtered down to the programming languages themselves. The four products described in this book (Borland's Pascal With Objects and C++, Microsoft's Visual C++ and Visual Basic) have, between them, 40 manuals and 57 high-density 3½" 1.44 Mb disks. The manuals combine into a pile 29 inches high, a daunting prospect for any programmer. To install all four packages in their entirety would require some 160 Mb of disk space – and that's not including DOS and Windows.

These packages contain vast ranges of options, most of which you will probably never use; of those that will one day be useful, most are best reserved for the experienced user. The aim of this chapter is to show you which options you should install when you fist get started and how you can create applications quickly, without having to wade through the wealth of information so generously provided by the language producers.

C++

C has been around for about 20 years but has only really become accepted as the standard programming language during the last five. Although it has a comparatively long history, it was only in 1989 that a standard – ANSI C – was finally defined. The advantage of the standard is that C code written for one compiler should work equally successfully for any other, regardless of the type of computer or operating system for which it is destined.

C++ first appeared in 1985 but its application for object-oriented programming only became genuinely useful with Release 2.0, in 1989, which allowed for multiple inheritance of classes.

A principle feature of C, and thus C++, is that it is a small language; ANSI C has only just over 30 keywords. Most of the functionality of a C program is provided by the C *functions*, which are held in external *libraries*. There are a number of libraries defined in the ANSI standard but others are often supplied and you can, of course, create your own. In a sense, the libraries are just collections of standard procedures.

The aim of C is to be close to the machine code into which it will ultimately be compiled. This results in compact, efficient code, without the redundancies of other high-level languages. The disadvantage is that C programming is not intuitive and requires considerable effort.

In the DOS world, C programs are fast and efficient; whether C++ programs under Windows are similarly ahead of their competitors remains to be seen.

MICROSOFT VISUAL C++

Microsoft C++ incorporates ANSI C, adding to it the constructions necessary for object-oriented programming.

Visual C++ includes an *integrated development environment* (IDE) for creating Windows applications based on the C++ language. Because it is an almost impossible task to build a new application from nothing, Visual C++ provides you with a framework from which to start and the tools necessary to build on that framework.

The framework is called the Microsoft Foundation Class Library. This is a hierarchy of classes that provide the basis for all the objects you are likely to need in a Windows application. You can either declare objects as instances of these classes or derive your own classes from them.

There are a number of Windows-based tools that combine together to make Visual C++:

- Visual Workbench is an IDE that provides the working environment in which you can develop Windows applications. Visual Workbench allows you to access the other tools.

- App Studio is a resource editor, which allows you to develop and edit dialogue boxes, controls, menus and other resources.

- AppWizard generates the application framework from the Foundation Class Library.

- ClassWizard allows you to update the methods for the classes that are being developed.

In addition to these tools (which work together to create an application), Microsoft supplies some additional tools:

- The CodeView debugger is a diagnostic utility used for tracking down bugs in a program.

- The Command-Line Utilities allow you to compile and link C++ programs from the DOS prompt, rather than from within Visual Workbench. These are useful when developing non-Windows applications.

- The Source Profiler lets you analyse the operation of a program, showing the frequency of calls to functions and the efficiency of the code.

Finally, C++ is bundled with the Microsoft Windows Software Development Kit (SDK). This comprises the set of functions that are necessary to communicate directly with Windows. The SDK is effectively the lowest level of programming available under Windows. While you can create C++ Windows programs using only the SDK, it is long and laborious to do so and the Visual Workbench gives you a tremendous headstart. Bear in mind that you can always incorporate some low-level programming in your C++ programs by calling Windows functions directly from within a method.

The SDK also includes a number of standard libraries to make life easier. For instance, there is a Common Dialog Box library (COMMDLG.DLL), which contains a set of templates for the dialogue boxes that frequently pop up in Windows applications: an Open box for selecting a file to open, a Save As box for saving files, a Color box for the user to choose a new colour, Find and Replace boxes for text searches, and so on.

Visual C++ Editions

There are two versions of Visual C++, the Standard Edition and the Professional Edition. The vast majority of Visual C++ features are included in both editions. The Professional Edition adds the CodeView debugger, the Source Profiler, the SDK tools and enhancements to other Standard Edition features.

The Standard Edition can be used to develop full Windows applications but the Professional Edition is needed if you want to create DOS applications.

BORLAND C++

Borland's C++ language is very similar to Microsoft's. It includes ANSI C and all the standard C++ keywords; in addition, it has a few of its own keywords (though using these will inevitably limit the portability of the code, supposedly one of C's principal attractions).

Borland C++ comes packaged with a range of programs, tools and utilities. The C++ library contains a large number of functions, suitable for programming under both DOS and Windows. The utility programs include WinSight (for debugging window-based programs) and a Windows help compiler.

As described for Microsoft C++, creating a Windows program from scratch is a non-starter. Borland provides two alternative application frameworks to give you a starting point: ObjectWindows and Turbo Vision. ObjectWindows is the framework to use when creating Windows applications; Turbo Vision is a similar framework for creating Windows-type applications that will run directly under DOS.

ObjectWindows saves you the trouble to writing your own C++ code to produce the objects that will represent windows, buttons, menus and so on. It provides the added advantages that you can be satisfied that the code is bug-free, that it will follow all the rules a Windows user has come to expect and that it will look just like any other Windows program. The downside of this is that you must sacrifice a considerable amount of individuality in the program but this a small price to pay for producing consistent programs with which your end users will be happy. ObjectWindows is described in more detail later.

Also supplied is the Resource Workshop, a Windows-based utility for creating Windows resource files. This is used in the creation of dialogue boxes, menus and so on.

Finally, there is Turbo Assembler, should you become fanatical enough about object-oriented programming to want to do it at assembler level, and Turbo Debugger, a tool for debugging any program created by the Borland products. Turbo Debugger is well worth learning when you reach the stage of producing large, complex applications.

The C++ package also comes with three weighty volumes that document the Windows API.

BORLAND PASCAL WITH OBJECTS

Borland's Pascal With Objects is an object-oriented version of their popular Pascal language. The language comes with a similar set of tools to those of Borland C++:

- ObjectWindows and Turbo Vision, the two alternative application frameworks

- WinSight, for debugging window-based programs

- The Windows help compiler

- Resource Workshop, for creating resource files

- Turbo Assembler and Turbo Debugger

The package also includes the Windows IDE, command-line compiler and run-time libraries.

MICROSOFT VISUAL BASIC

Microsoft's Visual Basic is more self-contained than the other packages described above. It is supplied as a complete programming language, containing all you need to create a fully-functioning standalone Windows .EXE application.

As for Visual C++, there are two versions: the Standard Edition and the Professional Edition. The Professional Edition offers some additional features, including:

- Custom controls

- Help compiler

- Data Access (for accessing common database structures)

- Crystal Reports (for creating custom reports from databases)

The Standard Edition for Version 3 onwards includes many of the features that were only available in the Professional Edition of earlier versions.

C PRELIMINARIES

This book cannot hope to provide a tutorial for any of the three languages used but some detail of the workings of the languages is necessary for the code examples to be meaningful, if not fully understood. (Interestingly, Borland do not even attempt to provide a C tutorial; rather, the user is directed to purchase a good book on the subject!)

C is a language of functions. Apart from a few basic mathematical operations (addition, multiplication, etc.), virtually anything you want to do must be achieved by calling functions. Unlike most languages, these functions are contained in *libraries*, rather than forming part of the language itself. A library is simply a file consisting of a group of independent functions, each function being a fragment of code (similar to a procedure) to perform some task. There are a number of standard libraries: for example, STDIO.H is the header file for the Standard Input/Output library. If you want to display a string of text on the screen, there is no statement built into C to perform this task, nor any built-in function; instead you must use the printf function from STDIO.H.

Every C program must have a main function. The entire body of the program is contained within this function and main is preceded by any definitions that are necessary. These definitions consist of variable declarations and #include statements for the libraries that are to be used. The following C program is the absolute minimum:

```
main()
{
}
```

This does nothing, as you will see if you compile and run it.

To compile the program, type the text into an ASCII file (say MAIN.C) and compile it with the Borland C++ command-line compiler:

```
BCC MAIN.C
```

This produces an executable file, MAIN.EXE, which is 4204 bytes long. This demonstrates that there is a certain amount of unavoidable overhead in any .EXE file. (A similar file would result from any other compiler.)

The following program, when run under DOS, does something a little more interesting:

```
#include <stdio.h>
main()
{
   printf("Printing text to the screen.\n");
}
```

If you compile and run this program – with any C compiler – the end product will be the text on the screen:

```
Printing text to the screen.
```

The #include statement declares that the functions in the library are to be made available to the program. The braces {} identify the start and end of a function definition (in this case the function is main). printf is a function defined in STDIO.H and the text in brackets is the argument passed to the function; printf interprets the \n as an instruction to start a new line at that point. Finally, the semi-colon (;) identifies the end of a statement; C statements are often spread across several lines for convenience, all spaces at the start of lines being ignored, so the semi-colon is essential to identify the end of the statement.

When the program is compiled, it should produce a program of the order of 6600 bytes. The program is only small because, although STDIO.H contains many functions, the compiler only includes in the .EXE file those that are used within the main body of the program.

Differences in C++

While this example is fine to get us going under DOS it is not suitable for a Windows environment. As will be explained in the next chapter, Windows takes full control of all communications with the hardware, including printing direct to the screen. Once you start Windows C++ programming, you must leave behind the direct access functions such as printf and let Windows do the work for you.

There is also another major distinction between programming in C under DOS and C++ under Windows. For C++, the primary function is WinMain(). This takes the place of the standard main() function and is obligatory in every Windows C++ program.

For C++, the WinMain function constructs the application object as an instance of the application class and then calls the object's Run function. When the program is executed, the application object is constructed, resulting in the automatic construction of the main window. The minimal C++ program is defined in more detail in Chapter 4.

Classes and Functions

In C, instances of *user-defined types* are called *variables*; in C++ the user-defined types are extended to become *classes*, and instances of classes are called *objects*.

To be accessible outside the class, a function or data item must be declared *public*; usually, the only public items are functions and all data is private. Therefore, the data held by an object can only be accessed via a public function.

All functions must be declared along with the class declaration. The function declaration is called the function *prototype*. When the function is defined, its name is in the form *class*:*:function*. This allows two classes to have functions of the same name. The function definition is outside the class declaration and does not necessarily have to be even close in the code (indeed, it is usual to put the declarations in the header file and the definitions in the source code file).

Private methods can only be called by other methods in the same class. In this case there is no need to refer to the class when either a private method or private data is used.

The redefinition of a method within a derived class may call the method of the base class. The call takes the form *baseclass*::*method*.

Header and Source Files

The usual practice when writing C++ applications is to put the class declarations in a header file, with a .H extension, and the function definitions in a source file, with a .CPP extension.

- The .H header file contains function prototypes, so another programmer can see what methods the class responds to, without having to worry about how the methods are implemented.

- The .CPP file source file contains the actual function definitions and places the detailed code in a location that isolates it from the declarations that tell another programmer what the class is all about.

The .CPP file has a #include statement that refers to the corresponding .H file. It also has #include statements for any other libraries whose functions are used internally by the class. (These #include statements may have to be put in the header file instead, if the function prototypes' parameters use structures that are defined in an external file.)

The advantage of separating the header and source file in this way is that another programmer has only to include the header file in an application; the corresponding .OBJ file must be available to be linked in when the program is compiled. If the code in the .CPP file is changed, a new .OBJ file is created, and other programmers need only relink their programs using the new object file.

As a general rule, there will be one header file and one source file for each class. If a group of classes are always used together, then they may be combined in a single pair of header and source files.

Friend Objects

For true encapsulation, there should be *no* public data; all data should be private and accessible to external objects only via a public function. This process of blocking direct access to data is often referred to as *data hiding*.

However, in certain cases you may want to allow access to one object's data from another specific object. In this case, the second object is declared to be a *friend* of the first. The friend keyword is included in the declaration of the first object. If one object is a friend of another, the reverse is not true unless explicitly declared so.

The use of friend classes should be kept to a minimum, since it dilutes the encapsulation of the data. If you subsequently make changes to a class, you may also have to alter the operation of friend classes.

Function Overloading

As well as allowing classes to redefine methods, C++ also has a process called *function overloading*. This allows the same name to be used for more than one function definition. The functions must have different numbers of arguments or, if two functions with the same name have the same number of arguments, the arguments must be of a different type. When a function is called, the one that has a set of arguments that exactly match the number and types of those in the function call will be used. For example, if a function compares two variables, there may be two functions, one for integers and the other for strings. Function overloading saves having to think up – and remember – a whole set of function names for doing the same thing with different combinations of variables.

Constructors and Destructors

Each class has a function, called a *constructor*, that creates instances of objects; similarly there is another function, called a *destructor*, that destroys objects when they are no longer needed.

The constructor function is called automatically each time a new instance of a class is declared. If you do not define one, the C++ compiler adds a default constructor that does nothing. The constructor is used to carry out any initialisations that are necessary for the object. The constructor must have the same name as the class. You may define more than one constructor as long as they have different sets of parameters; that is, the constructor can be overloaded in the same way as any other function.

Similarly, each class may have a destructor (again defaulting to a dummy one), which is called automatically when the object is destroyed. The destructor is used to tidy up when an object is destroyed (for instance, to release memory). The destructor's name consists of a tilde symbol (~) and the class name. There are no parameters, so there is no overloading and hence only one destructor.

The constructor for *local objects* (those declared within a function) is called when the object is declared; the destructor is activated on leaving the function. The constructor for *global objects* (declared outside all functions) is called at the start of the program; the destructor is called when the program ends.

When an object is created for a derived class its constructor is called. Clearly, since the derived class may include some of the methods of the base class, the base class data needs to be initialised as well. Therefore the constructor for the derived class must call the constructor for the base class. This is done by adding a colon (:) and base constructor function to the derived class constructor definition. The constructor therefore takes the form:

```
derivedclass::derivedclass(arguments) : baseclass(arguments2)
```

Examples of this structure are given in Chapter 4.

PROGRAM DESIGN

Most people who have programmed in procedural languages will be familiar with *top-down* design methods. These start with the main actions to be carried out by the program, then take each of the actions and break it down into a set of procedures. Each procedure is further broken down into more procedures at a lower level, until at last a stage is reached where each procedure can be coded. This is generally known as *procedural decomposition*. The result is a structured, procedural program.

Finding Classes

Procedural decomposition does not work with object-oriented programming. Here, the first task is to determine the objects that will be used within the program. You need to decide what display objects there will be – windows, buttons, lists, etc. – and what abstract objects will be needed for holding disk-file data, for printing and so on. For each distinct type of object, there will be a class. Often a class will provide the template for a single object but sometimes a class is used many times. Similar objects (e.g. dialogue boxes where only the text changes) will clearly be from the same class. Dissimilar objects will apparently be from different classes but may be surprisingly closely related; for instance, command buttons are usually defined as a special type of window! By examining the end product that you are hoping to achieve, it should be possible to determine the classes that will be needed. Don't worry about the hierarchy at this stage.

It should be noted that finding classes for a Windows application is generally fairly straightforward; most objects are intuitively obvious. If you go on to program in a non-Windows environment you will discover that finding objects becomes conceptually much more difficult. Often, the classes are modelled on real-world objects but sometimes classes are purely conceptual and, therefore, much harder to identify. The most important thing to remember is that a procedure is not a good starting point for a class; rather, a class is a collection of procedures with associated data. The data will usually have values that either remain the same throughout the application or are remembered from one use of the object to another. If a supposed object just has data that is initialised every time there is a call to the object, then what you probably have is a procedure (possibly with other nested procedures), which should form part of some other class. What you need to search for is objects that have a clearly defined *state*.

For instance, the template of a record from a database is a potential class. Its objects will have a set of data values; each record is an object, an instance of the class. Associated with it are procedures to change the value of a field, display a field value, perform a calculation on a field's value and so on.

Identifying Data and Methods

Once the classes have been found, you should decide the data that they will hold and the methods that they will act on. For example, a button will have as its data the height, width, position within the window, colour, text and so on; its methods may include Click and DragOver.

The types of data (height, colours, etc.) are usually called the *properties* or *attributes* of the class. Each of the properties can be given a *value*. For example, one of the properties for a button class will be Caption and its value for a particular object may be 'OK'.

The class's public methods should be identified next. The behaviour of an object – how it responds to user actions (such as clicking) and how it can be used by other objects – is determined by the methods that are defined for it.

The Class Hierarchy

When the classes, their behaviour and data have been identified, the next step is to build up the class hierarchy. To do this you need to determine the relationship between classes; this is done by comparing the methods and data of pairs or groups of classes.

- If one class has all the methods of a second, and adds a few more of its own, then the first class is probably derived from the second.

- If two classes have a common set of methods but each also has its own unique methods, then these classes may be derived from the same base class. You will probably have to define a new class to act as the base. The base class will include all the common methods (provided their definitions are identical for both derived classes).

- If two classes have the same set of methods, then they can be combined in a single class, as long as the definitions of the methods are the same in each case.

- If the methods of a class look as if they will have a number of CASE statements to determine behaviour according to the type of object, then it is likely that the class needs to be split into two or more classes derived from a single base class.

In this way, the hierarchy is built up. As you do this, your idea of what denotes a class within the application will probably change. This process of determining classes and fitting them into a hierarchy must continue until the classes have become firmly placed in relation to one another.

The final stage is to check that there is no redundancy and no ambiguity. *Redundancy* occurs when there are methods that are duplicated in derived classes (with identical code), when they could be moved up the hierarchy into a base class. Remember that methods can be overridden. For example, if three classes derived from the same base class have the same method and its implementation is identical in two of them, then the definition can be moved up to the base class; the third derived class can include a definition that overrides the base class definition.

Ambiguity occurs when the operation of a method depends on the object that has been created. The code will contain an IF or CASE statement. Without knowing what the object is, you cannot decide what the method will do. In this case, the class should be split to resolve the ambiguity. (The ambiguity at the design stage should not be confused with the polymorphism that occurs when the program is run; at run time, there may be a pointer to an unknown object and the program will not know how the method will respond but the appropriate method will be invoked.)

The most important thing is that this design should be completed before you start writing code. Of course, once the coding is underway, you will probably need to adjust the design as the application takes shape, the program is found to run in a different way to that expected or the requirements are found to be other than those originally anticipated.

This is where the flexibility of object-oriented programming pays great dividends. Often, when a program is run for the first time, it will be discovered that the designer has misinterpreted the requirements of the end user and changes need to be made. Because data and methods are encapsulated in independent classes, it is possible to make major changes to the coding of one class without the need to alter other classes and with the danger of knock-on effects carefully contained.

INSTALLATION

Before starting to install any of the programming packages described in this book make sure you have plenty of hard disk space free. To install the complete systems you need between 32 Mb and 52 Mb free; in order to compile a program you must also have plenty of free space, up to 12 Mb in the case of Visual C++. However, if space is short, considerable savings can be made by selective installation.

Installing Visual C++

When installing Visual C++ you should bear in mind the following points:

* Complete installation takes about 48 Mb of disk space; the bare minimum is about 25 Mb (omitting the on-line help files and the tools, and including only the MFC samples and limited libraries). If possible, include the on-line help.

* You should install libraries for at least the Small and Medium memory models.

* The target types for building libraries need include only the Windows .EXE option.

Before running Visual C++ you should check the following:

* In CONFIG.SYS, the FILES settings should be at least 50 and BUFFERS must be at least 30.

* There should be at least 12 Mb hard disk space free before creating a new application.

* The Windows temporary swap file size should be at least 2 Mb on a system with 4 Mb of RAM.

* You should run SHARE before running Windows.

The temporary swap file is set with the 386Enh section of SYSTEM.INI, which should look something like this:

```
[386Enh]
...
PagingFile=C:\WINDOWS\WIN386.SWP
MaxPagingFileSize = 2097156
```

It is esential to get your Windows system set up correctly in order to run Visual C++.

Installing Borland C++

The following points should be noted when installing Borland C++:

- Complete installation requires about 52 Mb of disk space; a minimum system (including ObjectWindows) needs 24 Mb. You will need the Class Libraries (in the Install options) and all the Windows options, apart from Turbo Debugger. The OWL examples should be included.

- At least the Small/Tiny and Medium library models should be installed.

- You should allow at least an extra 2 Mb of free disk space for use by the installation program (which will be freed again when installation is complete).

After installation, check the following:

- In CONFIG.SYS, the FILES setting should be at least 20.

- The DOS PATH should include C:\BORLANDC\BIN.

You will need at least 2 Mb free on the disk to compile any program.

Installing Borland Pascal With Objects

When installing Pascal With Objects, note the following:

- The complete system requires 28 Mb of disk space but an additional 5 Mb may be needed during the installation process for unarchiving the larger files.

- The minimum system – the Windows platform only, the Windows IDE help files, ObjectWindows Library (OWL), Windows 3.1 interface, Resource Workshop and some examples (Windows 3.1 and Resource Workshop) – needs 9.5 Mb. If necessary, you can save 5.7 Mb by scrapping the help files and a further 600 Kb on the example files, leaving just over 3 Mb.

Ideally, of course, you should install the entire system in order to make the most of its facilities. After installation, check the following:

- In CONFIG.SYS, the FILES setting must be at least 20.

- The DOS PATH should include C:\BP\BIN.

Only a small amount of hard disk space is needed for creating applications.

Installing Visual Basic

When installing Visual Basic, the following points should be noted:

- Complete installation takes about 32 Mb of disk space; the minimum system – just Visual Basic on its own – needs only 4.5 Mb.

- Of this, 2.7 Mb can be saved by deleting the help file, VB\VB.HLP.

From this, it can be seen that Visual Basic is a very compact system compared with the C++ applications.

3 | The Windows Environment

The Microsoft Windows environment has been around for many years but it is only relatively recently that it has become popular. Windows was bundled with PCs for years before people really started to take any notice of it; the environment was slow and prone to failure, and there were few applications written to take advantage of it. However, with the arrival of version 3, the drop in price in 386 and 486 machines, and the bundling of Windows with virtually every PC, Windows has now become the dominant environment for PC users.

This chapter outlines the main features of Windows, from a programming point of view, and describes the way in which Windows works.

WINDOWS FOR THE USER

From the user's point of view, Windows has the potential to offer some very desirable benefits:

- More than one application can be run at a time, and the user can suspend and restart any application at will. One application may still continue processing while the user is working with another one.

- All applications have a common appearance and behave in a similar way. If you know how to save a file in one Windows application you will almost certainly know how to do so in another application.

- The Windows clipboard allows you to move text, numbers and pictures from one application to another, using the same set of commands and shortcuts, no matter what applications you are using.

- Windows takes care of all communication with external devices: monitor, printer, modem, keyboard and mouse. Once you have set Windows up so that it communicates successfully with these devices you can be certain that any Windows application will also function correctly.

- More memory is available to programs (though Windows applications need a lot more memory to start with).

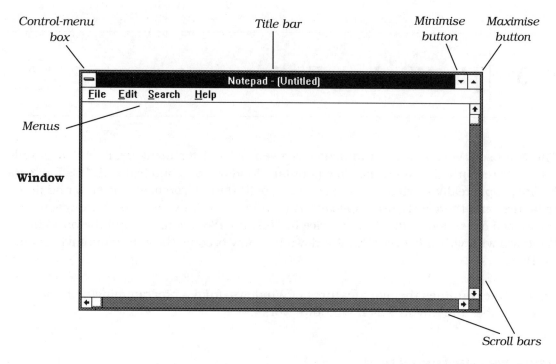

Figure 3.1 Components of a window

Of course, there are some disadvantages: notably, you need a fast machine for Windows programs to operate at a tolerable speed. Windows applications can also be rather boring – they all look the same and behave the same way – but that's the price you pay for not having to start learning all over again each time you get a new application.

The principle features of any Windows program are illustrated in Figure 3.1. The components are:

Window   A rectangle marked out on the screen, which contains a variety of objects and behaves in a predefined way

Title bar   A text string to identify the window to the user

Control-menu box   A button which, when clicked, results in the control menu popping up; this menu allows the user to switch to another application, close the window, etc.

Minimise button   Reduces the window to an icon

Maximise button   Expands the window to fill the screen

Menus	A hierarchy of options that activate procedures or lead to dialogue boxes; some menu options have shortcut keys or accelerators
Scroll bars	Devices for indicating the true size of the background window and the part of the window currently on display, and for moving the display around the background window

While these features provide a common interference for the user, they also place a substantial set of restrictions on the programmer.

WINDOWS FOR THE PROGRAMMER

Gone are the days when a programmer could sit down in front of a blank computer screen, type in a few instructions, and run the program instantly. Modern programming under Windows requires a very specialised form of software development. There are two alternatives to programming:

- Develop the program completely from scratch.

- Evolve the program from an existing Windows program.

Quite frankly, it is simply not feasible to develop a complex Windows application completely from scratch. Although it is possible to write your own procedures for displaying windows, dialogue boxes and controls, and for responding to events, it is an extremely complex task, prone to error and likely to result in applications that are sufficiently different to cause real problems for the user. And why bother repeating all this development work when someone else has already done it for you?

The purist may want to get down to the lowest level possible, creating an entire Windows application from nothing but for most developers the task is to produce a bug-free, working application in the shortest time possible. After all, just displaying a simple dialogue box on screen takes up a couple pages of C code (and that doesn't include the resource file that must be linked in to produce the functionality of the dialogue box).

Therefore, it is assumed that you will be starting with the frameworks provided by applications such as Visual C++ or ObjectWindows. The advantages of using a framework are:

- All the standard Windows functionality is supplied.

- The windows, controls and other objects are there waiting to be selected.

- Methods exist for all the events that are likely to occur.

- The applications will work within the restrictions imposed by the Windows environment.

- There is no need to worry about providing drivers for hundreds of different devices that users may have.

By far the easiest way of getting a Windows program up and running is to use one of the IDEs (integrated development environments) supplied with the programming languages.

Windows Restrictions

Another reason for deriving Windows applications from existing templates is the list of restrictions placed on any program that runs under Windows:

- The program can be run only under Windows; this is determined by creating a special type of .EXE file. Any attempt to run the program from the DOS prompt should result in a message that Windows is required.

- The program should follow all the standard rules for Windows behaviour and fit in with the accepted display guidelines.

- The program must be able to receive data from the clipboard and the user should be able to cut and copy data to the clipboard.

- It should be possible to run more than one copy of the program at a time.

If you use one of the frameworks as the basis for any new application, you will find that all of these requirements are met automatically.

WINDOWS COMPONENTS

Each of the frameworks – such as those of Visual C++ or ObjectWindows – provides the programmer with a set of standard classes as a starting point. These, in turn, call numerous Windows functions and provide methods to respond to the many Windows messages.

Any Windows program is comprised of calls to the 600 Windows functions. These functions are contained in the following files:

KERNEL.EXE	Disk file and memory functions, and communication with DOS
USER.EXE	Keyboard, mouse, sound, serial port and timer functions
GDI.EXE	Display and printer functions

(These three .EXE files cannot be run directly; instead, the functions they contain are called by Windows when required.)

These *external library modules* are held in the SYSTEM directory and must exist for all Windows systems to operate. Therefore there is no need to supply them with a Windows application; it is safe to assume that the end user's Windows system will have all these files.

Of course, this is not all there is to Windows; these three files make use of the .DRV files that are installed for each particular hardware configuration.

Windows is clearly made up of many components but, unlike more traditional programming methods, does not load everything it needs into memory at once. Instead, Windows loads functions as and when it needs them. The result is a large amount of disk swapping (and a disk cache becomes essential). This inevitably slows down applications but without it Windows programs would be impossibly large.

WINDOWS FUNCTIONS (API)

The three library modules (KERNEL.EXE, USER.EXE and GDI.EXE) together make up the Windows *Application Program Interface* (API). This is a set of about 600 functions that perform all the tasks of a standard Windows program. For example:

- DialogBox creates a modal dialogue box. (A modal dialogue must have a response before the user can move on; a modeless dialogue box can continue to exist while the user is working with other windows.) The parameters for the function specify the resource that will be used to build the dialogue box; this resource determines the size, colour and text of the box and the controls it will contain.

- InsertMenu inserts a new command at a specified position in a drop-down menu while DeleteMenu removes a menu item; DrawMenuBar redraws the menu bar at the top of the window.

- MoveWindow changes the width, height and position on screen of a window.

Any C++ program will be made up of calls to these functions. They can be thought of as analogous to the DOS interrupts that are called by DOS programs. When a DOS program wants to display text on screen, for example, it calls one of the interrupts that allow this to happen. In a similar way, a Windows program calls one of the API functions in order to draw text on a window.

However, just as most programmers rarely see the DOS interrupt calls (since these are hidden behind high-level language statements or in C standard library functions), so most Windows programmers need have little contact with the API functions. Most of the function calls are generated automatically for you by the IDE; when you indicate that a certain type of window or control is to be created, the IDE generates all the code necessary, including all the appropriate API function calls.

WINDOWS MESSAGES

When you want to tell Windows to perform some task (create a dialogue box, change a menu or move a window for example), you invoke an API function with the required parameters. When Windows wants to notify an application of some event it generates a *message*.

There are about 200 messages, covering all the events that might arise during the running of an application. Some of these messages are sent by Windows to an application when an event occurs. For example:

- WM_LBUTTONDOWN is sent when the user presses down the left mouse button and WM_LBUTTONUP indicates that the button has been released. The arguments that are passed with the message tell you whether other buttons or keys are currently being pressed and give the co-ordinates of the mouse pointer.

- WM_HSCROLL indicates that the horizontal scroll bar has been activated by the user; the parameters indicate the type of action (for instance, clicking on the arrows or outside the thumb block, or dragging the thumb block to a new position).

- WM_MOUSEACTIVATE occurs when the mouse button is clicked and the pointer is outside the active window.

- WM_TIMER indicates that a timer has reached its limit.

Each of these messages represents an *event*: some action by the user or change of state within the system to which the application may wish to respond. It is up to the programmer to decide which of the many possible events each object is going to respond to; if there is to be a response, then a piece of code must be written to carry out the required action.

Other messages are used by an application to send an instruction or make an enquiry. For example:

- BM_GETCHECK is an enquiry to see whether or not a radio button or check box is currently selected ('checked'). A non-zero value is returned if the button/check box is selected.

- LB_INSERTSTRING inserts a string item in a list box at a specified position; LB_GETCOUNT returns the number of items currently in a list box.

- EM_LINESCROLL scrolls the text in a control by a specified number of lines; EM_GETLINECOUNT returns the number of lines of text.

As for the functions, most of the time the sending and receiving of messages is hidden from the programmer.

RESOURCE FILES

Most of the objects that are visible in an application are 'resource' objects. A *resource* is an object that is defined in a file separate from the main application files. Resources include objects such as dialogue boxes, menu systems, icons, bitmaps and strings.

Resource files are developed independently of applications and combined with them during the final stages of the compilation process. This independence means that you can change the way a resource appears or behaves and then recompile the resource file, without having to recompile the entire application. Once a resource file has been completed satisfactorily it can be used again and again for new applications. This gives a common 'look and feel' to a set of applications.

Windows uses resources as part of its memory-management operations. Unless you specify that a resource is to be loaded when the application is run, Windows will not load a resource into memory until it is needed. For instance, the code for a dialogue box will not be loaded until the program specifies that the box is to be displayed. The resource is held in a part of memory that can be re-used for other purposes if necessary. Therefore, whether or not a resource needs to be reloaded from disk depends on whether or not the memory it occupied has been re-used.

Resources are defined in *resource script files*, with a .RC extension. These script files are compiled into binary .RES files, which are subsequently linked in to the application when the .EXE file is built.

The standard Windows libraries support the following resource types:

Dialogue box	A pop-up window that gives the user instructions or receives input
Menu	A drop-down menu bar that organises user options into logical groups

Accelerator table   A list of key presses for activating menu items (or other actions) directly from the keyboard

Bitmap   An image stored in binary format, with each pixel on screen represented by one or more bits of data

Cursor   A bitmap that indicates the current position of the pointer on the screen, as determined by movement of the mouse or other pointing device

Icon   A bitmap used to represent a program in the Program Manager or a window that has been minimised

String table   A list of text strings (titles, messages, etc.) to be used by the application

You can either use resources that have been supplied for you or create your own resources.

* Microsoft's Visual C++ provides some sample resources in a file called COMMON.RES, plus other resource files. These resources can be copied to your own .RC file using App Studio.

* Borland's ObjectWindows has a number of standard resource files, such as INPUTDIA.DLG (an input dialogue box) and FILEMENU.RC (a standard File Menu). Resources are created or amended with the Resource Workshop. (There is also the RC command-line compiler should you need to get down to the lowest level.)

Each resource is given a unique *resource ID*, consisting of an identifying string and integer. The resource is accessed by specifying either its name or number.

Resource files are not a concern if you are programming in Visual Basic; all this is handled for you.

4 | Creating an Application

Whatever programming language or development language you use, the Windows application that you end up with will look the same and behave in the same way. Indeed, much of the compiled code will probably be similar. However, the method by which you arrive at the final application will vary considerably, depending on the development route you have selected.

This chapter looks at the ways in which the basis is devised for a new application, using four development environments.

DEVELOPMENT DIRECTORIES

Before starting any new project you should create a directory to hold the many source files that will be generated during development. Regardless of the language or IDE that you are using, any Windows project will be comprised of many different files and it is essential that these are grouped together, well away from the language files or other projects.

As a general rule, it is a good idea to create the project directory as a subdirectory of a main development directory. Each new application will have its own subdirectory of this directory. In the examples in this book, the applications are all in subdirectories of a directory called C:\OOP. Avoid putting the projects in the language's own subdirectories, as this will lead to confusion later. In the case of Visual C++, all you need do is create the main development directory; the project subdirectories will be created for you. For the other languages, create a subdirectory of this directory for each new application.

When one project has been completed and you are starting another, you will probably want to re-use many of the windows, dialogue boxes and procedures that were developed for the first project. Create the new subdirectory and then copy across all the files that may be useful; then delete the redundant parts, modify anything that needs to be changed and add any references or procedures that are unique to the new project. That way, you will save a great deal of development time and also end up with projects that have a similar look and feel.

MICROSOFT'S VISUAL C++

Microsoft's Visual C++ is best tackled through the Visual Workbench, which provides access to the other tools and utilities.

Creating a new application is remarkably simple. With only a few steps Visual C++ sets up the skeleton of the application for you. As an example, consider the case of a program to record personal details of employees. The first task is to set up the outline of the application and then create a dialogue box where data can be entered or displayed.

The general procedure for creating the basic application is as follows:

1   Run Visual Workbench from within Windows, by clicking on the Visual C++ icon (Figure 4.1). The main window is displayed (Figure 4.2). This consists of a menu bar, with toolbar just below it and status line at the bottom of the window. The rest of the window is empty.

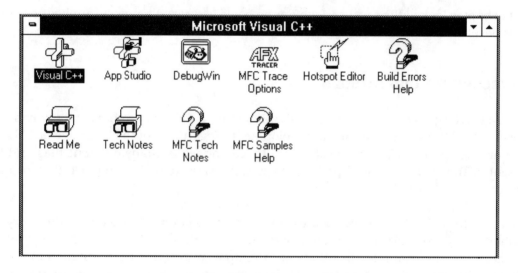

Figure 4.1 The Visual C++ group

2   To start a new project, select Project | AppWizard. This runs the AppWizard utility, which is used to set up the application.

3   The dialogue box asks for a project name and directory, and has a selection of command buttons (Figure 4.3). In the Directory box, select the base directory for your application. Type a name for the project at the top of the box (e.g. 'pers'); the Project Path is updated and the program suggests the name for a new subdirectory (Figure 4.4).

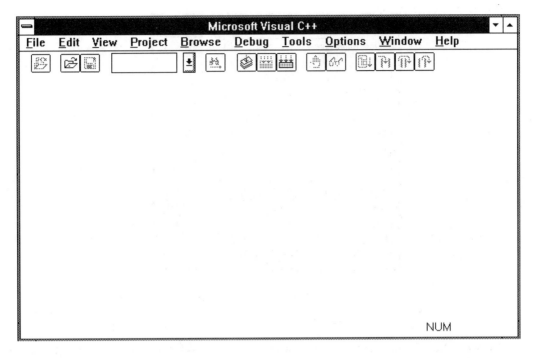

Figure 4.2 *Visual C++ main window*

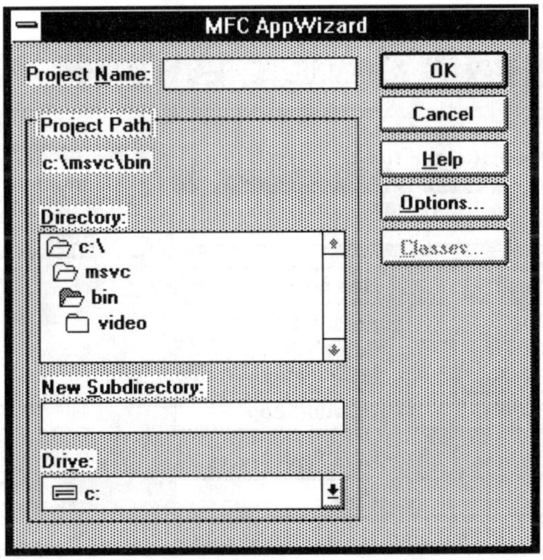

Figure 4.3 *AppWizard dialogue*

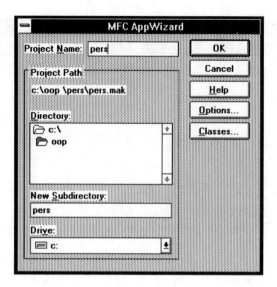

Figure 4.4 Selecting the project name and directory

4   Click on the Classes button. This shows that AppWizard will be creating four new classes, certain details of which can be changed (Figure 4.5). Click on CPersDoc (or equivalent). This has six items that can be changed. The File Extension will be used for new data files and an extension (e.g. 'per') should be entered. Click on OK.

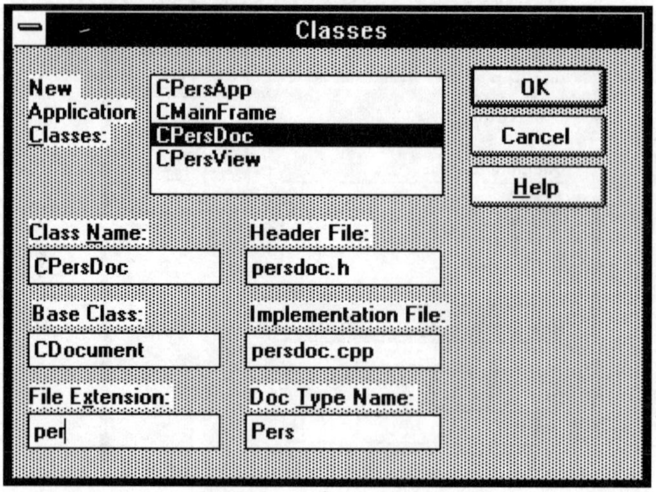

Figure 4.5 Application classes

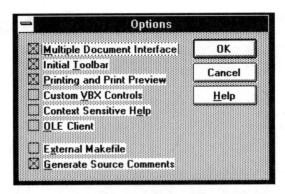

Figure 4.6 Application creation options

5   Click on the Options button. A list of features that may be included in the new application is given (Figure 4.6). For the current example, all of these should be turned off except 'Generate Source Comments'. Then click on OK.

6   You are now ready to generate the new application. Click on OK in the main AppWizard box. A list is given of the classes to be created and the application features (Figure 4.7).

7   Click on Create. The new files are created and you are returned to Visual Workbench. This is the only time in the development of an application when you will use AppWizard.

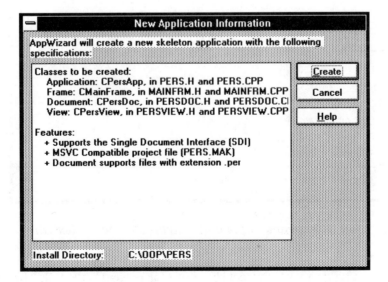

Figure 4.7 Application details

```
━    <1> Output                                    ▼ ▲
Compiling resources...
Compiling...
c:\oop\pers\stdafx.cpp
Compiling...
c:\oop\pers\pers.cpp
c:\oop\pers\mainfrm.cpp
c:\oop\pers\persdoc.cpp
c:\oop\pers\persview.cpp
Linking...
Binding resources...
Creating browser database...
PERS.EXE - 0 error(s), 0 warning(s)

← ▯                                                 →
```

Figure 4.8 Progress of compilation

It is now possible to build an EXE file for the application and run it. Click on Project | Build (or press Shift-F8). An Output window is displayed, which shows how the compilation is progressing (Figure 4.8). Even for a minimal application such as this, compilation takes some considerable time.

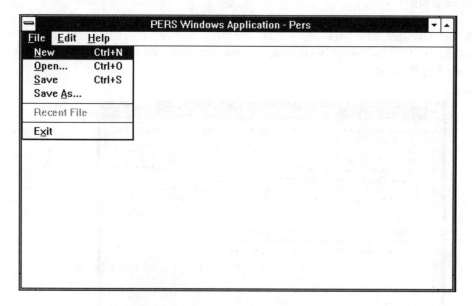

Figure 4.9 The minimal application (with File menu clicked)

The program can then be run with Project | Execute (or press CTRL-F5). The result is a blank window, with a menu bar containing three menus. Each of these has the usual options:

- The File menu has six standard options, with accelerator keys (Figure 4.9). Selecting File I Open brings up a standard File Open dialogue box, with everything you need for selecting the directory and drive, and even an option for restricting the file types (Figure 4.10). There is a similar dialogue box for File I Save As.

- The Edit menu has the usual Undo, Cut, Copy and Paste options, initially greyed out.

- The Help menu has an About option, which brings up an information box (Figure 4.11).

The main window responds to all the usual operations: resizing, minimising, maximising and moving. Clicking on the control-menu box leads to the standard menu, and ALT-F4 closes down the application. Without writing a single line of code, you have created a fully-fledged Windows application.

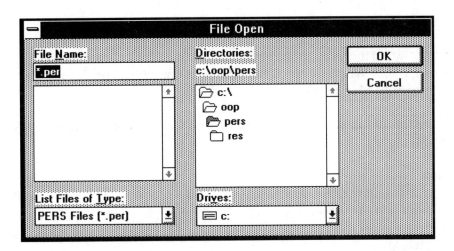

Figure 4.10 Standard File Open options

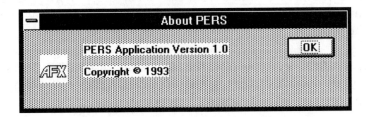

Figure 4.11 Help I About option

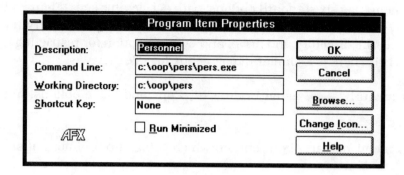

Figure 4.12 Setting up a new item

Returning to the Windows Program Manager you can set up a new program item for the application, using the default 'AFX' icon supplied with it (Figure 4.12).

The Default Application

Before going any further it is probably worth taking a look at the files that Visual C++ has created for you. When the EXE file has been compiled, the development directory will contain over 30 files, taking up some 3 Mb of disk space.

The names of the files depend on the name chosen for the application; the PERS example is described here.

PERS.MAK

The file that ties it all together is PERS.MAK, the project file. This file encodes details of all the other files that are used to build the final application. You do not have to do anything to the project file; it is updated automatically each time you add or remove files with Visual Workbench.

PERS.H

PERS.H is the main header file (Figure 4.13). This refers to RESOURCE.H, which defines a few constants, and declares a new CPersApp class, derived from CWinApp. Each application must have one and only one class derived from CWinApp. This class is central to the running of the program.

The main function, WinMain, is supplied by the Microsoft Foundation Class Library and is run automatically. (It doesn't appear in the application files.) WinMain registers the windows classes and then calls the following functions:

• CPersApp::InitInstance initialises the application.

```
// pers.h : main header file for the PERS application
//

#ifndef __AFXWIN_H__
    #error include 'stdafx.h' before including this file for PCH
#endif

#include "resource.h"            // main symbols

/////////////////////////////////////////////////////////////////////////
// CPersApp:
// See pers.cpp for the implementation of this class
//

class CPersApp : public CWinApp
{
public:
    CPersApp();

// Overrides
    virtual BOOL InitInstance();

// Implementation

    //{{AFX_MSG(CPersApp)
    afx_msg void OnAppAbout();
            // NOTE - the ClassWizard will add and remove member functions here.
            //    DO NOT EDIT what you see in these blocks of generated code !
    //}}AFX_MSG
    DECLARE_MESSAGE_MAP()
};

/////////////////////////////////////////////////////////////////////////
```

Figure 4.13 Main header file, PERS.H

- CWinApp::Run handles Windows messages. The application remains in the Run loop until the user closes down the main window.

- CWinApp::ExitInstance tidies up and closes down the application.

Therefore, your application class (e.g. CPersApp) must have at least one redefined function, InitInstance, to carry out the initial procedures before the main Run loop is executed. It is rarely necessary to redefine the Run function but you may want to add an ExitInstance function to CPersApp, which will carry out application-specific tidying up procedures before calling the standard ExitInstance function for CWinApp.

The application class, CPersApp, is a template for the application. The application object is created when the user runs the application; the user may have more than one instance of the application running at a time – and hence there may be more then one application object in existence.

The final block of PERS.H will contain functions for responding to user events; these will be added by ClassWizard.

PERS.CPP

PERS.CPP is the main source file (Figure 4.14). At the top of the file (after the #include statements) is the message map, which lists the Windows messages to which the application will respond. It can be seen that initially the application is set up to respond to three drop-down menu options: File|New, File|Open and Help|About App.

The CPersApp constructor and InitInstance are defined. Following on from these, a class called CAboutDlg is derived from CDialog, and its functions are defined. Finally, the OnAppAbout function (which is called when the user selects Help|About App) is defined. This function creates the AboutDlg object as an instance of CAboutDlg, and calls the object's DoModal function, which displays the dialogue box.

```
// pers.cpp : Defines the class behaviors for the application.
//

#include "stdafx.h"
#include "pers.h"

#include "mainfrm.h"
#include "persdoc.h"
#include "persview.h"

#ifdef _DEBUG
#undef THIS_FILE
static char BASED_CODE THIS_FILE[] = __FILE__;
#endif


/////////////////////////////////////////////////////////////////////////////
// CPersApp

BEGIN_MESSAGE_MAP(CPersApp, CWinApp)
    //{{AFX_MSG_MAP(CPersApp)
    ON_COMMAND(ID_APP_ABOUT, OnAppAbout)
        // NOTE - the ClassWizard will add and remove mapping macros here.
        //    DO NOT EDIT what you see in these blocks of generated code !
    //}}AFX_MSG_MAP
    // Standard file based document commands
    ON_COMMAND(ID_FILE_NEW, CWinApp::OnFileNew)
    ON_COMMAND(ID_FILE_OPEN, CWinApp::OnFileOpen)
END_MESSAGE_MAP()
```

Figure 4.14 Main source file, PERS.CPP (continues)

```
///////////////////////////////////////////////////////////////////////
// CPersApp construction

CPersApp::CPersApp()
{
    // TODO: add construction code here,
    // Place all significant initialization in InitInstance
}


///////////////////////////////////////////////////////////////////////
// The one and only CPersApp object

CPersApp NEAR theApp;

///////////////////////////////////////////////////////////////////////
// CPersApp initialization

BOOL CPersApp::InitInstance()
{
    // Standard initialization
    // If you are not using these features and wish to reduce the size
    //  of your final executable, you should remove from the following
    //  the specific initialization routines you do not need.

    SetDialogBkColor();        // set dialog background color to gray
    LoadStdProfileSettings();  // Load standard INI file options (including MRU)

    // Register the application's document templates.  Document templates
    //  serve as the connection between documents, frame windows and views.

    AddDocTemplate(new CSingleDocTemplate(IDR_MAINFRAME,
            RUNTIME_CLASS(CPersDoc),
            RUNTIME_CLASS(CMainFrame),      // main SDI frame window
            RUNTIME_CLASS(CPersView)));


    // simple command line parsing
    if (m_lpCmdLine[0] == '\0')
    {
        // create a new (empty) document
        OnFileNew();
    }
    else
    {
        // open an existing document
        OpenDocumentFile(m_lpCmdLine);
    }

    return TRUE;
}
```

Figure 4.14 (continued) Main source, PERS.CPP (continues)

```
/////////////////////////////////////////////////////////////////////////
// CAboutDlg dialog used for App About

class CAboutDlg : public CDialog
{
public:
   CAboutDlg();

// Dialog Data
   //{{AFX_DATA(CAboutDlg)
   enum { IDD = IDD_ABOUTBOX };
   //}}AFX_DATA

// Implementation
protected:
   virtual void DoDataExchange(CDataExchange* pDX);      // DDX/DDV support
   //{{AFX_MSG(CAboutDlg)
         // No message handlers
   //}}AFX_MSG
   DECLARE_MESSAGE_MAP()
};

CAboutDlg::CAboutDlg() : CDialog(CAboutDlg::IDD)
{
   //{{AFX_DATA_INIT(CAboutDlg)
   //}}AFX_DATA_INIT
}

void CAboutDlg::DoDataExchange(CDataExchange* pDX)
{
   CDialog::DoDataExchange(pDX);
   //{{AFX_DATA_MAP(CAboutDlg)
   //}}AFX_DATA_MAP
}

BEGIN_MESSAGE_MAP(CAboutDlg, CDialog)
   //{{AFX_MSG_MAP(CAboutDlg)
         // No message handlers
   //}}AFX_MSG_MAP
END_MESSAGE_MAP()

// App command to run the dialog
void CPersApp::OnAppAbout()
{
   CAboutDlg aboutDlg;
   aboutDlg.DoModal();
}


/////////////////////////////////////////////////////////////////////////
// CPersApp commands
```

Figure 4.14 (continued) Main source file, PERS.CPP

PERS.RC

The resources being used by the application are listed in the resource script file, PERS.RC (Figure 4.15). This file defines the icon to be used by the application, the menu, the accelerator keys, the definition of the About App dialogue box and the text strings to be used at various points in the application. The icon itself is in PERS.ICO, in the RES subdirectory.

```
//Microsoft App Studio generated resource script.
//
#include "resource.h"

#define APSTUDIO_READONLY_SYMBOLS
/////////////////////////////////////////////////////////////////////////////
//
// From TEXTINCLUDE 2
//
#include "afxres.h"


/////////////////////////////////////////////////////////////////////////////
#undef APSTUDIO_READONLY_SYMBOLS

#ifdef APSTUDIO_INVOKED


/////////////////////////////////////////////////////////////////////////////
//
// TEXTINCLUDE
//

1 TEXTINCLUDE DISCARDABLE
BEGIN
    "resource.h\0"
END

2 TEXTINCLUDE DISCARDABLE
BEGIN
    "#include ""afxres.h""\r\n"
    "\0"
END

3 TEXTINCLUDE DISCARDABLE
BEGIN
    "#include ""res\\pers.rc2""  // non-App Studio edited resources\r\n"
    "\r\n"
    "#include ""afxres.rc""  // Standard components\r\n"
    "\0"
END

/////////////////////////////////////////////////////////////////////////
#endif    // APSTUDIO_INVOKED
```

Figure 4.15 Resource script file, PERS.RC (continues)

```
/////////////////////////////////////////////////////////////////////////////
//
// Icon
//

IDR_MAINFRAME          ICON    DISCARDABLE      res\pers.ico


/////////////////////////////////////////////////////////////////////////////
//
// Menu
//


IDR_MAINFRAME MENU PRELOAD DISCARDABLE
BEGIN
    POPUP "&File"
    BEGIN
        MENUITEM "&New\tCtrl+N",              ID_FILE_NEW
        MENUITEM "&Open...\tCtrl+O",          ID_FILE_OPEN
        MENUITEM "&Save\tCtrl+S",             ID_FILE_SAVE
        MENUITEM "Save &As...",               ID_FILE_SAVE_AS
        MENUITEM SEPARATOR
        MENUITEM "Recent File",               ID_FILE_MRU_FILE1,GRAYED
        MENUITEM SEPARATOR
        MENUITEM "E&xit",                     ID_APP_EXIT
    END
    POPUP "&Edit"
    BEGIN
        MENUITEM "&Undo\tCtrl+Z",             ID_EDIT_UNDO
        MENUITEM SEPARATOR
        MENUITEM "Cu&t\tCtrl+X",              ID_EDIT_CUT
        MENUITEM "&Copy\tCtrl+C",             ID_EDIT_COPY
        MENUITEM "&Paste\tCtrl+V",            ID_EDIT_PASTE
    END
    POPUP "&Help"
    BEGIN
        MENUITEM "&About PERS...",        ID_APP_ABOUT
    END
END


/////////////////////////////////////////////////////////////////////////////
//
// Accelerator
//


IDR_MAINFRAME ACCELERATORS PRELOAD MOVEABLE
BEGIN
    "N",            ID_FILE_NEW,            VIRTKEY,CONTROL
```

Figure 4.15 (continued) Resource file, PERS.RC (continues)

```
    "O",              ID_FILE_OPEN,          VIRTKEY,CONTROL
    "S",              ID_FILE_SAVE,          VIRTKEY,CONTROL
    "Z",              ID_EDIT_UNDO,          VIRTKEY,CONTROL
    "X",              ID_EDIT_CUT,           VIRTKEY,CONTROL
    "C",              ID_EDIT_COPY,          VIRTKEY,CONTROL
    "V",              ID_EDIT_PASTE,         VIRTKEY,CONTROL
    VK_BACK,          ID_EDIT_UNDO,          VIRTKEY,ALT
    VK_DELETE,        ID_EDIT_CUT,           VIRTKEY,SHIFT
    VK_INSERT,        ID_EDIT_COPY,          VIRTKEY,CONTROL
    VK_INSERT,        ID_EDIT_PASTE,         VIRTKEY,SHIFT
    VK_F6,            ID_NEXT_PANE,          VIRTKEY
    VK_F6,            ID_PREV_PANE,          VIRTKEY,SHIFT
END


/////////////////////////////////////////////////////////////////////////
//
// Dialog
//

IDD_ABOUTBOX DIALOG DISCARDABLE  34, 22, 217, 55
CAPTION "About PERS"
STYLE DS_MODALFRAME | WS_POPUP | WS_CAPTION | WS_SYSMENU
FONT 8, "MS Sans Serif"
BEGIN
    ICON            IDR_MAINFRAME,IDC_STATIC,11,17,20,20
    LTEXT           "PERS Application Version 1.0",IDC_STATIC,40,10,119,8
    LTEXT           "Copyright \251 1993",IDC_STATIC,40,25,119,8
    DEFPUSHBUTTON   "OK",IDOK,176,6,32,14,WS_GROUP
END


/////////////////////////////////////////////////////////////////////////
//
// String Table
//

STRINGTABLE PRELOAD DISCARDABLE
BEGIN
    IDR_MAINFRAME            "PERS Windows Application\nPers\nPERS Document\nPERS
Files (*.per)\n.per"
END
STRINGTABLE PRELOAD DISCARDABLE
BEGIN
    AFX_IDS_APP_TITLE        "PERS Windows Application"
    AFX_IDS_IDLEMESSAGE      "Ready"
END
STRINGTABLE DISCARDABLE
BEGIN
    ID_INDICATOR_EXT         "EXT"
```

Figure 4.15 (continued) Resource file, PERS.RC (continues)

```
        ID_INDICATOR_CAPS          "CAP"
        ID_INDICATOR_NUM           "NUM"
        ID_INDICATOR_SCRL          "SCRL"
        ID_INDICATOR_OVR           "OVR"
        ID_INDICATOR_REC           "REC"
END


STRINGTABLE DISCARDABLE
BEGIN
        ID_FILE_NEW                "Create a new document"
        ID_FILE_OPEN               "Open an existing document"
        ID_FILE_CLOSE              "Close the active document"
        ID_FILE_SAVE               "Save the active document"
        ID_FILE_SAVE_AS            "Save the active document with a new name"
        ID_APP_ABOUT               "Display program information, version number and
copyright"
        ID_APP_EXIT                "Quit the application; prompts to save documents"
        ID_FILE_MRU_FILE1          "Open this document"
        ID_FILE_MRU_FILE2          "Open this document"
        ID_FILE_MRU_FILE3          "Open this document"
        ID_FILE_MRU_FILE4          "Open this document"
        ID_NEXT_PANE               "Switch to the next window pane"
        ID_PREV_PANE               "Switch back to the previous window pane"
        ID_EDIT_CLEAR              "Erase the selection"
        ID_EDIT_CLEAR_ALL          "Erase everything"
        ID_EDIT_COPY               "Copy the selection and put it on the Clipboard"
        ID_EDIT_CUT                "Cut the selection and put it on the Clipboard"
        ID_EDIT_FIND               "Find the specified text"
        ID_EDIT_PASTE              "Insert Clipboard contents"
        ID_EDIT_REPEAT             "Repeat the last action"
        ID_EDIT_REPLACE            "Replace specific text with different text"
        ID_EDIT_SELECT_ALL         "Select the entire document"
        ID_EDIT_UNDO               "Undo the last action"
        ID_EDIT_REDO               "Redo the previously undone action"
END


STRINGTABLE DISCARDABLE
BEGIN
        AFX_IDS_SCSIZE             "Change the window size"
        AFX_IDS_SCMOVE             "Change the window position"
        AFX_IDS_SCMINIMIZE         "Reduce the window to an icon"
        AFX_IDS_SCMAXIMIZE         "Enlarge the window to full size"
        AFX_IDS_SCNEXTWINDOW       "Switch to the next document window"
        AFX_IDS_SCPREVWINDOW       "Switch to the previous document window"
        AFX_IDS_SCCLOSE            "Close the active window and prompts to save the docu-
ments"
        AFX_IDS_SCRESTORE          "Restore the window to normal size"
        AFX_IDS_SCTASKLIST         "Activate Task List"
END
```

Figure 4.15 (continued) Resource file, PERS.RC (continues)

```
#ifndef APSTUDIO_INVOKED
/////////////////////////////////////////////////////////////////////////////
//
// From TEXTINCLUDE 3
//

#include "res\pers.rc2"  // non-App Studio edited resources

#include "afxres.rc"  // Standard components

/////////////////////////////////////////////////////////////////////////////
#endif    // not APSTUDIO_INVOKED
```

Figure 4.15 (continued) Resource script file, PERS.RC

This file should not be edited normally but will be updated by App Studio. Other resources can be added manually if necessary in PERS.RC2, in the RES subdirectory (Figure 4.16).

```
//
// PERS.RC2 - resources App Studio does not edit directly
//

#ifdef APSTUDIO_INVOKED
    #error this file is not editable by App Studio
#endif //APSTUDIO_INVOKED

/////////////////////////////////////////////////////////////////////////////
// Version stamp for this .EXE

#include "ver.h"

VS_VERSION_INFO      VERSIONINFO
  FILEVERSION        1,0,0,1
  PRODUCTVERSION     1,0,0,1
  FILEFLAGSMASK      VS_FFI_FILEFLAGSMASK
#ifdef _DEBUG
  FILEFLAGS          VS_FF_DEBUG|VS_FF_PRIVATEBUILD|VS_FF_PRERELEASE
#else
  FILEFLAGS          0 // final version
#endif
  FILEOS             VOS_DOS_WINDOWS16
  FILETYPE           VFT_APP
  FILESUBTYPE        0  // not used
```

Figure 4.16 User-defined resources, PERS.RC2 (continues)

```
BEGIN
    BLOCK "StringFileInfo"
    BEGIN
        BLOCK "040904E4" // Lang=US English, CharSet=Windows Multilingual
        BEGIN
            VALUE "CompanyName",      "\0"
            VALUE "FileDescription", "PERS MFC Application\0"
            VALUE "FileVersion",      "1.0.001\0"
            VALUE "InternalName",     "PERS\0"
            VALUE "LegalCopyright",   "\0"
            VALUE "LegalTrademarks", "\0"
            VALUE "OriginalFilename","PERS.EXE\0"
            VALUE "ProductName",      "PERS\0"
            VALUE "ProductVersion",   "1.0.001\0"
        END
    END
    BLOCK "VarFileInfo"
    BEGIN
        VALUE "Translation", 0x409, 1252
                // English language (0x409) and the Windows ANSI codepage (1252)
    END
END

/////////////////////////////////////////////////////////////////////////
// Add additional manually edited resources here...

/////////////////////////////////////////////////////////////////////////
```

Figure 4.16 (continued) User-defined resources, PERS.RC2

Other PERS.* Files

All other PERS.* files are either used by the Visual C++ tools for developing the application or were created when the application was built.

MAINFRM.*

The MAINFRM.H and MAINFRM.CPP files define the class CMainFrame, derived from CFrameWnd (Figures 4.17 and 4.18). From this class, the main frame window is created. This is the window within which all other screen objects will be displayed.

Initially, there is no special action or appearance specified for the main window. Therefore the default functions of CFrameWnd are used, with the result that the window has all the standard behaviour that you would expect of a window: resizing, moving, control-menu box and so on. The new class, CMainFrame, has an empty message map, and a constructor and destructor that do nothing, plus some diagnostic routines.

```
// mainfrm.h : interface of the CMainFrame class
//
/////////////////////////////////////////////////////////////////////////

class CMainFrame : public CFrameWnd
{
protected: // create from serialization only
   CMainFrame();
   DECLARE_DYNCREATE(CMainFrame)

// Attributes
public:

// Operations
public:

// Implementation
public:
   virtual ~CMainFrame();
#ifdef _DEBUG
   virtual      void AssertValid() const;
   virtual      void Dump(CDumpContext& dc) const;
#endif



// Generated message map functions
protected:
   //{{AFX_MSG(CMainFrame)
        // NOTE - the ClassWizard will add and remove member functions here.
        //    DO NOT EDIT what you see in these blocks of generated code !
   //}}AFX_MSG
   DECLARE_MESSAGE_MAP()
};

/////////////////////////////////////////////////////////////////////////
```

Figure 4.17 Main frame header, MAINFRM.H

```
// mainfrm.cpp : implementation of the CMainFrame class
//

#include "stdafx.h"
#include "pers.h"
#include "mainfrm.h"

#ifdef _DEBUG
#undef THIS_FILE
static char BASED_CODE THIS_FILE[] = __FILE__;
#endif

/////////////////////////////////////////////////////////////////////////
// CMainFrame

IMPLEMENT_DYNCREATE(CMainFrame, CFrameWnd)

BEGIN_MESSAGE_MAP(CMainFrame, CFrameWnd)
   //{{AFX_MSG_MAP(CMainFrame)
        // NOTE - the ClassWizard will add and remove mapping macros here.
        //    DO NOT EDIT what you see in these blocks of generated code !
   //}}AFX_MSG_MAP
END_MESSAGE_MAP()

/////////////////////////////////////////////////////////////////////////
// CMainFrame construction/destruction

CMainFrame::CMainFrame()
{
   // TODO: add member initialization code here
}

CMainFrame::~CMainFrame()
{
}

/////////////////////////////////////////////////////////////////////////
// CMainFrame diagnostics

#ifdef _DEBUG
void CMainFrame::AssertValid() const
{
   CFrameWnd::AssertValid();
}

void CMainFrame::Dump(CDumpContext& dc) const
{
   CFrameWnd::Dump(dc);
}

#endif //_DEBUG
```

Figure 4.18 Main frame source file, MAINFRM.CPP

PERSDOC.*

The data for the application is handled by the CPersDoc class, which is derived from CDocument. This class needs instructions to be added for loading and saving data; these instructions should be placed in the Serialize function, which is used for both operations.

The CPersDoc class and its functions are declared in PERSDOC.H and defined in PERSDOC.CPP (Figures 4.19 and 4.20).

```
// persdoc.h : interface of the CPersDoc class
//
/////////////////////////////////////////////////////////////////////////

class CPersDoc : public CDocument
{
protected: // create from serialization only
   CPersDoc();
   DECLARE_DYNCREATE(CPersDoc)

// Attributes
public:

// Operations
public:

// Implementation
public:
   virtual ~CPersDoc();
   virtual void Serialize(CArchive& ar);      // overridden for document i/o
#ifdef _DEBUG
   virtual     void AssertValid() const;
   virtual     void Dump(CDumpContext& dc) const;
#endif
protected:
   virtual     BOOL  OnNewDocument();

// Generated message map functions
protected:
   //{{AFX_MSG(CPersDoc)
        // NOTE - the ClassWizard will add and remove member functions here.
        //    DO NOT EDIT what you see in these blocks of generated code !
   //}}AFX_MSG
   DECLARE_MESSAGE_MAP()
};


/////////////////////////////////////////////////////////////////////////
```

Figure 4.19 Document header file, PERSDOC.H

```
// persdoc.cpp : implementation of the CPersDoc class
//

#include "stdafx.h"
#include "pers.h"

#include "persdoc.h"

#ifdef _DEBUG
#undef THIS_FILE
static char BASED_CODE THIS_FILE[] = __FILE__;
#endif

/////////////////////////////////////////////////////////////////////////////
// CPersDoc

IMPLEMENT_DYNCREATE(CPersDoc, CDocument)

BEGIN_MESSAGE_MAP(CPersDoc, CDocument)
    //{{AFX_MSG_MAP(CPersDoc)
        // NOTE - the ClassWizard will add and remove mapping macros here.
        //     DO NOT EDIT what you see in these blocks of generated code !
    //}}AFX_MSG_MAP
END_MESSAGE_MAP()

/////////////////////////////////////////////////////////////////////////////
// CPersDoc construction/destruction

CPersDoc::CPersDoc()
{
    // TODO: add one-time construction code here
}

CPersDoc::~CPersDoc()
{
}

BOOL CPersDoc::OnNewDocument()
{
    if (!CDocument::OnNewDocument())
        return FALSE;
    // TODO: add reinitialization code here
    // (SDI documents will reuse this document)
    return TRUE;
}

/////////////////////////////////////////////////////////////////////////////
// CPersDoc serialization

void CPersDoc::Serialize(CArchive& ar)
{
```

Figure 4.20 Document source file, PERSDOC.CPP (continues)

```
    if (ar.IsStoring())
    {
         // TODO: add storing code here
    }
    else
    {
         // TODO: add loading code here
    }
}



////////////////////////////////////////////////////////////////////////
// CPersDoc diagnostics

#ifdef _DEBUG
void CPersDoc::AssertValid() const
{
   CDocument::AssertValid();
}

void CPersDoc::Dump(CDumpContext& dc) const
{
   CDocument::Dump(dc);
}

#endif //_DEBUG

////////////////////////////////////////////////////////////////////////
// CPersDoc commands
```

Figure 4.20 (continued) Document source file, PERSDOC.CPP

PERSVIEW.*

The application data is made available to the user through the CPersView class, derived from CView. This class displays data in a child window which fills the *client area* of the frame window: that part within its border, below the menu bar (excluding the toolbar and status area, if any).

The main function is OnDraw, which is used to draw graphics or print text on the view. The class and its functions are declared in PERSVIEW.H and defined in PERSVIEW.CPP (Figures 4.21 and 4.22).

Other Files

The STDAFX files contain standard include files, which define the many other classes that are needed for defining objects such as command buttons, text boxes and scroll bars.

The README.TXT file gives a brief description of the files created by AppWizard.

Other files are used by Visual C++ to build the application or are for debugging purposes. Finally, of course, there is the executable file that results from the compilation process, PERS.EXE.

```
// persview.h : interface of the CPersView class
//
/////////////////////////////////////////////////////////////////////////////

class CPersView : public CView
{
protected: // create from serialization only
   CPersView();
   DECLARE_DYNCREATE(CPersView)

// Attributes
public:
   CPersDoc* GetDocument();

// Operations
public:

// Implementation
public:
   virtual ~CPersView();
   virtual void OnDraw(CDC* pDC);  // overridden to draw this view
#ifdef _DEBUG
   virtual void AssertValid() const;
   virtual void Dump(CDumpContext& dc) const;
#endif


// Generated message map functions
protected:
   //{{AFX_MSG(CPersView)
        // NOTE - the ClassWizard will add and remove member functions here.
        //    DO NOT EDIT what you see in these blocks of generated code !
   //}}AFX_MSG
   DECLARE_MESSAGE_MAP()
};

#ifndef _DEBUG // debug version in persview.cpp
inline CPersDoc* CPersView::GetDocument()
   { return (CPersDoc*) m_pDocument; }
#endif


/////////////////////////////////////////////////////////////////////////////
```

Figure 4.21 View header file, PERSVIEW.H

```
// persview.cpp : implementation of the CPersView class
//

#include "stdafx.h"
#include "pers.h"

#include "persdoc.h"
#include "persview.h"

#ifdef _DEBUG
#undef THIS_FILE
static char BASED_CODE THIS_FILE[] = __FILE__;
#endif

/////////////////////////////////////////////////////////////////////////////
// CPersView

IMPLEMENT_DYNCREATE(CPersView, CView)

BEGIN_MESSAGE_MAP(CPersView, CView)
    //{{AFX_MSG_MAP(CPersView)
        // NOTE - the ClassWizard will add and remove mapping macros here.
        //     DO NOT EDIT what you see in these blocks of generated code !
    //}}AFX_MSG_MAP
END_MESSAGE_MAP()

/////////////////////////////////////////////////////////////////////////////
// CPersView construction/destruction

CPersView::CPersView()
{
    // TODO: add construction code here
}

CPersView::~CPersView()
{
}

/////////////////////////////////////////////////////////////////////////////
// CPersView drawing

void CPersView::OnDraw(CDC* pDC)
{
    CPersDoc* pDoc = GetDocument();

    // TODO: add draw code here
}
```

Figure 4.22 View source file, PERSVIEW.CPP (continues)

```
///////////////////////////////////////////////////////////////////////////
// CPersView diagnostics

#ifdef _DEBUG
void CPersView::AssertValid() const
{
    CView::AssertValid();
}

void CPersView::Dump(CDumpContext& dc) const
{
    CView::Dump(dc);
}

CPersDoc* CPersView::GetDocument() // non-debug version is inline
{
    ASSERT(m_pDocument-IsKindOf(RUNTIME_CLASS(CPersDoc)));
    return (CPersDoc*) m_pDocument;
}

#endif //_DEBUG


///////////////////////////////////////////////////////////////////////////
// CPersView message handlers
```

Figure 4.22 (continued) View source file, PERSVIEW.CPP

BORLAND C++

Whether you are programming in Borland C++ or Pascal With Objects, you will probably elect to use ObjectWindows. This framework provides a hierarchy of classes that can be used as a starting point for the application, in much the same way as the Microsoft Foundation Class Library.

Like Visual C++, there is an IDE to do much of the hard work for you. The class structure is provided and then it is up to you to build up the actual C++ or Pascal program.

Each application must have the same basic structure. First, an *application object* must be defined; this object carries out the following tasks:

* Creates and displays the application's main window

* Receives and processes Windows messages

* Ends the application cleanly

ObjectWindows supplies a TApplication class from which the new application class must be derived. At the very least, the new class will redefine the InitMainWindow virtual function, which creates the main window object for the application.

The main window must be an instance of the ObjectWindows class, TWindow, or a class derived from TWindow.

To provide a direct comparison between Borland C++ and Visual C++, the same example is used.

The general procedures for creating a C++ ObjectWindows application are as follows:

1   Create the development directory (e.g. C:\OOP\PERS2).

2   The starting point should always be an existing program. Copy all the relevant files to the development directory. For example, to use the Borland STEP01 application as the basis, copy and rename the source file (from the DOS prompt) as follows:

```
copy c:\borlandc\owl\examples\steps\step1.cpp c:\oop\pers2\pers2.*
```

3   Run Borland C++ by clicking on the BCW icon (Figure 4.23). The main window is displayed (Figure 4.24). This contains a menu, toolbar and status line, with a text window ready to display a CPP source file.

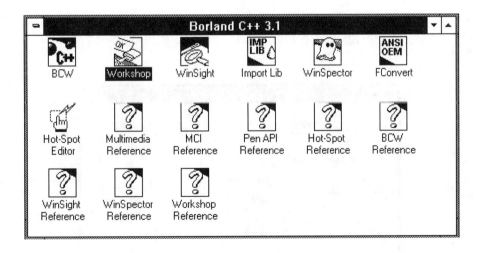

Figure 4.23 Borland C++ group

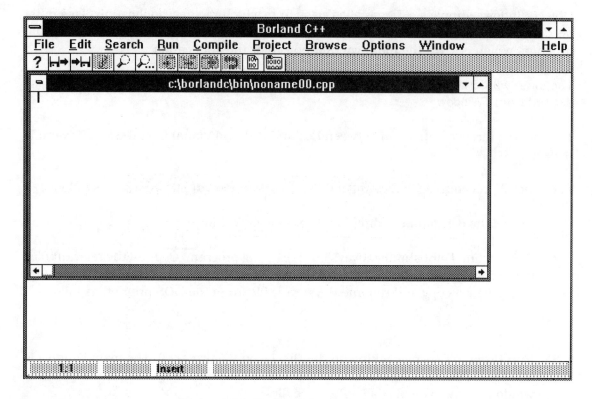

Figure 4.24 Borland C++ main window

4   Select Project|Open Project and set up the new project by choosing the development directory and giving the project a name (Figure 4.25). Click on OK. The project file is created.

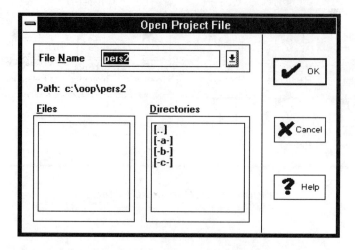

Figure 4.25 Opening a project

5 Identify the files to be included in the project, using Project | Add Item (Figure 4.26). Click on the source files and the Add button; click on Done when all files have been selected. The following files are needed:

> pers2.cpp   (in the current directory)
> c:\borlandc\owl\lib\owl.def

The files are listed in a box at the bottom of the window (Figure 4.27).

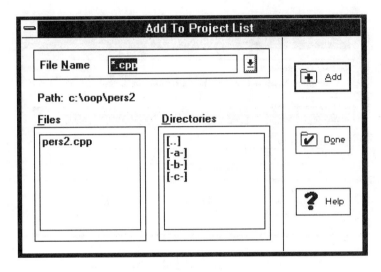

Figure 4.26 Adding files to the project

File Name	Lines	Code	Data	Location
pers2.cpp	26	183	61	.
owl.def	n/a	n/a	n/a	..\..\borlandc\owl\lib

Figure 4.27 List of files in the project

6   Using Options|Directories, identify the ObjectWindows include directories. The following directories are needed:

Include Directories	Library Directories
..\..\borlandc\owl\include	..\..\borlandc\owl\lib
..\..\borlandc\classlib\include	..\..\borlandc\classlib\lib
..\..\borlandc\include	..\..\borlandc\lib

The directories should be separated with semi-colons in each case (Figure 4.28).

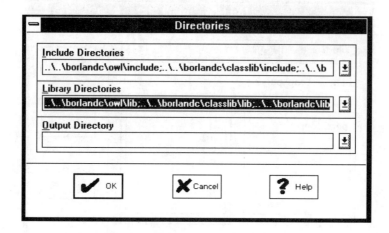

Figure 4.28 Include and library directories

7   Use File|Open to open a window containing the source file (Figure 4.29) and make any changes that are necessary. (At this stage, all you need do is change the comment at the top of the program and the text for the title bar.) Save the changes.

```
c:\oop\pers2\pers2.cpp

// ObjectWindows - (C) Copyright 1992 by Borland International

#include <owl.h>

class TMyApp : public TApplication
{
public:
    TMyApp(LPSTR AName, HINSTANCE hInstance, HINSTANCE hPrevInstan
        LPSTR lpCmdLine, int nCmdShow)
        : TApplication(AName, hInstance, hPrevInstance, lpCmdLine, n
    virtual void InitMainWindow();
};

void TMyApp::InitMainWindow()
{
    MainWindow = new TWindow(NULL, Name);
```

Figure 4.29 Source file window

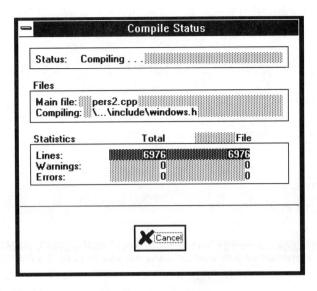

Figure 4.30 Compile status

You can build the .EXE file and run the program in a single step with Run | Run (or press CTRL-F9). A status window is displayed as the compile proceeds (Figure 4.30). Compilation is much faster than that of Visual C++.

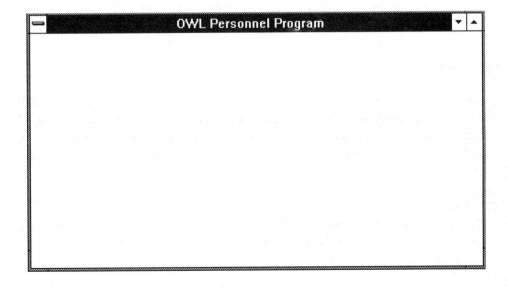

Figure 4.31 Minimal Borland C++ program

A blank window is displayed (Figure 4.31). As for the minimal Visual C++ application, this program follows all the usual Windows rules:

- The window can be resized, minimised, maximised and moved.

- There is a standard control-menu box.

- ALT-F4 (or the Close option) ends the application.

A new program item can be set up for the application, using one of the default Program Manager icons (Figure 4.32).

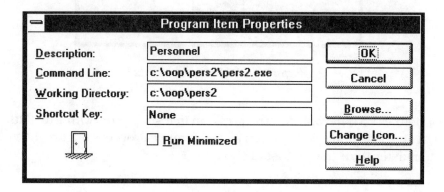

Figure 4.32   Creating a program item

Program Files

This version of C++ produces a much more modest set of files, compared with those of Visual C++. The development directory contains only six files, occupying just 700 Kb. The EXE file is 160 Kb, compared with the 1170 Kb for the Visual C++ version (though bear in mind that that version also includes a set of default menus and an About dialogue box).

PERS2.PRJ
The project file, PERS.PRJ, holds details of the files that make up the application and their locations. This file is maintained automatically by the system.

PERS2.CPP
This is the main source file for the project (Figure 4.33). A new application class is defined, TPersApp, derived from ObjectWindows' TApplication class. One function, InitMainWindow, is redefined for this class. This function generates the main window when the application is run.

```
// Minimal ObjectWindows program

#include <owl.h>

class TPersApp : public TApplication
{
public:
  TPersApp(LPSTR AName, HINSTANCE hInstance, HINSTANCE hPrevInstance,
    LPSTR lpCmdLine, int nCmdShow)
    : TApplication(AName, hInstance, hPrevInstance, lpCmdLine, nCmdShow) {};
  virtual void InitMainWindow();
};

void TPersApp::InitMainWindow()
{
  MainWindow = new TWindow(NULL, Name);
}

int PASCAL WinMain(HINSTANCE hInstance, HINSTANCE hPrevInstance,
  LPSTR lpCmdLine, int nCmdShow)
{
  TPersApp PersApp("OWL Personnel Program", hInstance, hPrevInstance,
             lpCmdLine, nCmdShow);
  PersApp.Run();
  return PersApp.Status;
}
```

Figure 4.33 Minimal source file, PERS2.CPP

The source file also contains the WinMain function. This function starts by creating an instance of the TPersApp class, PersApp, passing to it the title bar text and other necessary parameters. The Run function for the new object is called, resulting in the constructor function being invoked and the window being displayed. When the application ends a status value is returned.

Other Files
PERS2.DSK is the 'desktop' file, holding details of which windows are currently open, and other information relating to the way in which C++ is being used. The other files that are created are used in the compilation process.

BORLAND PASCAL WITH OBJECTS

The creation of a Pascal program using ObjectWindows follows very similar lines to that of the C++ application. The same classes are set up and the initial program has a very similar structure.

The general procedures are as follows:

1   Create the development directory (e.g. C:\OOP\PERS2P).

2   Start by copying an existing program, such as one of the example files. For instance, to use the STEP01 example, copy and rename the file as follows:

```
copy c:\bp\examples\docdemos\owl\step01a.pas c:\oop\per2p\pers2p.*
```

3   Run Borland Pascal by clicking on the BPW icon (Figure 4.34). The main window is displayed (Figure 4.35). The screen layout is similar to that of Borland C++.

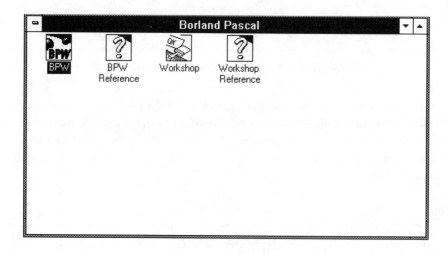

Figure 4.34 Borland Pascal group

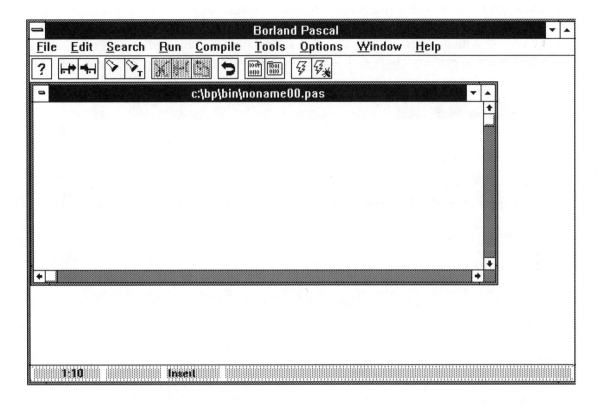

Figure 4.35 Borland Pascal main window

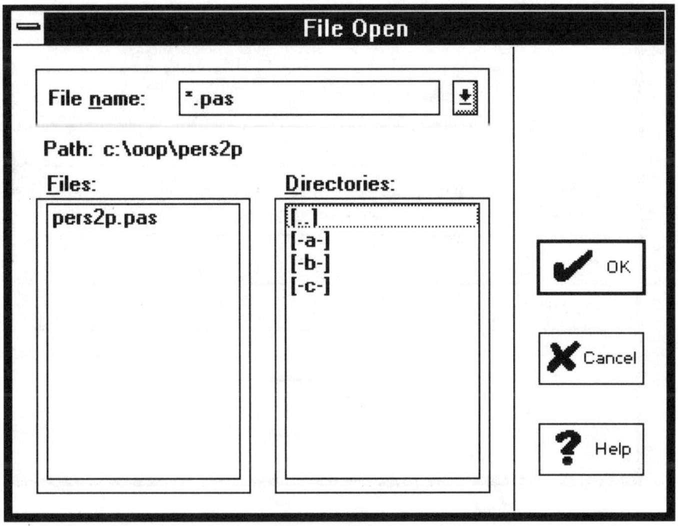

Figure 4.36 Opening a source file

4   There is no need to use projects in Borland Pascal. Each application has a primary Pascal file, which identifies the other files that are needed. Open the source file with File | Open (Figure 4.36). The file is displayed in a new window (Figure 4.37). Make any necessary changes (the comments and title bar text) and save the file.

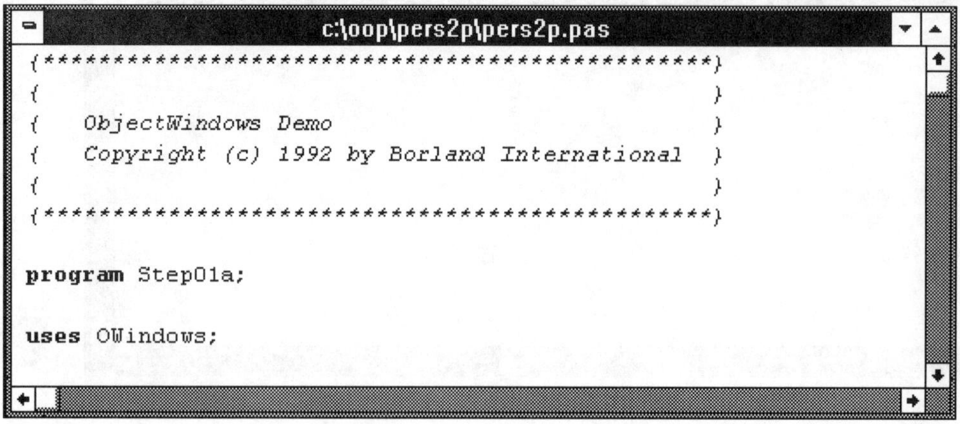

Figure 4.37 Source file window

The .EXE file is built and run with Run | Run (or press CTRL-F9). A status window is displayed during the very fast compilation (Figure 4.38) and the application looks just like the C++ version (Figure 4.39). The application behaves in the usual way and a Program Manager icon can be set up for it.

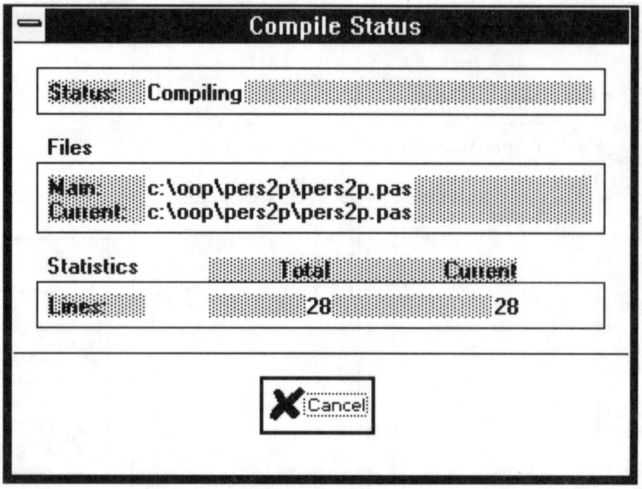

Figure 4.38 Compile status

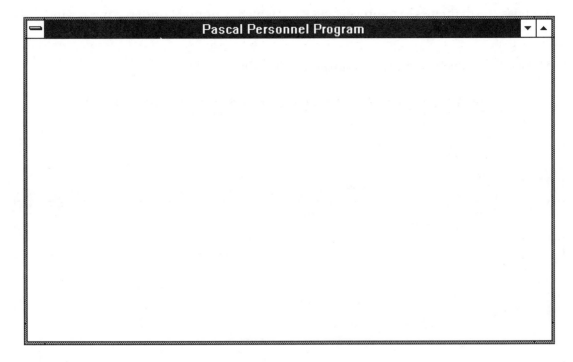

Figure 4.39 Minimal Pascal program

Program Files

These files are even more compact than the C++ equivalent. There are only two files:

- PERS2P.PAS is the source file and is only a few hundred bytes long.

- PERS2P.EXE is the executable file and is just 14 Kb.

The source file has the same structure as its C++ counterpart (Figure 4.40). The program name is identified at the top of the program, following which the uses keyword lists the other files to be included in the project. These are the equivalent of the C++ library files.

TPersApp is created as a new type descended from TApplication. Types in Pascal are the equivalent of C++ classes. The InitMainWindow procedure is declared. In the following section of the program, this procedure is defined. The new window object is created and a title for the window is given.

Finally, the application object, PersApp, is created as an instance of type TPersApp. Three procedures are called:

- Init is the constructor function; a name is supplied for the application.

- **Run** is the main message-processing loop, which continues until the main window is closed.

- **Done** is the destructor, which tidies up after the application.

This source file will be extended in a similar way to that of Borland C++.

```
{ * * * * * * * * * * * * * * * * * * * * * * * * * * * * * * * * * * * * * * * * * * * * * * * * * }
{                                                  }
{    ObjectWindows Minimal Program                 }
{                                                  }
{ * * * * * * * * * * * * * * * * * * * * * * * * * * * * * * * * * * * * * * * * * * * * * * * * * }

program pers2p;

uses OWindows;

type
  TPersApp = object(TApplication)
    procedure InitMainWindow; virtual;
  end;

procedure TPersApp.InitMainWindow;
begin
  MainWindow := New(PWindow, Init(nil, 'Pascal Personnel Program'));
end;

var
  PersApp: TPersApp;

begin
  PersApp.Init('Pers2p');
  PersApp.Run;
  PersApp.Done;
end.
```

Figure 4.40 Minimal Borland Pascal source file, PERS2P.CPP

VISUAL BASIC

In many respects, Visual Basic is like a simplified form of Visual C++. To start with, there is no complicated procedure to set up the project and the first window; these are provided automatically when Visual Basic is run. All you have to do is change the names, make any necessary changes and then run the program. The steps needed to reach the same stage as for the other environments above are as follows:

1   Create the development directory (e.g. C:\OOP\PERS3).

2   Click on the Visual Basic icon (4.41).

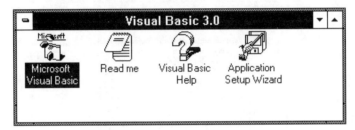

Figure 4.41 Visual Basic group

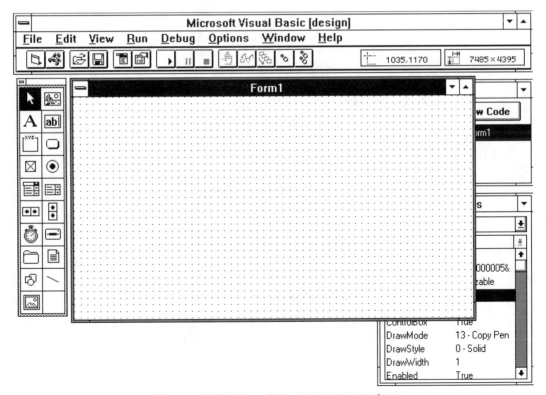

Figure 4.42 Visual Basic main window

3   The Visual Basic screen has a number of elements (Figure 4.42). At the top of the screen is the menu bar and toolbar. On the left is the toolbox, for adding controls to the window. The main part of the screen is taken up by a window titled 'Form1'; this is the main window for the new application. Behind this are two other boxes (Figure 4.43): the Project window, which shows the components of the project, and the Properties window, which sets attributes of windows and controls.

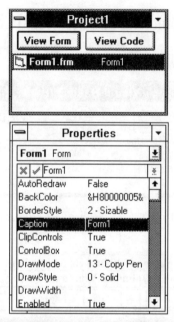

Figure 4.43 Project and Properties windows

4   In the Properties window, click on the Caption line and type a new name (Figure 4.44). As you do so, the name appears in the Form1 title bar.

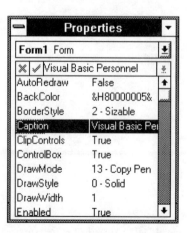

Figure 4.44 Changing the form title

5   Use File I Save File As to save the first window with a more imaginative name (Figure 4.45). Then use File I Save Project As to give the project a name (Figure 4.46). Store both files in the development directory. You can use the same name for both files; extensions of FRM and MAK are added automatically.

6   Run the program, with the Run I Start option.

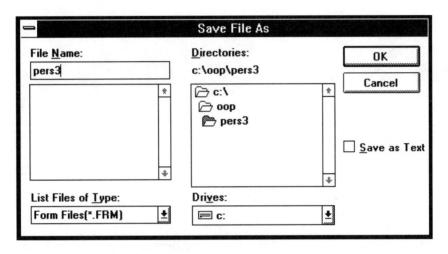

Figure 4.45 Saving the form

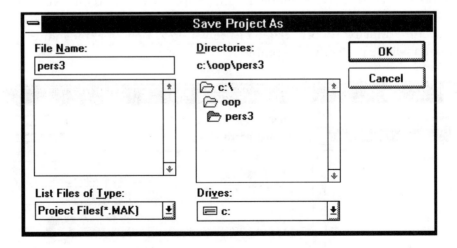

Figure 4.46 Saving the project

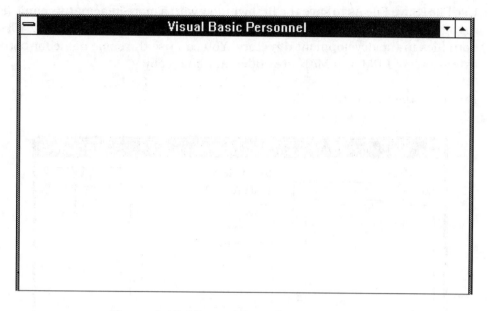

Figure 4.47 Minimal Visual Basic program

The application runs instantly and the main window is displayed (Figure 4.47). This window behaves exactly as expected.

Reaching this stage takes a fraction of the time required in the other environments, and results in no code at all being available to the programmer. Therefore, you cannot make silly mistakes in coding; but neither can you make subtle changes to the window that are not accounted for by its properties of the window. However, for many applications this approach will be perfectly acceptable.

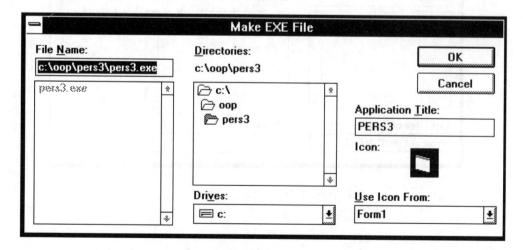

Figure 4.48 Creating a .EXE file

To create a .EXE file, use File | Make EXE File, giving it a filename of PERS3.EXE and the default Visual Basic icon (Figure 4.48). This program can then be run from Program Manager.

Visual Basic produces only three files for the minimal application:

- PERS3.FRM, holding details of the main window

- PERS3.MAK, the project file

- PERS3.EXE, the executable file

In all, these files take only 6 Kb of disk space.

5 | Windows and Dialogue Boxes

The basis of any Windows application is, not surprisingly, its windows and the actions that can be carried out within them. More surprisingly perhaps is the definition of the term 'window' and the impact of that on Windows programming.

This chapter looks at the logic behind window classes and their use in a project.

TYPES OF WINDOW

To most people, a 'window' is a rectangular area on the screen, with all the usual features (control-menu box, title bar, minimise and maximise buttons, scroll bars and so on). However, theoretically at least, all visual interface elements – windows, dialogue boxes and controls – are a type of window.

This is because all these elements are derived from the same base class: CWnd for the Microsoft Foundation Class Library and TWindow in ObjectWindows. Even though they are redefined in some way at each stage of the class hierarchy, they still all have some common features that can be traced back to their common ancestry. This is analogous to the natural world where trees, birds and people are all life forms, descended from a common beginning.

To avoid confusion, discussion in the remainder of this book will assumed that the term 'window' refers to the common-sense idea of a window: a rectangle displayed on screen, containing elements such as control-menu box, title bar, minimise and maximise buttons, scroll bars and interior controls.

In order to classify as a *window*, an object should have the ability to resize itself in some way:

- Resizing by dragging the window borders or corners

- Minimising to an icon or maximising to full-screen via the minimise and maximise buttons

- Showing a different portion of its client area by use of horizontal or vertical scroll bars

If a window can do none of these things, then it is probably a dialogue box. Of course, the taxonomy of windows objects is not particularly important in practical terms except that it tells you what sort of actions you can achieve with an object and what events it will respond to.

Ultimately, the distinction between a window and a dialogue box depends on the class from which it is derived. If it is a descendent of CWnd or TWindow it is a window; if from CDialog or TDialog then it is a dialogue box.

OVERLAPPING AND TILING

The fact that windows can be resized, either by the user or from within a program, results in a number of options being available for changing the display.

Overlapping

The user can drag a window anywhere on the screen, including over the top of another window. Thus windows can be made to *overlap*. The only restriction is for MDI child windows, which must remain within the boundaries of the MDI parent window. Within a program, you can offer a *cascade* option in one of the menus (usually a 'Windows' menu), which will reposition the windows so that the top left-hand corner of successive windows is a fixed distance below and to the right of the one above. This is achieved quite simply by changing the properties of the MDI child windows.

Tiling

Similarly, the user can vary the positions and sizes of the windows so that they fit neatly side-by-side; this same effect can be achieved within the program by offering a *tile* option. All you have to do is change the width, height and position of the windows so that they fit within the parent window's client area.

ACTIVE WINDOWS

At any time, only one of the windows on the display will be active. The *active* window is the one in which the user is currently working. It is indicated as active by the colour of the title bar. The active window is also said to have the *focus*.

Generally, the user can move the focus from one window to another by clicking on some other part of the screen, by closing the window or by opening another window. When a window is closed, the focus automatically transfers to another window. When a window is opened, it automatically receives the focus. In the case of modal dialogue boxes (as described below), the user cannot move the focus from the window until the dialogue box is closed.

The focus can also be shifted within a program by setting the properties of a window so that it has the focus.

When a window receives the focus (either as a result of user action or because the program directs it), a number of things happen:

- The window receiving the focus is brought to the top of the display.

- The title bar changes colour on both the window receiving the focus and (unless it is being closed) the window losing the focus.

- A LostFocus event is generated for the window losing the focus. (If the window is being closed, any procedure associated with the LostFocus event is executed before the window is closed.)

- A GotFocus event is generated for the window that is becoming active.

Therefore a program can build in a reaction to these events and specify actions for when a user starts to use a window and moves away from it.

THE MAIN WINDOW

Every Windows application must have a main window, which is displayed automatically when the application is run. Closing the window should have the knock-on effect of closing all other open windows and clearing up memory, before returning to the Program Manager.

The Visual C++ template files deal with the setting up the main window automatically. A new class, CMainFrame, is derived from CFrameWnd in MAINFRM.H; an object from this class becomes the main window for the application.

For ObjectWindows, the minimal program described in Chapter 4 created the main window as a TWindow object. However, the main window needs to behave slightly differently to the defaults offered by TWindow; for example, it must have a menu system attached. Therefore, a new window class, TPersWindow, must be derived from TWindow and the main window object must be an instance of this new class. The way in which the program is affected is shown in Figure 5.1 for Borland C++ and Figure 5.2 for Borland Pascal. Note that for the Pascal program additional units must be declared in the uses statement.

```
// PERS2 ObjectWindows program

#include <owl.h>

class TPersApp : public TApplication
{
public:
  TPersApp(LPSTR AName, HINSTANCE hInstance, HINSTANCE hPrevInstance,
    LPSTR lpCmdLine, int nCmdShow)
    : TApplication(AName, hInstance, hPrevInstance, lpCmdLine, nCmdShow) {};
  virtual void InitMainWindow();
};

// New window derivation here
_CLASSDEF(TMyWindow)
class TPersWindow : public TWindow
{
public:
  TPersWindow(PTWindowsObject AParent, LPSTR ATitle)
    : TWindow(AParent, ATitle) {};
};

void TPersApp::InitMainWindow()
{
//Main Window object is instance of derived class
  MainWindow = new TPersWindow(NULL, Name);
}

int PASCAL WinMain(HINSTANCE hInstance, HINSTANCE hPrevInstance,
  LPSTR lpCmdLine, int nCmdShow)
{
  TPersApp PersApp("OWL Personnel Program", hInstance, hPrevInstance,
              lpCmdLine, nCmdShow);
  PersApp.Run();
  return PersApp.Status;
}
```

Figure 5.1 Borland C++ program with new window class

```
{*************************************************}
{                                                 }
{    ObjectWindows Personnel Program              }
{                                                 }
{*************************************************}

program pers2p;

{ Identify new library files }
uses WinTypes, WinProcs, OWindows;

type
  { Declare pointer to window and new window type }
  PPersWindow = ^TPersWIndow;
  TPersWindow = object(TWindow)
    { Message handlers will be declared here }
  end;
  TPersApp = object(TApplication)
    procedure InitMainWindow; virtual;
  end;

procedure TPersApp.InitMainWindow;
begin
  { Define instance of new window type }
  MainWindow := New(PPersWindow, Init(nil, 'Pascal Personnel Program'));
end;

var
  PersApp: TPersApp;

begin
  PersApp.Init('Pers2p');
  PersApp.Run;
  PersApp.Done;
end.
```

Figure 5.2 Borland Pascal program with new window class

PARENT AND CHILD WINDOWS

The main window is linked to the application object in such a way that closing the main window has the effect of closing down the program. In a similar way, all other interface elements are related in some way to the main window. There may be other windows that are generated by actions in the main window; these are said to be *child* windows and the main window is their *parent* window. Closing the main window results in all the child windows being closed.

Similarly, any dialogue box is a child window of some other window; any control is a child window of a dialogue box or window. (Note that here the term 'window' is used in its broader sense, meaning an interface element.) In this way, there is a 'family' relationship between all interface elements in the application. An element can be the child of one element and the parent of another. Closing a parent window automatically closes all its child windows (and its child's child windows, and so on).

Do not confuse the parent-chlid relationship with the class hierarchy; a child window is not necessarily below its parent in the hierarchy and need not inherit any of its appearance or behaviour. Nor should this relationship be confused with the principles of MDI windows, for which a special parent-child relationship exists (see Chapter 15).

Every interface element has as one of its data members the identity of its parent; similarly, any element holds a list of its child windows (if any). Each interface element has a unique ID value that is used to link windows together in the parent-child relationships.

PROPERTIES

The appearance of any window and its behaviour are determined by the window's properties. The *properties* are a list of values that define the window. These values are also sometimes referred to as *style attributes*. Properties for a window include the following:

- The (X,Y) co-ordinates of the window's top left-hand corner in relation to the screen (for the main window) or the parent window

- The width and height of the window

- Whether or not it has minimise and maximise buttons, horizontal and vertical scroll bars; its initial state (minimised, maximised or normal size)

- The type of window: overlapping, pop-up, child, scrollable and so on

All of the properties are held as data members in the class definition. The values of the properties will be different for each instance of the class, i.e. for each object. These values change during the course of the program:

- When the user resizes the window the width and height data values change, moving the window changes its co-ordinates, etc.

- The program can change the property values, resulting in the window being redrawn according to the new properties.

Typically, the selection of an option by the user will result in the program changing properties; for example, clicking on a Tile option will result in the program changing the co-ordinates, height and width of each child window.

Note that these properties – defined when a particular object is created – are sometimes called *creation attributes*. Other attributes – *registration attributes* – are described below.

WINDOW HANDLES

When a Windows function is called, the arguments of the function call must identify the interface element to which the call relates. Windows has to be able to distinguish interface elements from each other. When an element is created, Windows allocates a *handle* to it. This is a unique integer, which links the new object with its interface element and acts as an identifier in all function calls.

You do not need to know the actual number associated with an element; Windows passes back the handle when the element is created and this is stored in a variable. In all future calls the variable is referenced by name; the numeric value is irrelevant.

Indeed, most of the time there is no need to have anything to do with the handle. The IDE protects the programmer from such basic details by breaking down the required operations into standard function calls. The handle is only needed if a Windows function is called directly by an event procedure.

WINDOW CLASSES AND REGISTRATION

Life for the programmer is made unnecessarily hard, especially when it comes to object-oriented programming under Windows, by the vast number of technical terms that have been devised and by the use of the same words, in different combinations, to mean completely different things.

A fine example of this confusion is the term 'window class', also known as 'Windows class'. This is not an OOP term and not to be confused with OOP classes (whether for Windows or otherwise).

A *window class* (or, according to Borland, *Windows class*) is the set of initial attributes that determine the appearance and behaviour of a window. The window class must be *registered* with Windows. This is done by filling in values for a WNDCLASS data structure and then calling the RegisterClass function; one of the arguments of this function is a pointer to the WNDCLASS structure.

When an OOP class is created, it will identify the window class that it is to use. All objects created for the OOP class will then share the same window class, and hence the same basic attributes. You do not have to have different window classes for different OOP classes – two OOP classes can share the same window class – but two objects from the same OOP class cannot use different window classes.

Registration Attributes

The attributes defined in the window class include the colours, the form of the mouse pointer and the icon to be used. These are called *registration attributes* and, unlike the *creation attributes* described above, cannot be changed when the window has been created. If you need a window with different attributes, then you need a new window class and therefore a new OOP class.

In general, you should not have to worry too much about window classes and registration attributes. All of this is dealt with by the IDE. If you are happy with the colours and other attributes provided by the framework you are working with, then there is no need to be concerned with any of this.

DIALOGUE BOXES

Dialogue boxes are a special type of window. Usually, they are temporary windows, placed on screen to display a message or to ask for information. As a general rule, they are fixed in size and may not be minimised or maximised, but may be moved to another part of the screen. Dialogue boxes are child windows of some other parent window.

There are two types of dialogue box:

- *Modal* dialogue boxes require input from the user before the application can do anything else. The user cannot click on any other window until the box is closed.

- *Modeless* dialogue boxes, although intended to be temporary in nature, are used to ask for information but do not have to be closed before any further action is taken.

Typically, modal dialogue boxes are used to give messages or to ask for information that is essential before any further action can be taken.

For instance, a modal dialogue box is used to ask for a filename when saving data. The user has either to give a filename and complete the process, or click on Cancel to abandon the save. It is not possible to return to the main part of the application, make changes and then continue with the save; the save process must be cancelled and then restarted. By default the position of modal dialogue boxes is fixed but this property can be changed.

Modeless dialogue boxes come somewhere in between modal boxes and fully-fledged windows. Remember that the classes for windows and dialogue boxes are both derived from the same base class, so it is not surprising that they share a lot of features in common. Modeless dialogue boxes are useful where the size and the content of the box are fixed and you do not want the user to be able to resize them. For example, they are used as data entry forms for databases or to set up the parameters for a search.

There is an important distinction in the way that dialogue boxes are set up:

- A modal dialogue box is *executed*; no further action can be taken until execution is complete.

- A modeless dialogue box is *created*; it does not have to be used immediately.

Windows supplies two functions for executing or creating dialogue boxes:

- DialogBox creates a modal dialogue box.

- CreateDialog creates a modeless dialogue box.

When either of these functions is called, Windows uses the dialogue box template from the application's executable file to create an overlaid Window that matches the template. The object is based on the dialogue box class. The template contains all the information needed to create a particular dialogue box (an instance of the class), and this template is usually added to the .EXE file from a resource file.

Like all windows, dialogue boxes can contain any number of controls.

MESSAGE BOXES

Although you can use dialogue boxes to give messages to the user there is a simpler method, if you are prepared to accept Microsoft's default messages boxes. Message boxes are a form of restricted dialogue box, with the following components:

- Control-menu box

- Title

- Icon

- Message text

- 1, 2 or 3 buttons

Rather than going to all the trouble of defining a dialogue box class and creating an object, this built-in box can be called directly using the Windows MessageBox function.

When the function is called, the box is displayed and the only option for the user is to click one of the buttons. The box then disappears, returning a value that indicates which button was pressed. (If there is insufficient memory to create the message box, zero is returned.)

In C++ and Pascal, this function has the form:

```
MessageBox(handle,message,title,buttons)
```

The handle is needed to identify the parent window for which the box is being created. The *buttons* value is a combination of the buttons to be displayed, the icon (if any) and the operating mode of the box. For example:

```
MessageBox(HWindow,"Abandon changes?","Abandon",MB_OKCANCEL|MB_ICONQUESTION)
```

The result is shown in Figure 5.3.

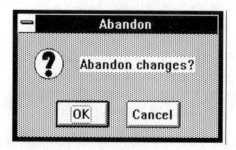

Figure 5.3 Example of a message box

Value for *buttons*
(Combine one value from each section)

	Visual Basic value	C++/Pascal constant[1]	Meaning
Buttons	0	MB_OK	OK
	1	MB_OKCANCEL	OK, Cancel
	2	MB_ABORTRETRYIGNORE	Abort, Retry, Ignore
	3	MC_YESNOCANCEL	Yes, No, Cancel
	4	MB_YESNO	Yes, No
	5	MB_RETRYCANCEL	Retry, Cancel
Icon	0		No icon
	16	MB_ICONSTOP	Critical message
	32	MB_ICONQUESTION	Warning query
	48	MB_ICONEXCLAMATION	Warning message
	64	MB_ICONINFORMATION	Information message
Default	0	MB_DEFBUTTON1	Ist button
	256	MB_DEFBUTTON2	2nd button
	512	MB_DEFBUTTON3	3rd button
Type	N/A[2]	MB_APPLMODAL	Modal box (the default – therefore may be omitted)
		MB_SYSTEMMODAL	Used to indicate serious error (e.g. out of memory) – all applications suspended
		MB_TASKMODAL	Used for errors such as no window handle available

Return values (key pressed)

1	IDOK	OK (or ENTER key)
2	IDCANCEL	Cancel (or ESC key)
3	IDABORT	Abort
4	IDRETRY	Retry
5	IDIGNORE	Ignore
6	IDYES	Yes
7	IDNO	No

Notes
1 First two characters of Pascal constants are lower case 'mb'.
2 All Visual Basic message boxes are normal modal boxes.

Figure 5.4 Message box parameters

In Visual Basic, the function has a similar form:

```
variable = MsgBox(message, buttons, title)
```

The return value is to be found in the *variable*. There is no need for a handle, since the box is included in code that is attached to a particular window. The *buttons* value is the sum of the numbers represented by the constants used for C++. For example, the same message box as above could be displayed with:

```
RetVal = MsgBox("Abandon changes?",33,"Abandon")
```

The message box options are listed in Figure 5.4.

The advantage of this approach is that Windows takes full responsibility for creating and destroying the message boxes.

CREATING DIALOGUE BOXES IN VISUAL C++

The method for creating windows or dialogue boxes varies, depending on the development environment that has been selected.

When working in Visual C++, new windows are created as dialogue boxes in App Studio.

Run App Studio by selecting the Tools|App Studio option from the Visual Workbench menu bar. The App Studio window is displayed (Figure 5.5). The main dialogue box shows the resources currently available to the application. Clicking on one of the resource types on the left results in the matching resources being listed on the right. For example, click on 'Dialog' and App Studio will show you that the only dialogue box at present is IDD_ABOUTBOX (Figure 5.6).

Adding a new dialogue box is very simple:

1   Click on the New button or select the Resource|New option.

2   From the list of resource types, choose Dialog (Figure 5.7). Click on OK.

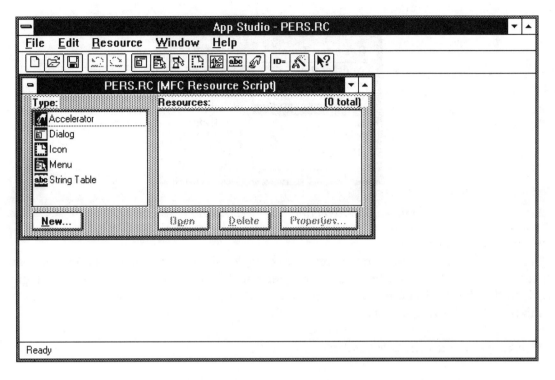

Figure 5.5 App Studio display

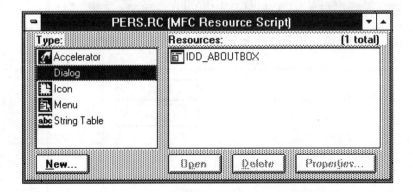

Figure 5.6 List of dialogue resources

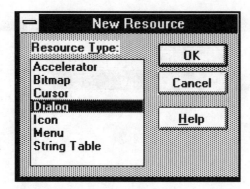

Figure 5.7 Selecting a new dialogue resource

The screen becomes a little confusing at this stage. Overlaid on the screen is a dialogue box, showing that the new box has been given the default name of IDD_DIALOG1 (Figure 5.8). In the client area of this box is a representation of the dialogue box you are creating. This has the following features:

- A title bar, with the title 'Dialog'

- A control-menu box

- OK and Cancel buttons (with OK being the default button)

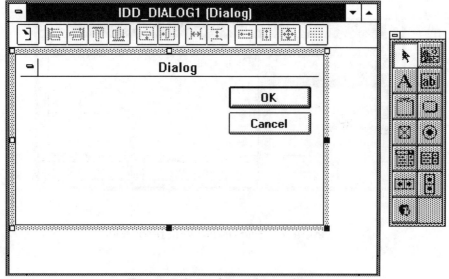

Figure 5.8 Dialogue box editor

Also added to the screen is the App Studio toolbox, showing the controls that can be added to the new dialogue box. You can make this collection of boxes easier to interpret by moving them around the main window.

The size, position, title and other properties of the dialogue box are changed with the Properties box. To bring up this box, double-click anywhere on the dialogue box. There are two sets of properties – General and Styles – which can be selected by clicking on the arrow of the combo box in the top right-hand corner of the window. The contents of the Properties box change, depending on the property that has been selected.

The General properties determine the overall appearance of the box (Figure 5.9):

- The Caption is the title of the box. This can be changed to something like 'Employee Details'. As you enter the new caption, the dialogue box itself is updated.

- The position of the box is given by a pair of (X,Y) co-ordinates. This position can either be changed by amending the two co-ordinate properties or by dragging the title bar of the dialogue box to a new position. The current position is shown in the App Studio status bar, at the bottom of the App Studio main window. The position is shown in the left-hand box.

- In a similar way, the size of the box is changed by resizing the dialogue box itself. The width and height are shown in the right-hand box on the status bar (by default, 185 x 92).

- The Font button lets you change the Font Name and Font Size.

- The Menu property allows you to attach a menu bar to the dialogue box (see Chapter 8).

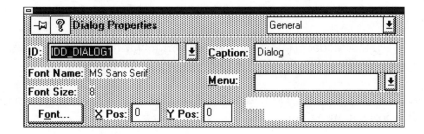

Figure 5.9 Dialogue General properties

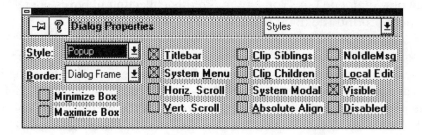

Figure 5.10 Dialogue Styles properties

All measurements are given in terms of *dialogue box units* (DLUs). The DLU is calculated from the standard 8-point font. A box enclosing an average character will be 8 DLUs high and 4 DLUs wide (there are about 60 DLUs per inch).

The Styles properties let you change the type of Window being created (Figure 5.10).

- The box can be overlapped, pop-up or child window.

- Various types of border are available (no border, thin line, resizable box, fixed box with normal border).

- Minimise and maximise boxes can be added.

- The title bar can be turned off.

- The control-menu box can be removed (determined by the System Menu property)

- Horizontal and vertical scroll bars can be added.

- The Clip properties determine the way in which windows are redrawn.

- Setting the System Modal property turns the window into a modal dialogue box (one which must be closed before any further action can be taken).

- The Absolute Align property, if set, aligns the window relative to the screen rather than the application's main window.

- The NoIdleMsg property turns off the Windows WM_ENTERIDLE message which is normally sent to the dialogue box when there are no other messages waiting.

- The LocalEdit property is set if you want the dialogue box to use memory in the application's data segment.

• The Visible property is turned off if you do not want the box to be visible when first called, while the Disabled property temporarily disables the box.

Using these properties, you can create any type of window. The dialogue box in Figure 5.11 has had the following properties changed:

Caption	Employee Details
X,Y	50,50
Width x Height	250 x 180
Minimize Box	True

Other controls are added to this box in Chapter 7. The dialogue box is linked in to a menu option in Chapter 9.

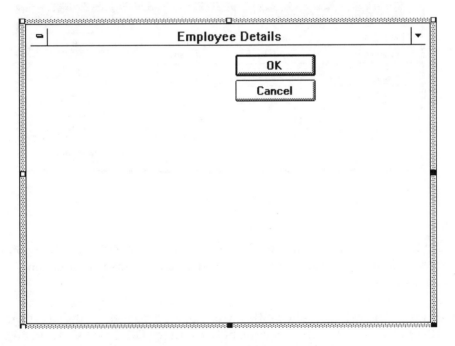

Figure 5.11 Revised dialogue box

Creating the New Class

The next stage is to create a new class for the dialogue box, derived from CDialog. This is done using ClassWizard, as follows:

1   Invoke ClassWizard by selecting Resource I ClassWizard or pressing CTRL-W. The Add Class box is displayed.

2   Fill in the new Class Name (e.g. EmpDetails). As you do so, the names of the header and source files are filled in (Figure 5.12). The Class Type is shown as CDialog.

3   Click on Create Class. The files are set up, providing a template for the new class. You are turned to the main ClassWizard dialogue box, from which clicking on OK takes you back to App Studio.

You can now leave App Studio and return to Visual Workbench.

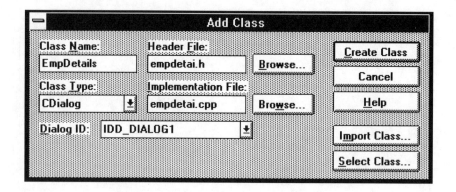

Figure 5.12 Adding a new class

ClassWizard has created two new files, EMPDETAI.H and EMPDETAI.CPP. Since these files are independent of the main program, a dialogue box, once created, can be re-used in other applications.

The header file, EMPDETAI.H, shows that the class EmpDetails is derived from CDialog (Figure 5.13). It also identifies the dialogue box resource (IDD_DIALOG1) and declares the DoDataExchange function. This is a CDialog function (originally defined in CWnd) that provides the means for getting data into and out of dialogue box fields. The new class will override the original definition, providing specific functions for each of the dialogue box fields; these must be set up via ClassWizard (as described in Chapter 9).

```
// empdetai.h : header file
//

/////////////////////////////////////////////////////////////////////
// EmpDetails dialog

class EmpDetails : public CDialog
{
// Construction
public:
   EmpDetails(CWnd* pParent = NULL);   // standard constructor

// Dialog Data
   //{{AFX_DATA(EmpDetails)
   enum { IDD = IDD_DIALOG1 };
         // NOTE: the ClassWizard will add data members here
   //}}AFX_DATA

// Implementation
protected:
   virtual void DoDataExchange(CDataExchange* pDX);      // DDX/DDV support

   // Generated message map functions
   //{{AFX_MSG(EmpDetails)
         // NOTE: the ClassWizard will add member functions here
   //}}AFX_MSG
   DECLARE_MESSAGE_MAP()
};
```

Figure 5.13 Dialogue header file, EMPDETAI.H

EMPDETAI.CPP defines the constructor function, EmpDetails::EmpDetails, which initially does nothing (Figure 5.14). The source file also has a definition of DoDataExchange; it is here that ClassWizard will add specific functions. Finally, there is a template for the message map (described further in Chapter 9).

To link the dialogue box in to the application, the following line must be included in the first section of PERS.CPP:

```
#include "empdetai.h"
```

The new functions are then available to the main application. (Instructions to call the EmpDetails constructor will be added later.)

```
// empdetai.cpp : implementation file
//

#include "stdafx.h"
#include "pers.h"
#include "empdetai.h"

#ifdef _DEBUG
#undef THIS_FILE
static char BASED_CODE THIS_FILE[] = __FILE__;
#endif

/////////////////////////////////////////////////////////////////////////////
// EmpDetails dialog

EmpDetails::EmpDetails(CWnd* pParent /*=NULL*/)
   : CDialog(EmpDetails::IDD, pParent)
{
   //{{AFX_DATA_INIT(EmpDetails)
       // NOTE: the ClassWizard will add member initialization here
   //}}AFX_DATA_INIT
}

void EmpDetails::DoDataExchange(CDataExchange* pDX)
{
   CDialog::DoDataExchange(pDX);
   //{{AFX_DATA_MAP(EmpDetails)
       // NOTE: the ClassWizard will add DDX and DDV calls here
   //}}AFX_DATA_MAP
}

BEGIN_MESSAGE_MAP(EmpDetails, CDialog)
   //{{AFX_MSG_MAP(EmpDetails)
       // NOTE: the ClassWizard will add message map macros here
   //}}AFX_MSG_MAP
END_MESSAGE_MAP()

/////////////////////////////////////////////////////////////////////////////
// EmpDetails message handlers
```

Figure 5.14 Dialogue source file, EMPDETAI.CPP

ClassWizard has already updated the PERS.RC resource file. This includes the definition of the new dialogue box in the Dialog section (Figure 5.15).

The relationship between the dialogue box properties and the entries in this file are easy to see. However, you must not edit PERS.RC yourself. To create new dialogue boxes manually, use RES\PERS.RC2.

The dialogue box name has also been assigned a constant value in RESOURCE.H:

```
#define IDD_DIALOG1       101
```

A similar dialogue box can be created with the other development environments.

```
/////////////////////////////////////////////////////////////////////////////
//
// Dialog
//

    ...

IDD_DIALOG1 DIALOG DISCARDABLE  50, 50, 250, 180
STYLE DS_MODALFRAME | WS_MINIMIZEBOX | WS_POPUP | WS_CAPTION | WS_SYSMENU
CAPTION "Employee Details"
FONT 8, "MS Sans Serif"
BEGIN
    DEFPUSHBUTTON    "OK",IDOK,129,6,50,14
    PUSHBUTTON       "Cancel",IDCANCEL,129,23,50,14
END

/////////////////////////////////////////////////////////////////////////////
```

Figure 5.15 Additions to PERS.RC

OBJECTWINDOWS FOR C++ AND PASCAL

A dialogue box is created in ObjectWindows using the Resource Workshop. The procedures are identical, whether you are creating a resource for C++ or Pascal. The dialogue
box is set up as follows:

1   Click on the Workshop icon to load the program. This has a very simple interface
    (Figure 5.16) compared with the equivalent Microsoft program, App Studio.

2   Create a new resource file with File | New Project.

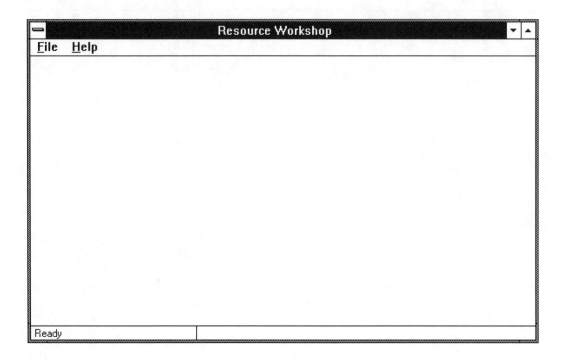

Figure 5.16 App Studio display

3   In the New Project window, select the RC file type (Figure 5.17). Other options allow for cursor files, bitmaps, binary resource files, icons and font files.

4   A small dialogue box appears (Figure 5.18). This will hold details of the resource file components. Use File | Save Project to save the new resource file with the name EMPDETAI.RC.

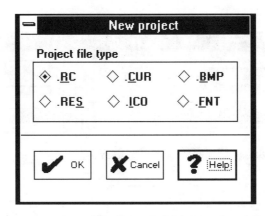

Figure 5.17 Project file types

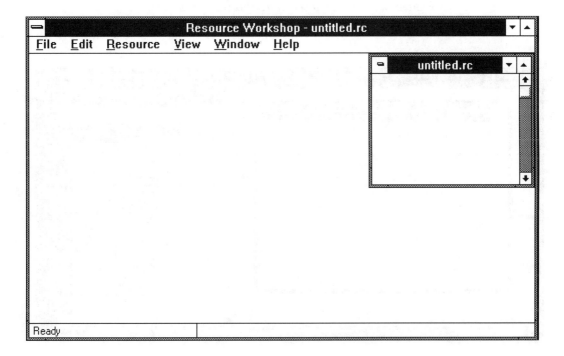

Figure 5.18 Resource editor

5   Choose Resource | New to create the new dialogue resource. Click on the DIALOG
    option (Figure 5.19), then on OK.

6   The Dialogue Editor is displayed (Figure 5.20).

You can now change the dialogue box to fit your requirements. The box can be moved to
a new position, and its size and shape can be altered by dragging the border around the

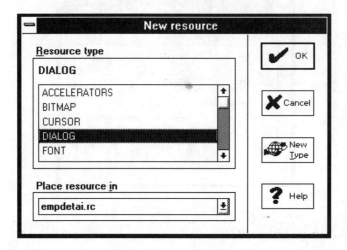

Figure 5.19 Selecting a new dialogue resource

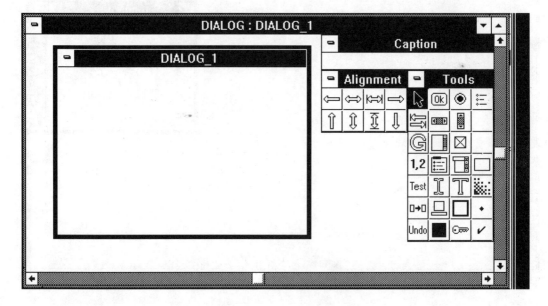

Figure 5.20 The dialogue editor

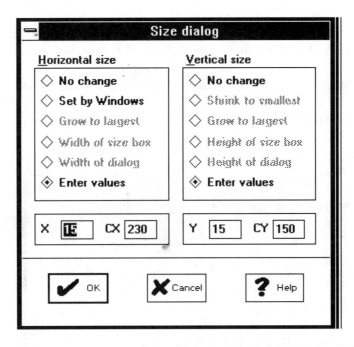

Figure 5.21 Changing the size of the dialogue box

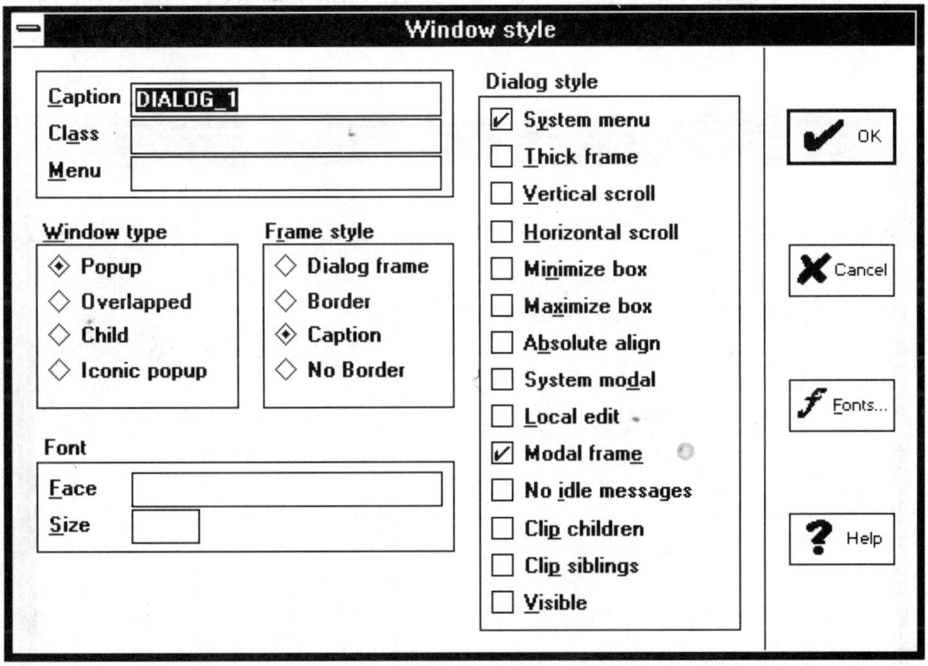

Figure 5.22 Dialogue box properties

edges of the box. For precise settings, select Align | Size. The position of the upper left corner is given by the X and Y values, the width and height by CX and CY (Figure 5.21).

The style of the box is determined by the Window Style options. These are displayed by double-clicking on the new box's title bar (Figure 5.22). A new Caption should be typed in (e.g. 'Employee Details').

The other options are similar to those described for Visual C++. The following options should be selected:

- Popup window type, to make this a pop-up window

- Caption frame style, to give a single-line border and title bar

- System Menu, to include the control-menu box

- Minimize Box, to add a minimise button

- Modal Frame, to make this a modal dialogue box

The dialogue box is shown in Figure 5.23. Save the changes with File | Save Project. The dialogue box is described in the resource file, EMPDETAI.RC (Figure 5.24). The

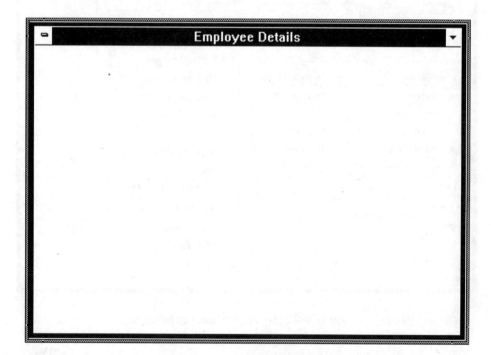

Figure 5.23 New dialogue box

```
DIALOG_1 DIALOG 15, 15, 230, 150
STYLE DS_MODALFRAME | WS_POPUP | WS_CAPTION | WS_SYSMENU | WS_MINIMIZEBOX
CAPTION "Employee Details"
BEGIN
END
```

Figure 5.24 Application resource file, EMPDETAI.RC

similarities between this and the Visual C++ version are immediately obvious. The definition is shorter because there are not buttons yet.

VISUAL BASIC

The creation of a window in Visual Basic is very fast. Select File | New Form. This generates a blank 'form' – a window. The window is given a default name of Form2 (or similar) and a default size.

As for Visual C++, the properties are changed with the Properties box. Select one of the properties and then supply a new value, either by typing or by clicking on one of the available options.

- The Left and Top properties determine the position of the top left-hand corner of the window on the screen.

- The Width and Height properties determine its size.

- The Caption property sets the form's title.

The Visual Basic toolbar has co-ordinate and size boxes that are identical to those of C++ but note that the units here are *twips* (of which there are 1440 per inch). One DLU is about 24 twips.

The following changes should be made to the new form:

- Change the position by dragging the form's title bar or altering the Left and Top properties (to 1200, 1200 for example).

- Change the size by dragging the edges or altering the Width and Height properties (to 7000 x 5000 twips).

- Change the Caption to 'Employee Details'.

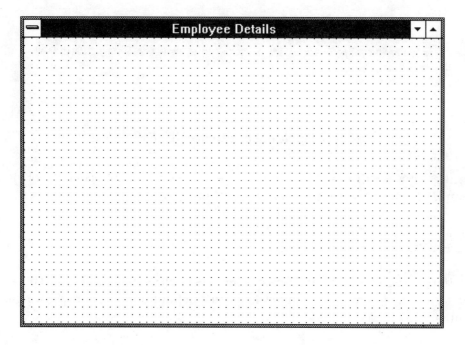

Figure 5.25 Initial Visual Basic dialogue box

- Change the Name to 'EmployeeDetails' (this is needed in the procedures).

- Set the MaxButton properly to False, so that the box cannot be expanded to full-screen size. Note that the maximise button will still be shown on the dialogue box during development but will disappear when the program is run.

Save the form as EMPDETAI.FRM. The window is as shown in Figure 5.25.

Note that none of the Visual Basic files created so far can be viewed or edited.

6 | Controls

Creating windows and dialogue boxes is the first stage in the development of any application. The next stage is to add items to each window so that it has some practical functions. This chapter looks at controls: the buttons, list boxes and other features that are added to any standard Windows application.

CONTROL DEFINITION

The many different types of object that are placed on windows are described under the general term *control*. There are a number of standard controls with which any Windows user will be familiar:

- Command buttons
- Labels
- Text boxes
- Check boxes
- Option buttons
- List boxes
- Combo boxes
- Scroll bars
- Drive lists

- Directory lists
- File lists
- Timers
- Picture boxes
- Image controls
- Frames
- Shapes
- Lines

These types are described below. In addition, you can use *custom controls*, additional types that you can design yourself or are supplied by third-party software developers.

Technically speaking, controls are types of windows. Each of the standard controls listed above has a class that is derived from the CWnd or TWindow class (or similar classes in other development environments). Although a command button may not look like a window, in fact it shares many properties. Command buttons have a position (a pair of co-ordinates), height, width, background colour and caption text; they respond to some of the same events as normal windows, such as clicking, or receiving and losing the focus. As far as Windows is concerned, a control is a child window.

This may appear confusing at first but if you consider windows, dialogue boxes and controls as just different types of interface elements, derived over several generations from the same base class, then handling of all these types of object becomes much easier.

CREATING CONTROLS

It is in the creation of controls that the distinction between dialogue boxes and windows becomes important:

- The controls on a dialogue box are defined in the resource file. As such, they are not necessarily objects in the true sense and may appear on the dialogue box as a result of direct calls to the Windows functions.

- The controls on a window are objects, instances of some class, and are treated by Windows as child windows.

The method by which Windows and dialogue boxes are populated with controls varies, depending on the development environment you are using.

Visual C++

When working with Visual C++, controls are added using App Studio. App Studio has a palette of tools (also called a *toolbox*) for adding a number of standard controls (Figure 6.1). These may be added to any dialogue box, and stored in a resource file that defines the box and all its controls.

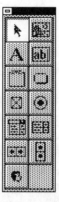

Figure 6.1 App Studio toolbox

When you have created a dialogue box (as described in Chapter 5) you can add controls in a number of ways:

- Click on a control on the palette, then click on the dialogue box. A control appears at the point where you clicked. The control has a default size, suited to the type of control chosen.

- Drag the pointer from the control on the palette to the required position. The effect is the same as for clicking.

- Click on the control on the palette. Then hold down the mouse button when the pointer is on the dialogue box; drag the pointer down and to the right to mark out the shape of the control, and release the mouse button. This gives you the ability to determine the size of the control.

Any of these methods has the same effect: a control is added to the dialogue box with a set of default values for its properties. Some of these properties can be changed using the mouse. Click on the pointer tool in the top left of the tool palette and then click on a control. The selected control has small square boxes, called *sizing handles*, displayed on the corners and sides. The position and size of the control are changed as follows:

- To move the control to a new position, place the mouse pointer inside the control and then drag.

- To change either the height or width, drag one of the sizing handles on the sides of the control.

- To change both height and width at the same time, drag one of the sizing handles on the corners of the control.

The App Studio status bar shows the current position (relative to the top left-hand corner of the dialogue box) and size of the selected control. If no control is selected, the values relate to the dialogue box. Controls can be deleted, copied or moved to a new dialogue box using the options of the Edit menu.

Other properties for the control are changed in the same way as for the dialogue box; double-click on the control to bring up the Properties window and then give the properties new values (Figure 6.2). There are many more properties for some controls than for others. In some cases, a new value can be typed in directly (for example, the caption that is displayed on the control). For other properties, a list is given from which you can select a value; in many cases, properties are simply turned on or off by clicking on a check box.

When you save the resource file, the full definitions of the dialogue box and all its controls are saved.

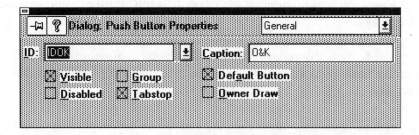

Figure 6.2 App Studio Properties window

Borland C++ and Pascal

If you are programming in either Borland C++ or Borland Pascal With Objects the easiest way of creating dialogue boxes is to use Resource Workshop. This program creates resource files that contain complete definitions of dialogue boxes and their component controls.

Resource Workshop provides an interface that is similar in many respects to App Studio. Controls are provided on a tollbox, which has similar icons to those of App Studio (Figure 6.3). Two other small windows appear to the left and above the toolbox:

• The Alignment window offers eight alternative ways of aligning the controls on the dialogue box (for example, so that they all line up on the left or are all centred in the box).

• The Caption window provides another way of changing the window title.

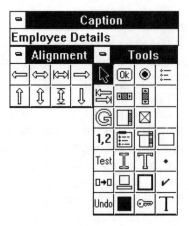

Figure 6.3 Resource Workshop toolbox

Double-clicking on a control brings up a Properties window for that particular type of control (Figure 6.4). The values and choices made in this window determine the appearance and behaviour of the control.

The operation of Resource Workshop is identical for both C++ and Pascal With Objects. Controls are added in a similar way to App Studio.

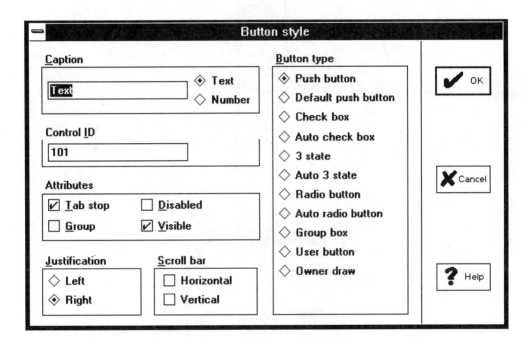

Figure 6.4 Resource Workshop Properties window

Visual Basic

The Visual Basic approach to controls is almost identical to that of App Studio for Visual C++. Visual Basic offers a few more controls in the tool palette (notably those relating to disks) but other than that the actions required for creating, deleting, moving and copying controls are the same as those of C++. The tool palette is shown in Figure 6.5.

The setting of properties also follows similar lines; the property names tend to be different but their effect is the same. The main difference is that the property window is visible on screen at all times (unless switched off via the Window menu). The properties listed depend on the type of control that is selected (Figure 6.6).

The controls are saved when you save the form file.

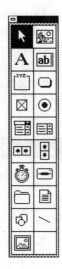

Figure 6.5 Visual Basic toolbox

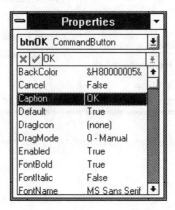

Figure 6.6 Visual Basic Properties window

THE FOCUS

In the same way that only one window can be current at any time, so only one control on the current window or dialogue box can be current. This control is said to have the *focus*. This is indicated in a number of different ways:

- Command buttons are given a thicker border and a dotted line appears around the caption.

- A vertical-bar cursor appears in text boxes.

- A dotted line is put around the captions of check boxes and radio buttons.

The focus can be moved from one control to another in several ways:

- Clicking on a different control

- Tabbing from one control to the next

- Pressing the access key for a control

- Forcing the focus to move from within the program

The focus also moves when you make another window current.

When an object – window or control – gets the focus an event is generated. This is a good place to set initial values; for instance, text can be initialised in a text box. Similarly, losing the focus generates another event. Here you can check that the entry made by the user is valid.

You can also send a message to Windows to force it to move the focus from one control to another (for example, CDialog::GotoDlgCtrl shifts the focus to a specific control).

CO-ORDINATE SYSTEM

By this stage it will have become apparent that, though the general principles of programming are the same regardless of the language and environment you choose, some of the implementation details are quite different. One of the differences that can cause some confusion, especially when moving from one environment to another, is the co-ordinate system.

Every window, dialogue box and control has attributes that determine its position either directly on the screen or relative to the window borders. All these objects also have a width and height. In all cases, the co-ordinates are given as an (X,Y) pair, where X measures the distance across the screen and Y the distance down. The (0,0) point is the top left-hand corner of the screen or window in all cases. However, the units of measurement vary from one system to another:

- For Visual C++ and Borland C++, measurements are in *dialogue box units* (DLUs). The DLU is based on an average character from the standard font, 8-point MS Sans Serif. Horizontally, 1 DLU is the average width of a character divided by 4; vertically, 1 DLU is the average height of a character divided by 8.

- For Visual Basic, the default system uses *twips* (of which there are 1440 per inch, i.e. 20 per character *point*). However, there are properties for choosing other units – such as points (72 per inch), pixels, characters (12 per inch horizontally, 6 vertically), inches, millimetres or centimetres – or for setting a user-defined co-ordinate system.

The Windows API has its own functions for converting the selected co-ordinate system into standard screen co-ordinates. For example, ClientToScreen converts the selected co-ordinates to screen co-ordinates. Windows itself uses a *logical* co-ordinate system, which is independent of the number of pixels on the output screen. When it displays a graphic representation it converts the logical co-ordinates to *physical* co-ordinates, which are device-dependent. Two functions, LPtoDP and DPtoLP, convert from *logical points* to *device points* and vice versa.

As a general rule, when changing co-ordinates as part of the program code, it is a good idea to use constants rather than actual values, with the co-ordinates defined in terms of fixed X and Y values. A change to the co-ordinate system can then be implemented by a simple change to the basic X and Y constants.

THE TAB ORDER

On any window or dialogue box containing more than one control, one of the controls will always have the *focus*. This is the control that is currently being used. Usually, the focus is moved from one control to another by clicking on a control; when the user clicks, the control under the pointer receives the focus, and the previously selected control loses the focus. The control with the focus is highlighted by having a thicker border, a flashing cursor or in some other way.

Sometimes the user will want to move the focus from one control to another using the keyboard. One approach is to use the TAB key to move between controls. In order to do this, the controls must be put in sequence. This is known as the *tab order*.

The user can move the focus in either direction:

- Pressing TAB moves the focus up the tab order (0,1,2,...)

- Pressing SHIFT-TAB moves the focus down the order (7,6,5,...)

When the last control is reached, pressing TAB takes the focus back to the beginning again (or SHIFT-TAB on the first takes the focus to the end of the order). Therefore, repeated pressing of TAB cycles the focus round the controls.

Each control is assigned a number – the *tab index* – that is its order in the sequence. The first control has tab index 0 and the others are numbered sequentially from 1. When creating controls, the tab order is the order in which the controls were created.

You can change the tab order in App Studio with Layout I Set Tab Order (or press CTRL-D). Then set the order by clicking on the controls in the required order (Figure 6.7), and press ENTER when finished. To change just part of the order, hold down CTRL and click on the control immediately before the changed part of the order, then click on each of the controls in the changed sequence. For example, to change control number 7 to control number 4, CTRL-click on control number 3 and then click on the new numbers 4 to 7.

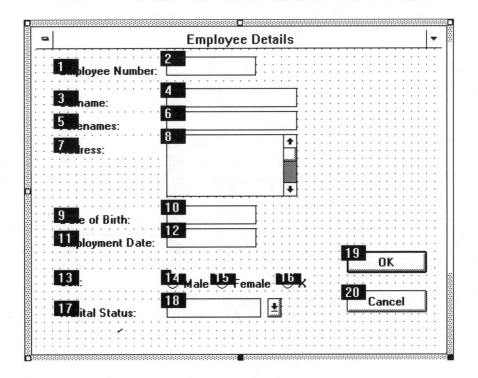

Figure 6.7 Changing the tab order in App Studio

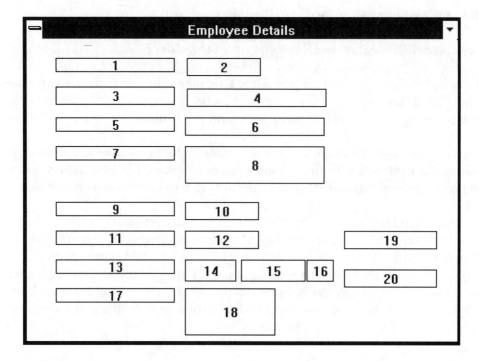

Figure 6.8 Changing the tab order in Resource Workshop

For Borland C++, the Resource Workshop has a tool, marked with '1,2', for changing the tab order. The tab numbers are shown on the controls and can be changed by clicking on each control in order (Figure 6.8).

In Visual Basic, properties are used. Each control has a TabIndex property. Changing this property for any control results in the controls that come later in the order being renumbered automatically. For example, changing an index of 7 to 4 results in the index values 4, 5 and 6 being renumbered as 5, 6 and 7.

All controls should be included in the tab order, even if they cannot receive the focus. For instance, labels should be included; this is particularly useful when a label is to be used for the shortcut key for a text box (see below).

Although all controls are in the tab order, they do not necessarily have to receive the focus. Each control is set to be either affected or unaffected by the tab order, so the order can be restricted to just those controls where the TAB key is to be effective.

ACCESS KEYS

In some circumstances it is useful for the user to be able to move the focus to a particular control with the keyboard rather than the mouse. This may be because it is simpler (particularly when typing text, where pressing a key is easier than having to move over to the mouse); alternatively, the mouse may not be functioning. Full keyboard control is achieved by assigning *access keys* to the controls (sometimes called *mnemonic keys*).

The access key is assigned to a control by putting an ampersand (&) in front of the access key in the control's caption. For example, a button with the caption '&Cancel' has C as the access key; the access key for 'O&K' is K. It doesn't matter whether the access keys are upper or lower case. The effect is as follows:

- The access key is underlined when displayed on screen.

- When the user presses the letter key corresponding to the access key, the focus is transferred to that control

Make sure you do not allocate the same access key to more than one control on the dialogue box or window.

To include an '&' in the caption, use a double ampersand (e.g. 'Save && E&xit': the access key is X).

To be consistent with other Windows applications, access keys should be applied to all controls which may receive the focus. Another form of access key (accelerators or shortcut keys) is discussed in Chapter 8, *Menus*.

Access Keys for Text Boxes

Text boxes do not have a caption but an access key can still be used:

1   Put a label control on the window next to the text box (usually immediately to the left or above the text box, though proximity is not important).

2   Give the label an access key by including an ampersand in the caption.

3   Change the tab order so that the label immediately precedes the text box.

When an access key is pressed and the corresponding control is not able to receive the focus, the focus passes to the next control in the tab order. So pressing the access key for a label will move the focus to the next control: in this case, the text box.

In the example (Figure 6.9), each of the labels has been given an access key, apart from Sex (which doesn't need one). The radio buttons and command buttons also have access keys. This dialogue box is built up in Chapter 7.

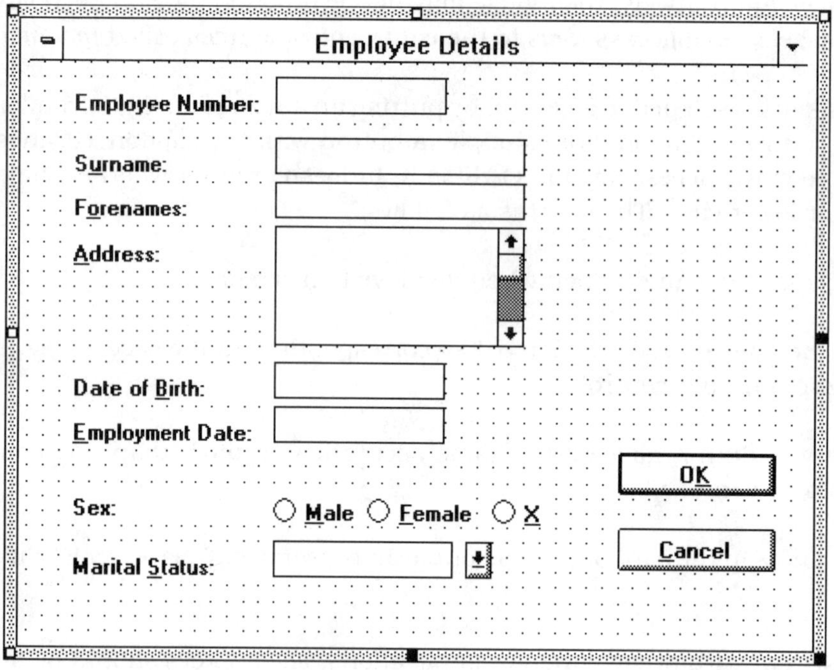

Figure 6.9 Dialogue box with access keys

GROUP BOXES

It is often useful to collect together a set of controls into a recognisable group. This is done with a group box. A *group box* (or *frame* in Visual Basic terms) appears on screen as a rectangle with a title set into the top line. Other controls are put inside the group box.

In most cases, group boxes are used for purely cosmetic purposes, grouping controls together for convenience. However, there are some situations where it is essential to put controls into a group. This is particularly the case with radio buttons. Without group boxes, only one radio button on a dialogue box can be checked at any time. With group boxes, one radio button can be checked within each group. Therefore, the user can make a selection from several groups of radio buttons on a single dialogue box.

Within a group, the user can move between controls using the arrow keys.

App Studio and Visual Basic provide a group box/frame control, identified on the toolbox by a rectangle overlaid with 'XYZ'. The controls that are to be included in the group must be added *after* the group box and must be drawn inside it; you cannot move a control into a frame after it has been created (it will actually be placed on top of the frame, overlapping it).

For App Studio, controls are identified as being in a group by setting the Group property of the first control to True and all others to False. The controls must all be together within the tab order. The end of the group is signified by the next control with a Group property of True; this is the start of another group. (If there are no groups, the Group property for all controls will be True.)

7 | Standard Controls

This chapter describes the standard controls that are available in all the environments under consideration. In each case, the class of the control is given for both the Microsoft Foundation Class Library and the ObjectWindows class library. The controls described below can be set up automatically through Visual C++ App Studio or Visual Basic, and are included on both toolboxes; they are also included on the Borland C++ Resource Workshop toolbox. The App Studio toolbox is shown in the illustrations.

Each control has a number of properties that determine its appearance and behaviour; the most important of these are detailed. The main events to which the control responds are also described. All of these controls respond to standard events, such as receiving and losing the focus and mouse activities in the immediate area of the controls.

If these controls are included on a dialogue box, as part of an external resource, then they will be created automatically when the dialogue box is created and destroyed when the box is closed. Alternatively, controls that are created with the new keyword must be destroyed with delete when no longer needed.

COMMAND BUTTONS

Command buttons give the user the opportunity to initiate an event. For example, the familiar OK and Cancel buttons are signals from the user that details in a dialogue box are correct or that an action is to be abandoned. Buttons are also used to provide other choices for a user and a series of buttons may be placed on a toolbar to give the user fast access to actions that must otherwise be activated through the menu system. The class of command buttons is the base class for derivatives such as check boxes and option boxes.

Command buttons consist of a rectangle with a caption. Usually, command buttons are created in such a way that a mouse click temporarily changes the button picture, giving the impression of a button being pressed, then released.

Command buttons respond to two major events: the mouse button click and double-click (though Visual Basic restricts this to click events only). In addition, you can code for events such as the mouse button being pressed or released, dragging the pointer over the button's 'airspace', or receiving and losing the focus.

There is a special property that can be applied to one (and only one) button on a dialogue box or window. This is determined by the BS_DEFPUSHBUTTON style, which identifies the control as the *default* button. The default button has a thicker border and pressing the ENTER key has the same effect as clicking the button. Visual Basic also has a Cancel property; pressing the ESC key is the same as clicking the key that has the Cancel property set.

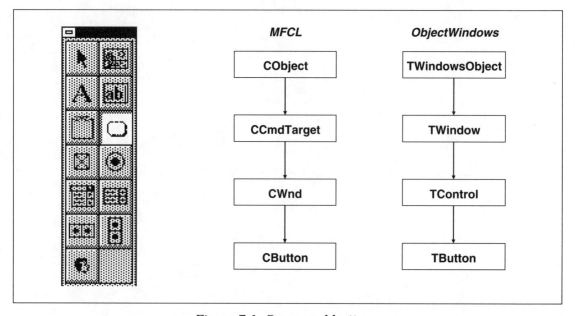

Figure 7.1 Command buttons

Visual C++

For Visual C++, command buttons are objects from the CButton class, which is derived from CWnd. Apart from the button style (the type of button and features such as the Default property) parameters to this class determine the size and position of the button and the caption that is displayed on it. App Studio and Visual Basic have a command button on their toolboxes, signified by a rounded rectangle (Figure 7.1).

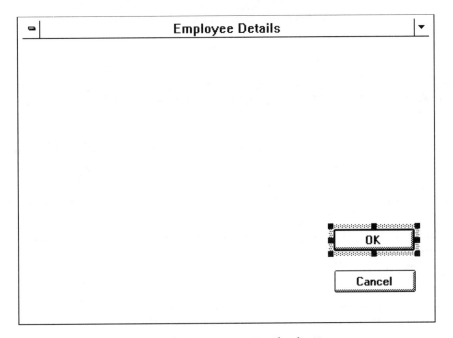

Figure 7.2 Repositioning the buttons

Note that the CButton class is used for creating check boxes and radio buttons, as well as command buttons. The type of control is determined by attributes; these are set automatically by App Studio, depending on the selection made from the toolbox.

The OK and Cancel buttons on the App Studio sample dialogue box can be dragged to a new position, at the bottom of the box (Figure 7.2).

Double-clicking on one of the buttons displays its properties (Figure 7.3). For command buttons, these are very simple and determine the following:

• The control ID

• The caption displayed on the button

• Whether the button is visible when the dialogue box is first displayed and, if it is, whether it has been disabled

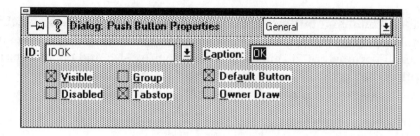

Figure 7.3 Button properties

- Whether the button is part of a group, and included in the tab order (described in Chapter 6)

- Whether the button is the *default* button, activated by the user pressing ENTER (only one default button is allowed per dialogue box, in this case the OK button)

- Whether this is an *owner-draw* button (one with a customised appearance)

Properties affecting the size and shape of a button are changed by dragging the button or its borders.

ObjectWindows
ObjectWindows gets its command buttons from the TButton class, which is derived directly from TControl. The data for this class is similar to that of Visual C++. Properties relating to check boxes and radio buttons are set in separate classes.

Before adding OK and Cancel buttons, switch on the grid with Align | Grid, giving a grid size of 5 x 5 (Figure 7.4). Click on the command button tool on the toolbox (marked with an OK button) and then mark out the button area on the grid.

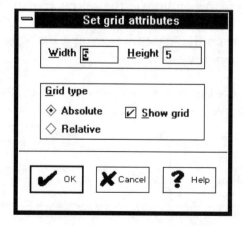

Figure 7.4 Setting the grid

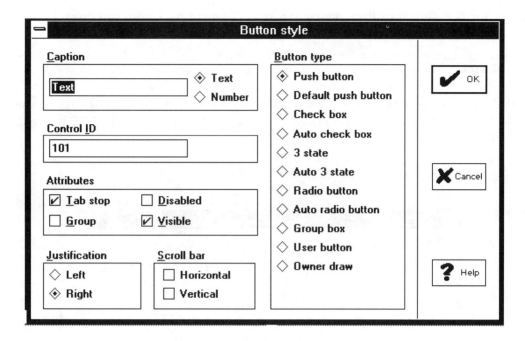

Figure 7.5 Borland button properties

To change the control's properties, double-click on the button. The Button Style window is displayed (Figure 7.5). For the OK button, the Caption should be set to 'OK' and the Default Push Button style should be selected.

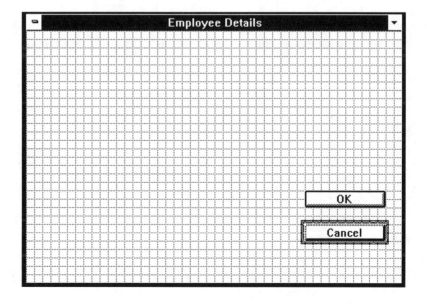

Figure 7.6 Borland dialogue box

Repeat for the Cancel button, giving it a new Caption but leaving the Push Button style checked. The dialogue box now looks like Figure 7.6.

Visual Basic

Mark out the two command buttons in the same way as for Visual C++. Set the Caption to 'OK' and 'Cancel' respectively. For the OK button, set the Default property to True; for the Cancel button, set the Cancel property to True (so that pressing the ESC key activates the button).

The dialogue box is as shown in Figure 7.7.

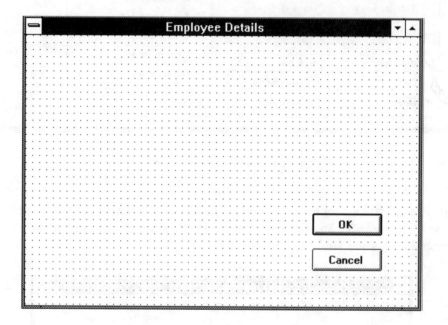

Figure 7.7 Visual Basic dialogue box

LABELS

Labels are fixed items of text that are displayed on windows. The text may be changed within a program but not by the user. Labels are used for titles (excluding those in the title bar or the captions on buttons), instructions and other explanatory text. They are particularly useful when attached to text boxes (used for data entry). The fact that they can be changed by the program means that they can also be set up to display messages (with the label text initially blank) or to show status information. Labels consist of an item of text in a rectangle. There are no special user-activated events for labels.

Visual C++

For Visual C++ labels are derived from the CStatic class. The parameters determine the positions of the text within its rectangle, and the colour of the rectangle and its background. App Studio and Visual Basic have label tools, identified by a capital 'A' (Figure 7.8).

In the example application, labels can be added to the dialogue box at each point where data is to be entered.

1   First of all, switch on the *grid* with Layout I Grid Settings, selecting the Snap to Grid option. The effect is that all new controls have their corners on grid points, ensuring that they can be aligned with a minimum of difficulty.

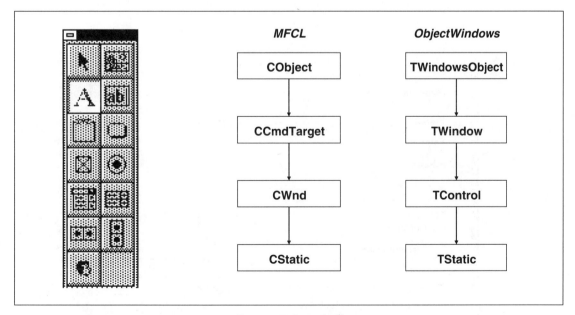

Figure 7.8 Labels

2   Drag the label tool to the dialogue box to put the first label on the box. Move the label to a suitable position (e.g. (15,10) for a point near the top left-hand corner) and make it a suitable size (e.g. 650 x 10 DLUs).

3   Use Edit I Copy to copy the control to the clipboard and Edit I Paste to add further controls. This method ensures that all the labels are the same size. They can be lined up with the grid.

4   Double-clicking on a control brings up the Properties box (Figure 7.9). The only item you need to change is the Caption, which gives the text to be displayed on the box.

When labels have been added the box will look something like Figure 7.10.

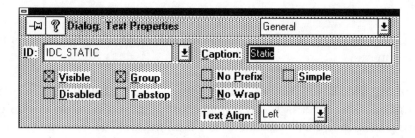

Figure 7.9 Label properties

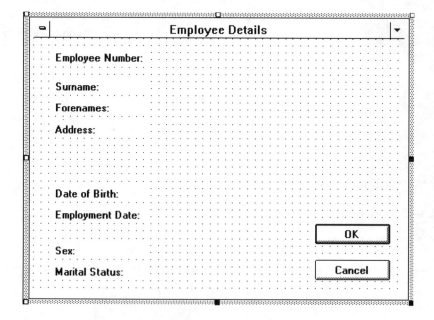

Figure 7.10 Dialogue box with labels

Properties new to labels are:

- No Prefix, which allows the use of ampersands (&) in label names (see *Access Keys* in Chapter 6).

- No Wrap, which stops text wrapping onto the next line and clips text that is too long.

- Text Align, which gives the choice between left-aligned, right-aligned and centred text.

- Simple, which gives left-aligned, non-wrapping text.

Note that for any control, a help window describing the properties can be brought up by clicking on the '?' button in the top left of the Properties box.

ObjectWindows

For ObjectWindows, labels are derived from the TStatic class. This class has only the maximum text length as a parameter, apart from those parameters defining position and size, text value, parent windows and control ID.

The labels are added in the same way as for Visual C++. (The label is identified by a large 'T' on the toolbox.) Double-clicking on a label brings up the Properties window (Figure 7.11). After the labels have been added, the dialogue box will look like Figure 7.12.

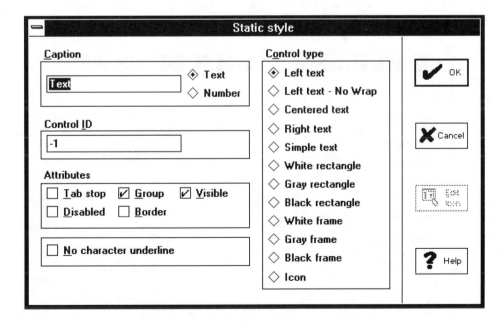

Figure 7.11 Borland label properties

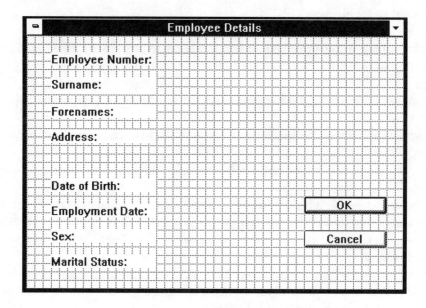

Figure 7.12 Borland dialogue box with labels

Visual Basic

Visual Basic labels are added in a similar way to those of Visual C++ and have an equivalent set of properties. The text of the label is determined by the Caption property. When labels have been added the dialogue box will look like Figure 7.13.

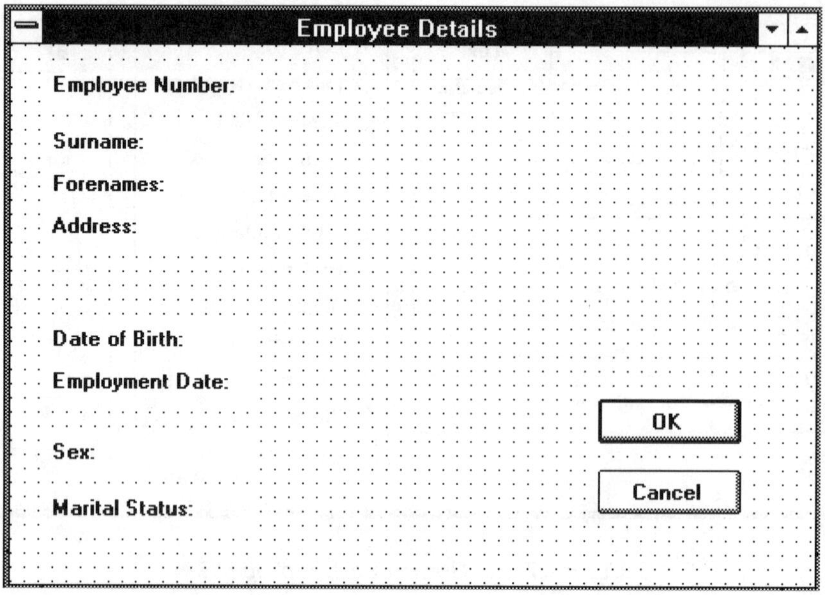

Figure 7.13 Visual Basic dialogue box with labels

TEXT BOXES

The *text box* is the means by which a user can enter any type of information into the application. The box is added in the same way as for a button or label.

The text box is surrounded by a rectangle (which may be made invisible by changing its colour) and may cover one or more lines. Text boxes are used for all types of data entry: single- or multi-line text, integers, real numbers, dates, times and so on. *Single-line* boxes are used for individual data entries while *multi-line* boxes allow the entry of free-form text. Text boxes are also referred to as *edit controls*. The text box on the App Studio and Visual Basic toolboxes is represented by 'ab' in a rectangle (Figure 7.14).

As far as the user is concerned, when a text box has the focus a vertical bar appears at the end of the existing text (if any). The user can enter any value into the text box and all the usual editing keys are available.

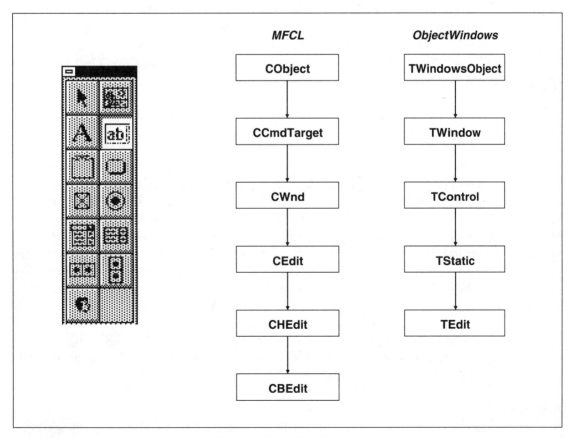

Figure 7.14 Text boxes

The user completes the entry in a number of ways:

- Tabbing to the next control

- Clicking on another control

- Pressing ENTER to activate the default button or ESC to activate the Cancel button

- Clicking on another window or ending the current application

It is up to the programmer to decide what happens when the control loses the focus. Normally, some sort of validation is carried out. It is one of the drawbacks of the text box that once the user starts to type in a text box, the programmer almost loses control of what is happening. The easiest approach is to wait until the user has finished and then act according to what has been entered; for example, in the case of non-numeric entry in a text box where only numeric values are allowed, the program might be made to beep and then either clear the entry or, more sympathetically, force the user to re-enter by putting the focus back on the text box. Be careful here, however, that you do not create a situation where a user who doesn't know the rules cannot get out of the text box. At the very least, you should ensure that the user can get out of the box and clear the entry by pressing the ESC key.

Visual C++ allows you to set a range for the entries while in Borland C++ you can set an option for numeric validation or force the case of text entries.

When the text box is created, its properties determine features such as the size and position, number of lines, maximum number of characters allowed and whether there are scroll bars. The text box classes have methods for returning the current line and current character position (from the start of the text). Note that the first character is character 0 and that paragraph ends require two characters (carriage return/line feed). When determining the maximum size you should also allow 1 for the terminator character; a value of 0 or 1 for the maximum length allows an unlimited number of characters to be entered. Even an empty text box has a length of 1 (the terminator character).

By default, all text is left-aligned. This can be changed to centred or right-aligned text. There is no automatic justification of text; this you must do for yourself or leave it to the printer to achieve when the text is output.

Scrolling
Scroll bars can be added, either vertically or horizontally (or both). For vertically scrolling text, the box can be used for text entry where there are more lines than will fit in the space allowed by the text box. All the usual cursor-control keys are available, including the following:

- PgUp to move up one boxful

- PgDn to move down one boxful

- CTRL-HOME to move to the start of the text

- CTRL-END to move to the end of the text

In addition, the operation of the scroll bars is built into the class definition, so use of scroll bars is also handled automatically.

If horizontal scrolling is allowed, then the text behaves as follows:

- The user can enter unlimited text on any line.

- To start a new line of text, the user must press CTRL-ENTER (to avoid confusion with ENTER, which activates the default button).

The more usual approach on multi-line boxes is to prohibit horizontal scrolling, which has the following effects:

- When the user types over the end of a line, the word being typed is automatically wrapped over to the next line.

- Pressing CTRL-ENTER starts a new paragraph and inserts a carriage return/line feed pair of characters.

- Changing the size of the text box results in the text being reformatted to fit.

Note that if there is no default control on the dialogue box or window, pressing ENTER has the same effect as CTRL-ENTER.

You can only supply one line of text as the default if you use the control properties. To fill a new box with several lines of text, the text needs to be put into the box either when it is created or – if it is empty – when it gets the focus.

Cut and Paste
The text box classes automatically provide for the user to mark out a block of text by dragging the pointer over the text. The colours of selected text are reversed as the pointer is dragged over the text.

The classes have methods that allow for the selected text to be cut or copied to the clipboard, or for clipboard text to be pasted in at the cursor position. These methods can be tied in to the standard Edit menu options of Cut, Copy and Paste, if this menu is included on the menu bar. (For details of this and other menus, see Chapter 8; for information on the clipboard, see Chapter 11.) If the usual shortcut key combinations are included on the menus, then the user can cut, copy and paste without having to use the menus directly.

Text Box Events

Events are generated when the text box gets or loses the focus, or when the user clicks or double-clicks on it. Events also occur when the user tries to move around the text: in both cases the event is notified before the display is updated. The EN_MAXTEXT event occurs when the text goes over a maximum of some sort:

- When the maximum number of characters is exceeded

- When the new text will not fit in a single-line box with no horizontal scrolling

- When the new text would result in wordwrap that would require more lines than are available on a box that does not scroll vertically

In all of these cases, the text is truncated and the surplus text ignored. It is usual to make the computer beep when this happens.

Text Box Implementation

Adding text boxes is very simple in all three environments and most of the expected functionality is already built in to the boxes.

Visual C++

The Visual C++ implementation of text boxes is based on the CEdit class, which is derived from CWnd. Apart from the usual text box features, CEdit allows the use of a text box for entering passwords (see below).

For the example application, text boxes can be placed next to the first six labels; there is no need for labels and text boxes to be paired in this way but it is often convenient to do so. Text boxes are added in the same way as the other controls. In this case, some boxes will need to be different widths and one box – for the Address – will need to be several lines deep.

The text box has two sets of properties: General and Styles (Figure 7.15 and 7.16). The General properties have all been seen before; the Styles set includes a few new properties. Some of these determine the way in which the text appears and the use of the box:

- Password displays all characters as asterisks as they are entered (single-line text only).

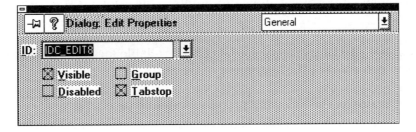

Figure 7.15 Text box General properties

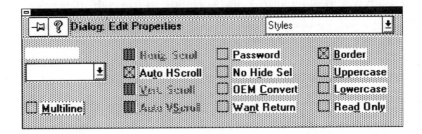

Figure 7.16 Text box Styles properties

- No Hide Sel affects the way in which text is displayed when the box loses or regains the focus.

- OEM Convert converts entries to the OEM character set and back to Windows characters again, to ensure that characters are being entered that can be recognised by Windows (particularly important for filenames, for example).

- Want Return, if selected, interprets the ENTER key as a carriage return, rather than a click on the default button; this is useful for multi-line text. (If the property is not switched on, the user must press CTRL-ENTER to start a new line.)

- Border shows or hides the lines around the edge of the box.

- Uppercase and Lowercase convert all entries to upper or lower case letters respectively.

- Read Only shows text but does not allow the user to change it.

Scrolling is mainly applied to multi-line boxes:

- Auto HScroll allows the user to enter text that extends beyond the right-hand edge of the box, and can be scrolled using the cursor-control keys.

- Horiz Scroll takes this a stage further by adding a horizontal scroll bar (multi-line text only).

Similar properties affecting vertical scrolling are available for multi-line text. For multi-line boxes, you can also set the alignment of the text.

In the current example, the following properties should be changed:

- The Employee Number should have Uppercase switched on, so that any lower-case letters are automatically translated to capitals.

- The Address should have Multiline, Auto HScroll and Vert Scroll switched on, to add a vertical scroll bar and allow horizontal scrolling to the right if necessary.

The dialogue box now looks like Figure 7.17.

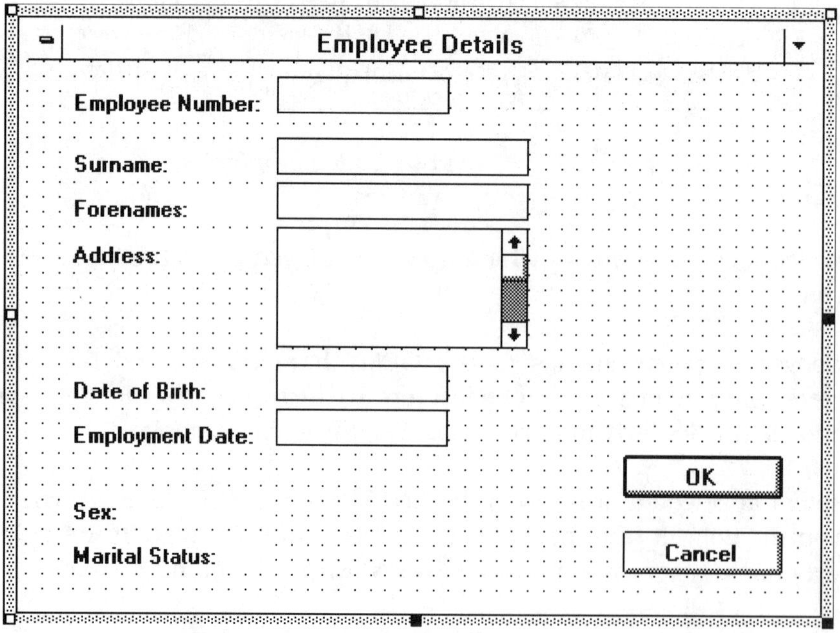

Figure 7.17 Dialogue box with text boxes

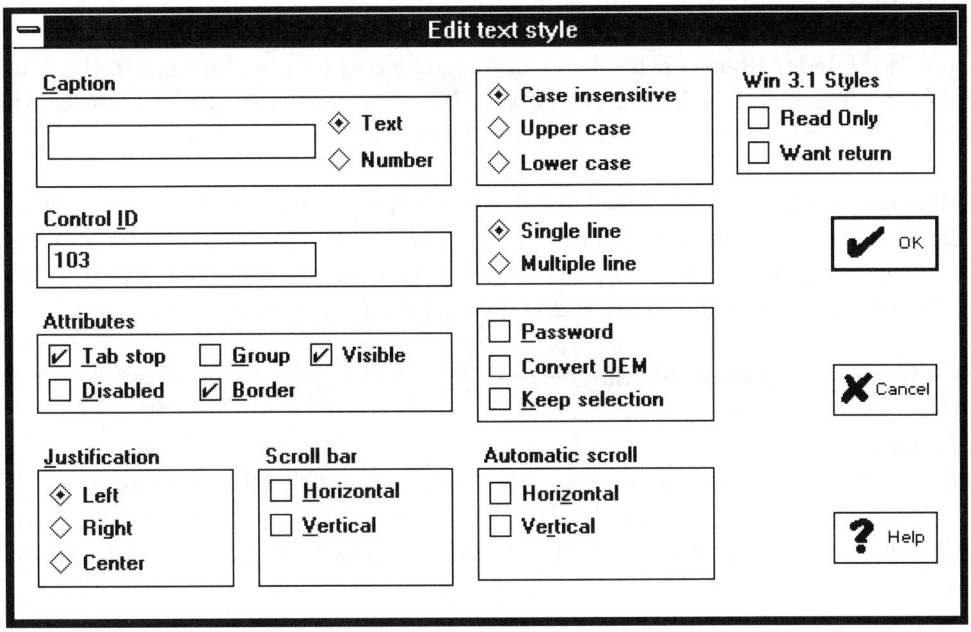

Figure 7.18 Borland text box properties

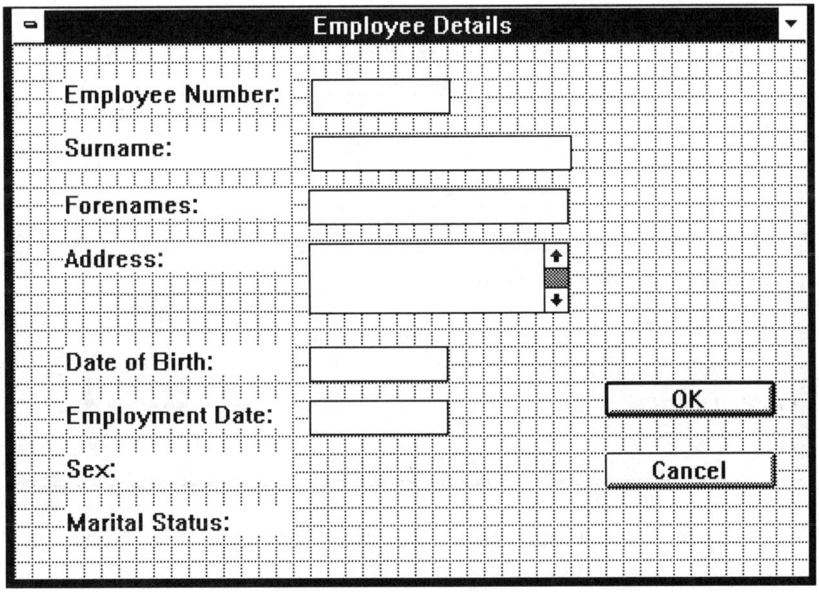

Figure 7.19 Borland dialogue box with text boxes

ObjectWindows

ObjectWindows has a slightly different approach, deriving its TEdit class from TStatic, the class used for labels. However, the behaviour of the text box is identical to the Microsoft text boxes, similar events are catered for and there are corresponding methods. The text box tool is to the left of the label tool on the Resource Workshop toolbox.

The properties window for text boxes combines all the properties found in the two Visual C++ property boxes (Figure 7.18 above). The default settings are all right for most of the text boxes. For the Employee Number, switch on the Upper Case option; in the case of the address box, turn on the Multiple Line style and add a vertical scroll bar.

Figure 7.19 shows the revised dialogue box.

Visual Basic

For each of the Visual Basic text boxes, the Text property should be cleared, so that the boxes are empty. For the address box the MultiLine property should be set to True and ScrollBars should be set to 2-Vertical. The updated dialogue box is shown in Figure 7.20.

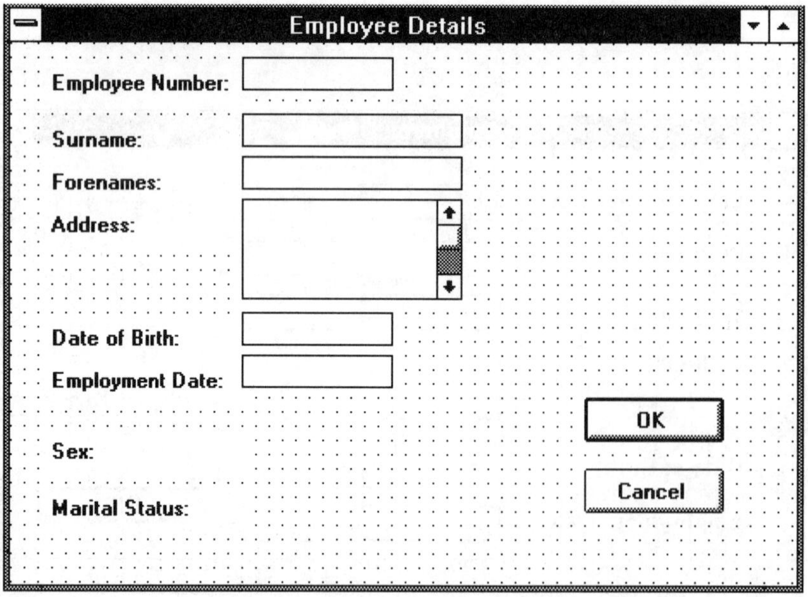

Figure 7.20 Visual Basic dialogue box with text boxes

Tab Stops

Visual C++ allows you to set *tab stops* for multi-line text boxes. These are measured in terms of dialogue units. When a tab character (ASCII 09) is encountered in the text, the cursor moves to the next tab stop to the right. Tab stops are set with the SetTabStops method.

Passwords

The entry of a password is simplified if you are using Visual C++. If the ES_PASSWORD property is set, any characters typed are replaced with an asterisk (*). The password character can be changed with the SetPasswordChar method. Although a string of asterisks is displayed, the programmer can recover the contents of the textbox in the usual way.

Pen-based Systems

The Microsoft Foundation Class Library provides another type of edit control, CHEdit, which is derived from CEdit. This control provides handwriting-recognition routines. A program built from the MFCL automatically detects that a system is equipped with a pen device and will do its best to recognise the text. You can improve recognition by specifying the type of text that is expected (upper case, numeric, etc.) Usually, you will also provide a label control where the recognised text is displayed as it is entered.

A further class, CBEdit, derived from CHEdit, restricts the areas where the user can write characters. Individual character positions are separated by vertical lines and the user is only allowed one character for each box that is created in this way. The layout of the box is controlled by parameters.

Text Boxes and OOP

The use of text boxes is an excellent example of the advantages of object-oriented programming. Most programmers have struggled at one time or another to create text-entry or data-entry procedures using some other programming environment. Providing all the editing and cursor movement functions is a laborious task and, inevitably, results in data entry facilities that are subtly different to anyone else's, so that the end user has to learn how to use the entry boxes of each individual package.

Programming within the frameworks of Visual C++, ObjectWindows or Visual Basic means that the standard text-editing facilities are provided for you, with the added benefit that the user will know how to use the text boxes without any special training.

Text boxes illustrate the main principles of OOP:

- The class encapsulates the standard methods and the text or data itself, with all the parameters needed to define the boxes built into the objects that are created.

- The text box class does not have to define every aspect of text-box appearance and behaviour. Many of the display features and methods are inherited from the base class, so need no further explanation within the class.

- The same methods are provided that can be found in other objects (clicking, dragging, etc.) but have unique definition and different effects: an example of polymorphism.

The other advantage of the OOP approach is that you can define your own classes simply by deriving them from the standard class. For example, you may define a numeric data entry box as a derivative of the standard text box, where the behaviour is the same as for a normal box except that the entry is restricted to certain numeric characters.

CHECK BOXES

When the user is required to switch a feature on or off, the usual approach is to provide a *check box*. This is a special type of command button, consisting of a caption with a rectangle to the left. When the user clicks on the rectangle, an 'X' is put in the box; clicking again removes the 'X'. For example, a check box may be used in a text search dialogue box to determine whether or not the search should be case sensitive.

There are two types of check boxes:

- 2-state check boxes can either be on (checked) or off (unchecked). Each click toggles between these two states.

- 3-state check boxes have an additional *grey* state. This is usually selected by the program when the feature offered by a check box is either not available or not applicable.

Usually, if there is more than one check box on a dialogue box, the boxes will behave independently of each other. If you want the boxes to be related in some way (for instance, clicking on one box automatically checks another box), then this must be dealt with in the event-handling methods. Check boxes are often included in groups.

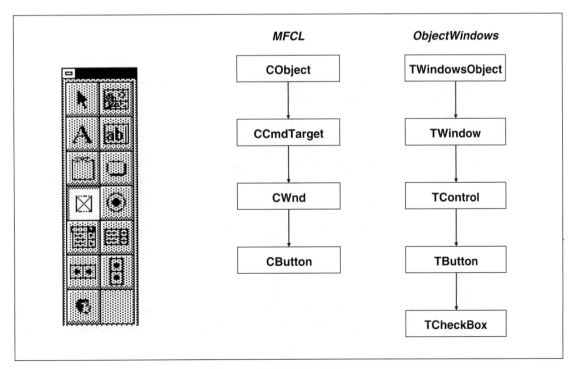

Figure 7.21 Check boxes

The events recognised by check boxes are the same as for ordinary buttons. There are special methods for setting the state of the check boxes.

Visual C++

Visual C++ includes check boxes in the CButton class. The button becomes a check box if one of the check box styles is selected. The properties allow you to choose between 2-state and 3-state boxes; the check box may also be set to change its state automatically when the user clicks on the box (rather than being determined by specially-written methods).

App Studio distinguishes between ordinary command buttons and check boxes by providing a 2-state automatic check box on the toolbox (Figure 7.21). When a check box is created with App Studio the BS_AUTOCHECKBOX property that defines this type of box is automatically set.

The App Studio properties are very simple (Figure 7.22). In addition to those covered alone, the following properties can be set:

- Auto determines whether or not clicking on the box toggles between checked and unchecked states (by default, switched on).

- Left Text puts the caption on the left of the box, rather than the right.

- Tri-State produces a three-state check box.

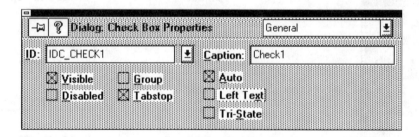

Figure 7.22 Check box properties

ObjectWindows

ObjectWindows distinguishes between command buttons and check boxes by deriving a TCheckBox class from TButton. By default, this class produces 2-state automatic check boxes; for other types of check box, the properties must be changed and a new class derived.

The check box properties from Resource Workshop are shown in Figure 7.23.

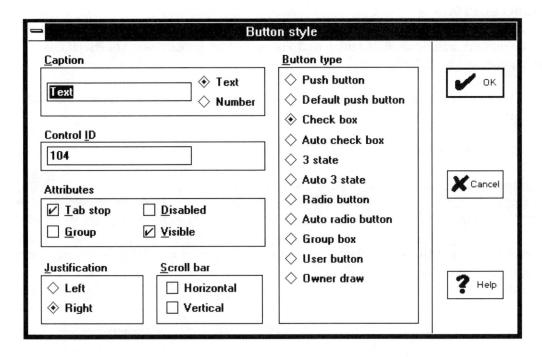

Figure 7.23 Borland check box properties

Visual Basic

Visual Basic provides a simple 2-state automatic check box.

RADIO BUTTONS

Radio buttons, also known as *option buttons*, are a further extension of check boxes. The differences are as follows:

* The button is symbolised by a circle to the left of the caption. When checked, the button is filled in.

* There are only two states: checked and unchecked.

* Radio buttons are almost always used in groups.

* When a button is clicked, it is checked and all others in the group are unchecked.

Therefore radio buttons are affected by the same events as check boxes (though behave slightly differently) and have similar methods.

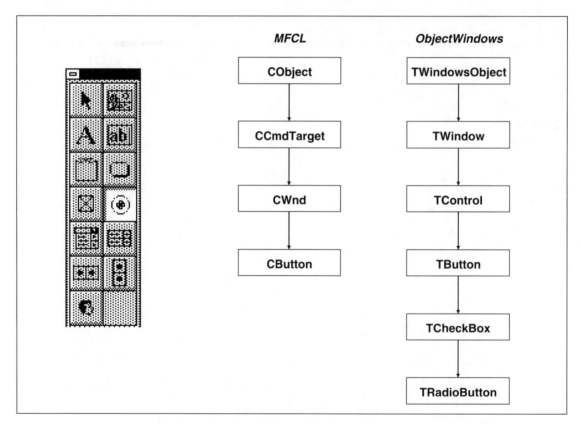

Figure 7.24 Radio buttons

Visual C++

Radio buttons in Visual C++ are implemented as part of the CButton class. A button is defined as a radio button by setting one of the BS_RADIOBUTTON or BS_AUTORADIOBUTTON properties.

App Studio offers an automatic radio button in the toolbox, as does Visual Basic (Figure 7.24).

Radio buttons have similar properties to check boxes (Figure 7.25). Three radio buttons can be added to the example dialogue box to choose between Male, Female and X (Unknown) as the Sex of the employee (Figure 7.26). For each of these, the Tabstops property should be turned on, so that they will receive the focus when the TAB key is used to move around the screen.

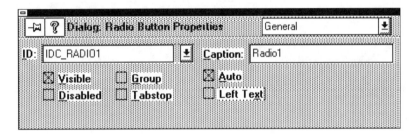

Figure 7.25 Radio button properties

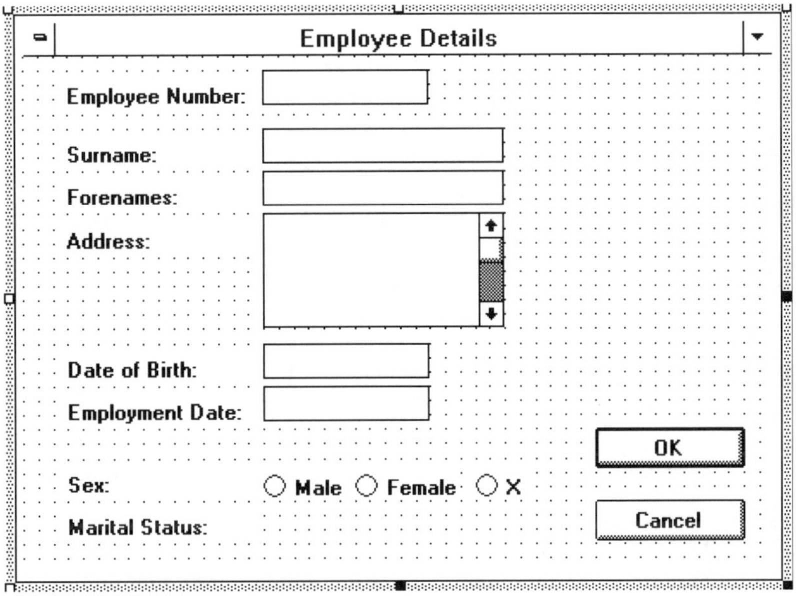

Figure 7.26 Dialogue box with radio buttons

ObjectWindows

ObjectWindows has a special class, TRadioButton, derived from TCheckBox, which provides an automatic radio button. The same properties sheet as for the command button and check box is used. To make a group of radio buttons dependent on each other (so that only one can be selected at a time), turn on the Auto Radio Button style.

Visual Basic

The Visual Basic radio buttons are automatic buttons and operate in the same way as those of the other environments.

LIST BOXES

So far, the user's options for making entries have ranged from choosing from a simple list of radio buttons to entering a value in a text box. However, in many cases you want to provide the user with a fixed list of options from which to select. Neither the radio buttons nor the text box are really suitable:

- A large list of radio buttons becomes difficult to manage and is impractical for very large lists. Deciding which item has been selected requires a considerable amount of code.

- Having to type the choice makes the process long-winded for the user and is prone to error.

The answer is to use a *list box*. A simple list box consists of a rectangle in which a list of text items is shown. If the box is not wide enough for some of the items, then only part of the text will be visible. If there are more items that can be fitted in the list, a vertical scroll bar is added automatically. Unless specified otherwise, Windows will always amend the height of the list box so that a whole number of items are displayed.

List boxes are useful in any situation where the available options can be determined by the program. For example, in a database program you can use a list box for choosing a

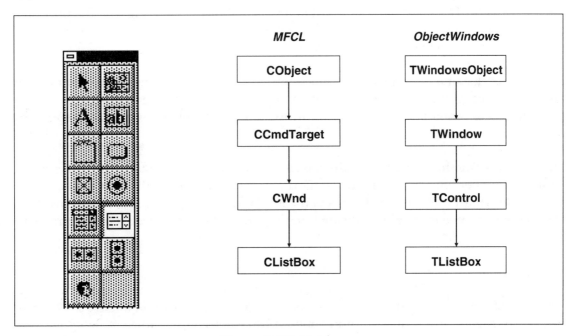

Figure 7.27 List boxes

record by listing the key fields. (Note that applications more frequently use combo boxes, described below.)

Several types of simple list boxes can be created by setting properties when the list is created:

- Single or multiple columns

- Items sorted alphabetically or unsorted

- Single or multiple selection

The usual list box is a sorted single list, with single selection. If you choose a multiple-selection box, there are two ways of allowing the user to make the selections:

- Clicking on an item selects or deselects it.

- Extra items are added when the user clicks with the SHIFT key held down; clicking without the SHIFT key deselects all previous selections.

List boxes respond to Click and Double-click events. A Click event is generated whenever the user clicks the pointer on an item; the selected item is highlighted. A Click event is also generated if the user moves the highlighting up or down through the items using the cursor keys. Therefore the Click event is not a good way of deciding that the user has made a choice. The usual approach is to decide that the selection process is complete when the user double-clicks on an item.

The list box class has a number of public methods for manipulating the list: adding or removing items, getting the selected string, finding a specified string in the list, checking the number of items in the list and returning the length of the string at a specified position, for example.

There are also methods relating to the position of an item in the list. Each item is given an index number, starting with index 0 for the first item in the list. The index of the last item is 1 less than the number of items in the list. When getting the index of the currently selected item, a negative value indicates that no item has been selected or an error has occurred.

Visual C++

Visual C++ has a CListBox class, derived from CWnd. The parameters determine the size and style of the box. App Studio and Visual Basic have a list box tool (Figure 7.27), that will create single- or multiple-column lists; multiple selection can be set using list box properties.

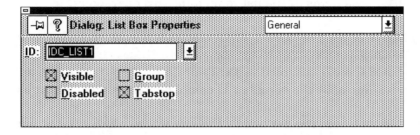

Figure 7.28 List box General properties

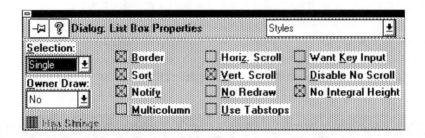

Figure 7.29 List box Styles properties

For App Studio, the General properties are similar to those already covered but there are some new Styles properties (Figures 7.28 and 7.29). The Selection property lets you choose between the following types of box:

Single   Only one item selected at a time

Multiple   Multiple selection by clicking

Extended   Multiple selection by using the mouse with the SHIFT and CTRL keys

Other properties are used as follows:

- Sort lists items in alphabetical order.

- Notify notifies the parent window when an item is selected.

- Multicolumn provides multiple columns in the box.

- No Redraw does not update the box when changes are made.

- Use Tabstops allows items in the list to include TAB characters.

- Want Key Input lets you check each character as it is entered.

- Disable No Scroll shows a disabled vertical scroll bar when there are insufficient items to fill the box. (Normally the scrollbar is completely missing on short lists.)

- No Integral Height leaves the list box as the size it was when created; by default, the box is resized to show complete items only.

ObjectWindows

For ObjectWindows, the TListBox class is derived from TControl and behaves in a similar way to the Visual C++ class. The properties shown in Figure 7.30.

There are some special types of list box, used for drive, directory and file lists, and the principle of list boxes can be extended to create combo boxes. The file-related controls are described in Chapter 13. Combo boxes are described below.

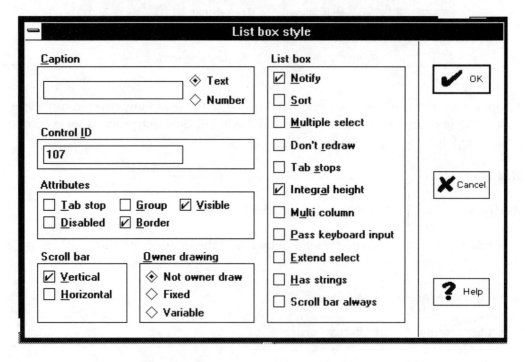

Figure 7.30 Borland list box properties

Visual Basic

The Visual Basic list boxes are identical to those of Visual C++, offering multiple selection and multi-column lists, as well as simple single-column lists.

COMBO BOXES

In principle, a *combo box* is a combination of a list box and a text box. The combo box is used for selecting an item from a list, in the same way as for a list box, but in this case the item may be typed in by the user in the attached text box.

The combo box consists of a list box with a text box immediately above it. To the right of the text box is a button with a down-pointing arrow. Items are selected from a combo box in one of two ways:

- Click on the down-pointing to display the list (if not already shown) and then click on an item.

- Type an entry directly into the text box (either an existing item or a new item).

The way in which the combo box can be used is determined by the style of the box, which is set when the box is created:

- A *simple* combo box displays the list at all times. An item is selected by clicking or entering in the text box; when an item is clicked, it is displayed in the text box.

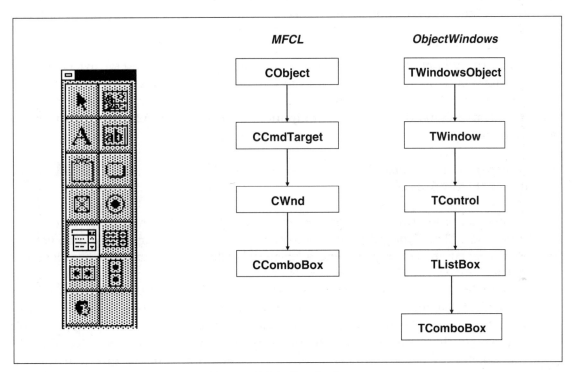

Figure 7.31 Combo boxes

- A *drop-down* combo box works in a similar way to the simple box but the list is only displayed when the user clicks on the arrow button.

- A *drop-down list* combo box requires the user to click on the arrow button to display the list, from which an item may be selected. However, an entry cannot be made in the text box, the sole purpose of which is to display the currently selected item (i.e. it is effectively a label box rather than a text box).

If the simple or drop-down styles are selected, it is up to the programmer to validate any input in the text box. If you want to restrict selections to the items already in the list, then you must provide a routine to reject new entries and request a new item. If new text entries are to be added to the list, the routine must do this when it has been established that this is a new item.

As far as the user is concerned, the difference between drop-down and drop-down list combo boxes is the relationship of the arrow button to the text box. For drop-down boxes there is a small gap between the two; for drop-down list combo boxes the two are joined together.

The events recognised by the combo box and its methods are similar to those of list boxes, as would be expected. There is an additional event, generated whenever there is a change in the text of the text box, and an event occurs when the user clicks the arrow button.

Visual C++

Curiously, the Visual C++ class hierarchy contains parallel classes for list boxes and combo boxes; both are derived directly from CWnd. The combo box class is CComboBox. Much of its functionality is copied from CListBox. (Of course, for a programmer, this duplication makes no difference, the only interest being the public methods that are available.)

App Studio and Visual Basic have a combo box tool, shown to the left of the list box on the toolbox (Figure 7.31).

The combo box properties in App Studio are a subset of those for the list box (Figures 7.32 and 7.33). The Type property lets you choose between simple, drop-down and drop-down list combo boxes. The General properties allow you to enter the default values for the list.

The drop-down list type of combo box is ideal for situations where the user is to be restricted to a preset list of items, as is the case with Marital Status on the example dialogue box. In this case, turn the Sort property off, so that the items are listed in the order in which they were originally entered. You should also make sure that there is enough space at the bottom of the dialogue box to allow a reasonable portion of the list to drop down (Figure 7.34).

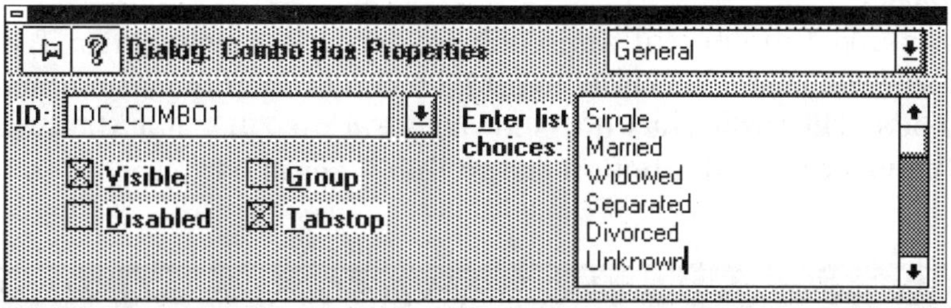

Figure 7.32 Combo box General properties

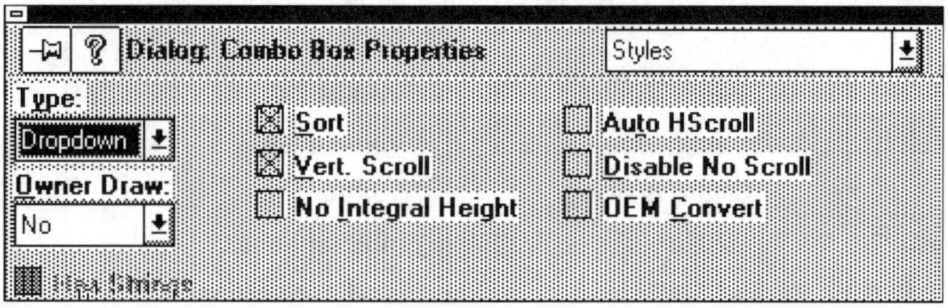

Figure 7.33 Combo box Styles properties

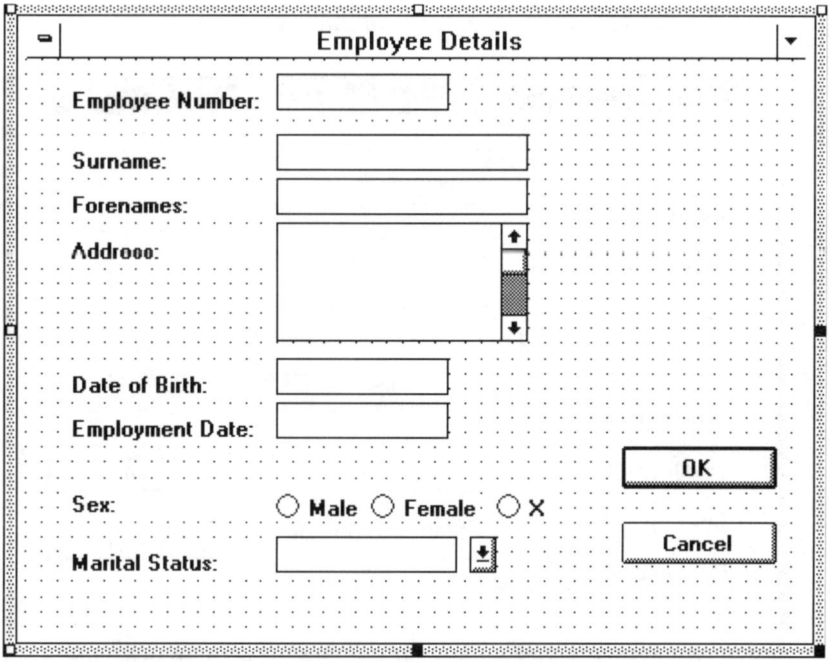

Figure 7.34 Dialogue box with combo box

ObjectWindows

ObjectWindows takes a different approach by deriving a new class, TComboBox, from TListBox. This means that it has only to add a few new methods and amend some of the existing methods. The properties are shown in Figure 7.35. For the example dialogue box, switch the Vertical Scroll function on, so that a scroll bar appears to the right of the

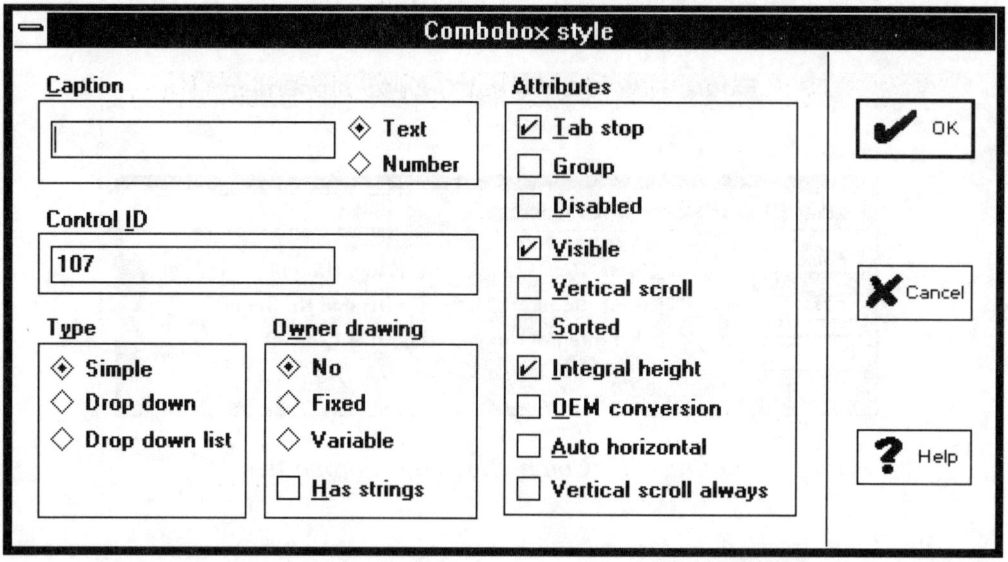

Figure 7.35 Borland combo box properties

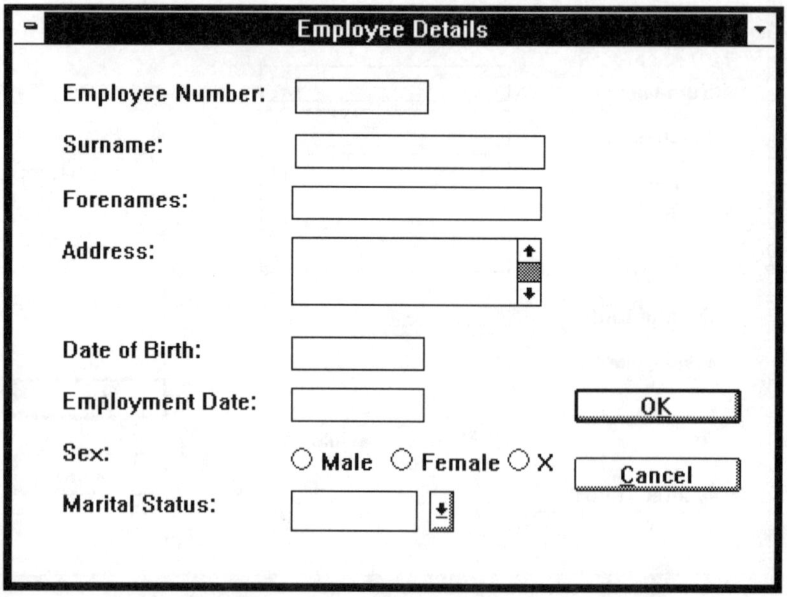

Figure 7.36 Borland dialogue box with combo box

combo box list. The entries for the combo box list must be made in the code. The completed dialogue box is shown in Figure 7.36.

Visual Basic

The Visual Basic combo box can be of any of the three types offered by the other environments. The Text property should be cleared (initial values must be entered when the program is run). The finished dialogue box is shown in Figure 7.37).

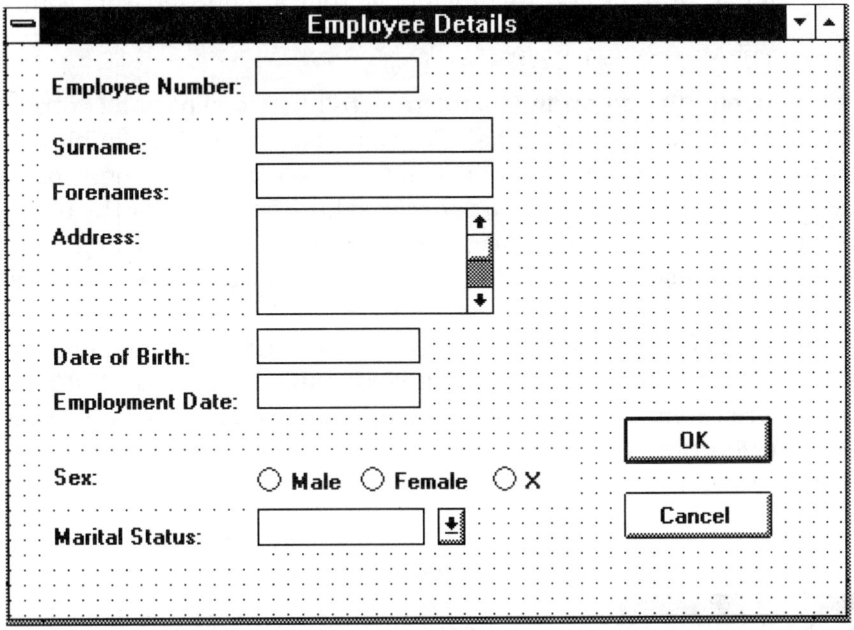

Figure 7.37 Visual Basic dialogue box with combo box

SCROLL BARS

Windows frequently have *scroll bars* on the right or at the bottom to allow the user to scroll to parts of the window that are not currently visible. Similarly, text controls that allow for more text than can be shown in the control have scroll bars and long lists result in scroll bars being added to list and combo boxes. All these scroll bars have a fixed position and size; the programmer may be able to decide whether or not they are displayed but frequently they are added automatically when the window or control is created. These scroll bars are all part of some control or window; they are not separate controls in their own right.

Sometimes it is useful to add an independent scroll bar, a separate control that is not connected to any window, text box or list. For example, the mouse double-click speed is adjusted in the Windows Control Panel using a scroll bar. The scroll bar provides a pictorial method of entering a value in a range and is often easier for the user than a text box. The use of a scroll bar also reduces the amount of error checking that is needed; using a scroll bar, the user cannot enter a value that is outside the allowed range.

A scroll bar consists of a long thin box, with an arrow button at each end. Between the buttons is a 'grey' area, in which is a *scroll box*, a small rectangle that can be moved anywhere in the grey area. The scroll box is also referred to as the *thumb* position. Scroll bars can be either horizontal or vertical.

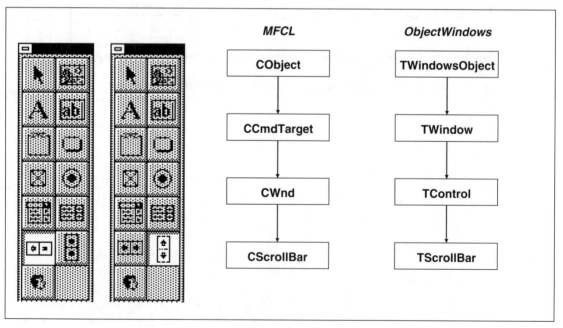

Figure 7.38 Scroll bars

The position of the control box on the scroll bar represents a value in a specified range. When creating the scroll bar, the following parameters are specified:

- The *minimum* value, returned when the scroll box is on the left of a horizontal scroll bar or at the top of a vertical bar

- The *maximum* value, returned when the scroll box is on the right of a horizontal scroll bar or at the bottom of a vertical bar

- The *small change* value, which is the amount by which the return value changes when an arrow button is clicked

- The *large change* value, which is the amount by which the return value changes when the grey area of the scroll bar is clicked

The small change and large change values are also sometimes referred to as the *line magnitude* and *page magnitude* respectively. (On a text box or window, clicking an arrow button usually scrolls the text one line whereas clicking the grey area scrolls the text by one 'page', i.e. one boxful.)

By default, the range of the scroll bar is 0-100, the small change is 1 and the large change 10.

There are events for the various scroll bar activities: clicking on an arrow button or the grey area, or dragging the scroll box. The methods allow you to change the range or other parameters, move the scroll box to a new position, or retrieve the current position (as a value in the current range).

Visual C++ has a CScrollBar class, derived from CWnd. App Studio and Visual Basic have horizontal and vertical scroll bars on their toolbars (Figure 7.38).

The scroll bars have very simple properties in App Studio (Figure 7.39). The Align property determines whether or not the scroll bar is fixed to one edge of the dialogue box.

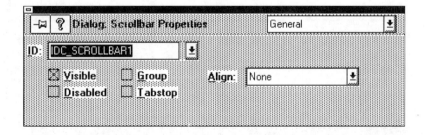

Figure 7.39 Scroll bar properties

ObjectWindows has a TScrollBar class, derived from TControl.

Figure 7.40 illustrates a Visual Basic form where a scroll bar is used as an alternative to a text box for entering a percentage value. The procedures for transferring values between the two controls are shown in Figures 7.41 and 7.42.

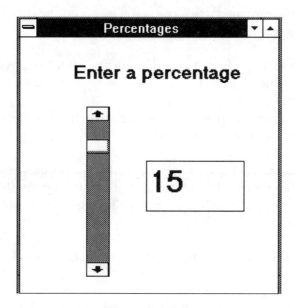

Figure 7.40 Scroll bar example

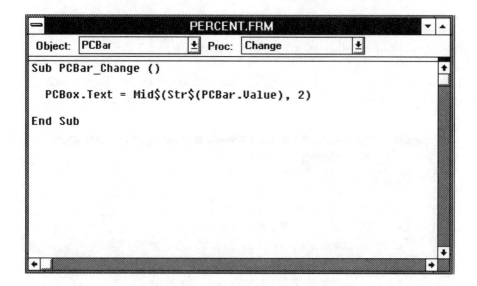

Figure 7.41 Scroll bar example: scroll bar procedure

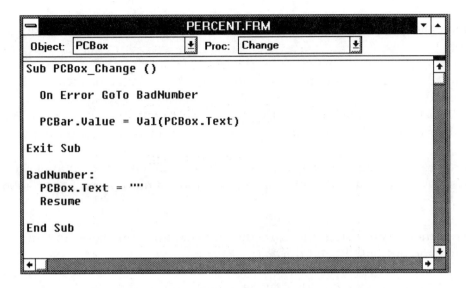

Figure 7.42 Scroll bar example: text box procedure

TESTING THE DIALOGUE BOX

To complete the dialogue box, add access keys and decide the tab order, as described in Chapter 6.

In Visual C++, you can check on the way in which the dialogue box will work with the App Studio Resource I Test option (press CTRL-T). In Borland's Resource Workshop, use Options I Test Dialog or click on the Test button on the toolbox. For Visual Basic, an individual form cannot be tested until it is linked in to the main window in some way.

The box appears on screen exactly as it would when run as part of an application. The text boxes can be filled in, radio buttons selected and options chosen from combo boxes (Figure 7.43).

You can test the entry of values, the use of the TAB key and access keys, and the operation of the command buttons. To end the test:

- In App Studio, clicking on either OK or Cancel, pressing ENTER or ESC, or clicking on Close in the control-menu box, ends the test.

- In Resource Workshop, the OK and Cancel buttons do not yet have any code attached, so you must use the control-menu box or ALT-F4 to end the test.

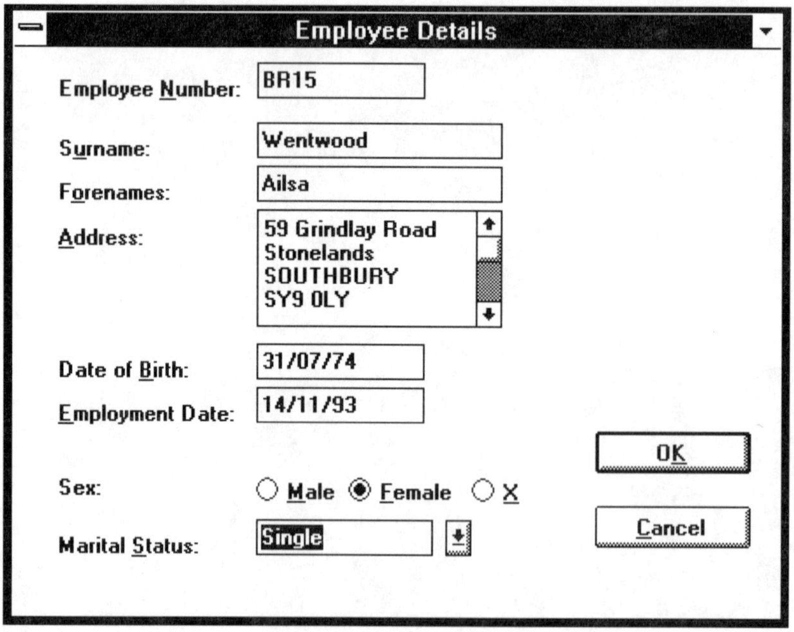

Figure 7.43 Testing the dialogue box

DIALOGUE BOX CODE

Inspecting the PERS.RC file for the Visual C++ application, you can see that the dialogue information has changed. The altered sections are shown in Figure 7.44. There is a line for each object, giving the type of control, plus its ID, co-ordinates, size and any properties that have been set to True. Initialisation information is also given.

In addition, new constant definitions are added to RESOURCE.H for the extra control IDs (Figure 7.45).

The revised ObjectWindows resource file, PERS2.RC, is shown in Figure 7.46.

In the case of Visual Basic, there is still no code available for inspection.

```
/////////////////////////////////////////////////////////////////////////
//
// Dialog
//

...

IDD_DIALOG1 DIALOG DISCARDABLE  50, 50, 250, 193
STYLE DS_MODALFRAME | WS_MINIMIZEBOX | WS_POPUP | WS_CAPTION | WS_SYSMENU
CAPTION "Employee Details"
FONT 8, "MS Sans Serif"
BEGIN
    LTEXT           "Employee &Number:",IDC_STATIC,15,10,65,10
    EDITTEXT        IDC_EDIT1,80,5,55,12,ES_UPPERCASE | ES_AUTOHSCROLL
    LTEXT           "S&urname:",IDC_STATIC,15,30,65,10
    EDITTEXT        IDC_EDIT3,80,25,80,12,ES_AUTOHSCROLL
    LTEXT           "F&orenames:",IDC_STATIC,15,45,65,10
    EDITTEXT        IDC_EDIT4,80,40,80,12,ES_AUTOHSCROLL
    LTEXT           "&Address:",IDC_STATIC,15,60,65,10
    EDITTEXT        IDC_EDIT2,80,55,80,40,ES_MULTILINE | ES_AUTOHSCROLL |
                    WS_VSCROLL
    LTEXT           "Date of &Birth:",IDC_STATIC,15,105,65,10
    EDITTEXT        IDC_EDIT5,80,100,55,12,ES_AUTOHSCROLL
    LTEXT           "&Employment Date:",IDC_STATIC,15,120,65,10
    EDITTEXT        IDC_EDIT7,80,115,55,12,ES_AUTOHSCROLL
    LTEXT           "Sex:",IDC_STATIC,15,145,65,10
    CONTROL         "&Male",IDC_RADIO1,"Button",BS_AUTORADIOBUTTON |
                    WS_TABSTOP,80,145,30,10
    CONTROL         "&Female",IDC_RADIO2,"Button",BS_AUTORADIOBUTTON |
                    WS_TABSTOP,110,145,35,10
    CONTROL         "&X",IDC_RADIO3,"Button",BS_AUTORADIOBUTTON | WS_TABSTOP,
                    150,145,20,10
    LTEXT           "Marital &Status:",IDC_STATIC,15,165,65,10
```

Figure 7.44 Alterations to PERS.RC (continues)

```
      COMBOBOX          IDC_COMBO2,80,160,70,30,CBS_DROPDOWN | WS_VSCROLL |
                        WS_TABSTOP
      DEFPUSHBUTTON     "O&K",IDOK,190,130,50,14
      PUSHBUTTON        "&Cancel",IDCANCEL,190,155,50,14
END

/////////////////////////////////////////////////////////////////////////////
//
// Dialog Info
//

IDD_DIALOG1 DLGINIT
BEGIN
    115, 0x403, 7, 0
0x6953, 0x676e, 0x656c, "\000"
    115, 0x403, 8, 0
0x614d, 0x7272, 0x6569, 0x0064,
    115, 0x403, 8, 0
0x6957, 0x6f64, 0x6577, 0x0064,
    115, 0x403, 10, 0
0x6553, 0x6170, 0x6172, 0x6574, 0x0064,
    115, 0x403, 9, 0
0x6944, 0x6f76, 0x6372, 0x6465, "\000"
    115, 0x403, 8, 0
0x6e55, 0x6e6b, 0x776f, 0x006e,
    0
END

/////////////////////////////////////////////////////////////////////////////
```

Figure 7.44 (continued) Alterations to PERS.RC

```
#define IDC_EDITEMPNO            102
#define IDC_EDITADDRESS          103
#define IDC_EDITSURNAME          104
#define IDC_EDITFORENAMES        105
#define IDC_EDITDOB              106
#define IDC_EDITEMPDATE          109
#define IDC_RADIOMALE            111
#define IDC_RADIOFEMALE          112
#define IDC_RADIOX               113
#define IDC_COMBOSTATUS          115
```

Figure 7.45 Additions to RESOURCE.H

```
DIALOG_1 DIALOG 15, 15, 230, 157
STYLE DS_MODALFRAME | WS_POPUP | WS_CAPTION | WS_SYSMENU | WS_MINIMIZEBOX
CAPTION "Employee Details"
BEGIN
   LTEXT "Employee &Number:", -1, 15, 10, 65, 8, WS_CHILD | WS_VISIBLE | WS_GROUP
   EDITTEXT 103, 86, 10, 40, 10, ES_LEFT | WS_CHILD | WS_VISIBLE | WS_BORDER |
        WS_TABSTOP
   LTEXT "S&urname:", -1, 15, 25, 65, 10, WS_CHILD | WS_VISIBLE | WS_GROUP
   EDITTEXT 103, 86, 26, 75, 10, ES_LEFT | WS_CHILD | WS_VISIBLE | WS_BORDER |
        WS_TABSTOP
   LTEXT "F&orenames:", -1, 15, 41, 65, 8, WS_CHILD | WS_VISIBLE | WS_GROUP
   EDITTEXT 103, 85, 41, 75, 10, ES_LEFT | WS_CHILD | WS_VISIBLE | WS_BORDER |
        WS_TABSTOP
   LTEXT "&Address:", -1, 15, 56, 65, 8, WS_CHILD | WS_VISIBLE | WS_GROUP
   CONTROL "", 103, "EDIT", ES_LEFT | ES_MULTILINE | WS_CHILD | WS_VISIBLE |
        WS_BORDER | WS_VSCROLL | WS_TABSTOP, 85, 56, 75, 20
   LTEXT "Date of &Birth:", -1, 15, 85, 65, 8, WS_CHILD | WS_VISIBLE | WS_GROUP
   EDITTEXT 103, 85, 85, 40, 10, ES_LEFT | WS_CHILD | WS_VISIBLE | WS_BORDER |
        WS_TABSTOP
   LTEXT "&Employment Date:", -1, 15, 100, 65, 8, WS_CHILD | WS_VISIBLE | WS_GROUP
   EDITTEXT 103, 85, 100, 40, 10, ES_LEFT | WS_CHILD | WS_VISIBLE | WS_BORDER |
        WS_TABSTOP
   LTEXT "Sex:", -1, 15, 115, 65, 8, WS_CHILD | WS_VISIBLE | WS_GROUP
   CONTROL "&Male", 104, "BUTTON", BS_AUTORADIOBUTTON | WS_CHILD | WS_VISIBLE |
        WS_TABSTOP, 85, 115, 28, 12
   CONTROL "&Female", 105, "BUTTON", BS_AUTORADIOBUTTON | WS_CHILD | WS_VISIBLE |
        WS_TABSTOP, 115, 115, 35, 12
   CONTROL "&X", 106, "BUTTON", BS_AUTORADIOBUTTON | WS_CHILD | WS_VISIBLE |
        WS_TABSTOP, 150, 115, 15, 12
   LTEXT "Marital &Status:", -1, 15, 130, 65, 8, WS_CHILD | WS_VISIBLE | WS_GROUP
   CONTROL "Single", 107, "COMBOBOX", CBS_DROPDOWNLIST | WS_CHILD | WS_VISIBLE |
        WS_TABSTOP, 85, 130, 49, 25
   DEFPUSHBUTTON "O&K", 101, 170, 100, 50, 10, WS_CHILD | WS_VISIBLE | WS_TABSTOP
   PUSHBUTTON "&Cancel", 102, 170, 120, 50, 10, WS_CHILD | WS_VISIBLE | WS_TABSTOP
END
```

Figure 7.46 Alterations to PERS2.RC

8 | Menus

Menus are a feature of most Windows applications. All Windows users are familiar with menus and their use, and they provide a convenient way for grouping together related procedures. The creation of menu systems is surprisingly easy, and it is also possible to expand or reduce menus at run-time. This chapter discusses the issues involved in setting up a menu system.

DROP-DOWN MENUS

Most Windows programs have a *menu bar* along the top of the window. The bar contains a row of menu names, associated with each of which is a *drop-down menu*. This is a list of menu items that appear below the menu name when the name is clicked. The term *menu* is usually taken to mean the menu name and its associated list of items. Therefore a menu bar consists of a number of separate menus.

Somewhat confusingly, drop-down menus are also sometimes called *pop-up menus*. This term is also used in other circumstances. Sometimes clicking on a menu item will result in a *sub-menu* appearing to the right of the main menu. Sub-menus are also referred to as pop-up menus or *cascading menus*. Here, the terms 'drop-down menu' and 'sub-menu' are used.

The operation of a menu system is very simple:

- Clicking on a menu name brings up the menu.

- Clicking on an item in the menu executes the related procedure or brings up a sub-menu.

- Clicking on any other part of the window removes the drop-down menu from the window.

Menus have a number of other features:

- When a menu has been clicked, the arrow keys can be used to move around the menu system, an item being selected by pressing ENTER.

- Menu names may have access keys, underlined in the name, which activate the menu when pressed following the ALT key (the ALT key and access key do not have to be pressed simultaneously).

- Menu items may also have access keys, for which ALT is not necessary.

- Menus items may have *shortcuts*, or *accelerator keys*, which allow the menu item to be called directly without bringing up the menus.

- Check marks (ticks) can be placed against menu items.

- Menu items that are temporarily unavailable can be 'greyed out'.

- Menus can be subdivided by the inclusion of *separator bars*.

All of these features are implemented quite simply.

CREATING AND EDITING A MENU

The methods for creating menus are very different from one development environment to another.

Visual C++

The Microsoft Foundation Class Library has a CMenu class, which is derived directly from CObject. The class allows you to create a menu object and has procedures for adding menu items and changing their properties (disabled, greyed, checked, etc.)

The easiest way to create a Visual C++ menu is through App Studio. Selecting the Resource | New option gives a list of resource types (Figure 8.1). Selecting Menu gives you a blank menu, with an empty box for a new menu name. When you start to type a name in this box, the Properties window pops up. In here you type the caption for the menu and give it other attributes (as described below).

When a menu has been created, you can add a new item by filling in the empty box that appears below the menu. The process is the same as for the original menu name but you should also enter a prompt to be displayed on the status line (Figure 8.2). The system

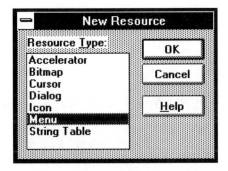

Figure 8.1 Selecting the menu resource

Figure 8.2 Menu item properties

will give it a unique ID consisting of the text 'ID', the menu name and option name, separated by underscores: e.g. ID_FILE_OPEN.

Clicking on any existing menu name displays the menu and new items can be added at the bottom. New menu names can be added to the menu bar at any time.

Menu names and items are inserted by clicking on any existing name and pressing the INS key. A menu or item is removed by clicking on it and pressing DEL. Items can be moved from one menu to another by dragging them.

Choosing the File | Save option updates the resource file with the changes. If you want to save the menu in a different resource file, start by opening the file or creating a new one *before* you add the new menu.

You can also load and edit an existing menu. App Studio is supplied with a default menu system (IDR_MAINFRAME), which includes standard File, Edit and Help menus (Figure 8.3). The Resource | Open option allows you to load any Menu resource.

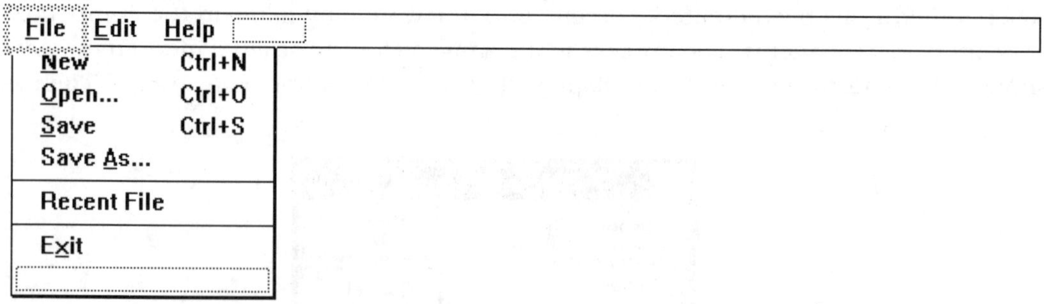

Figure 8.3 The default menu system

In the example program, you can add a new menu option to bring up the data entry dialogue box:

1   Insert a new Employees menu in front of the Help menu, by clicking on the Help menu and then pressing the INS key. In the gap that is created, type 'Employees'. The Properties box is displayed (Figure 8.4). Note that the menu expands to make room for the name as it is typed in.

2   Click on the blank box under the Employees menu and type 'Enter Details...'. The three dots indicate that the option leads to a dialogue box. For the Prompt, type 'Enter details of new employees' (Figure 8.5). When you next inspect the Properties box you will see that the system has added an ID of ID_EMPLOYEES_ENTER-DETAILS.

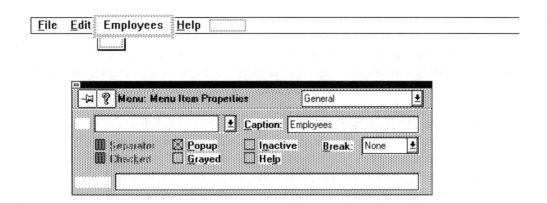

Figure 8.4 Adding a new menu

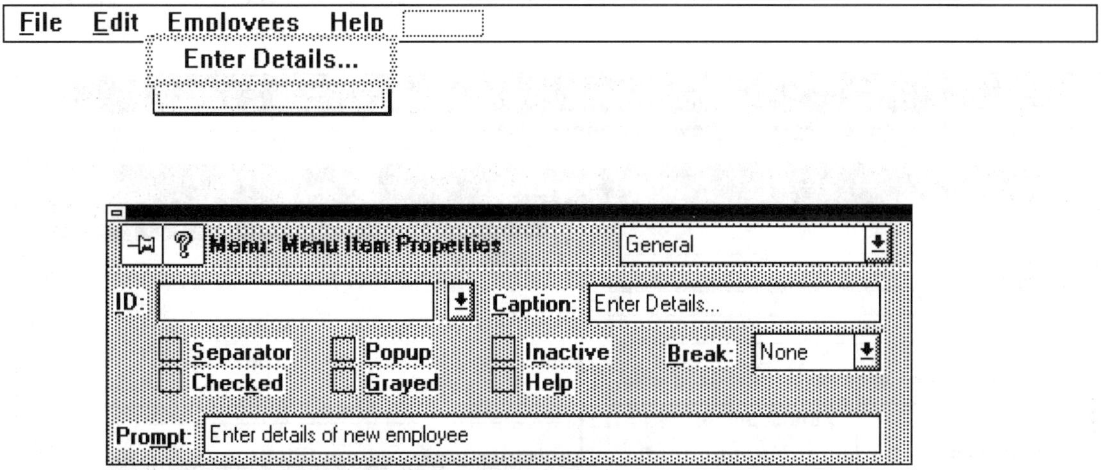

Figure 8.5 Adding a menu item

Press CTRL-S to save the changes. The code to bring up the dialogue box will be attached in the next chapter.

ObjectWindows

Menus for Borland C++ and Pascal are held in a resource file, as for Visual C++, This file must be compiled using a resource editor, such as Resource Workshop, or the command-line resource compiler, RC. The compiled file is than included in the project. If you need to change a menu later, all you need to do is change the resource file and then relink the project.

Within the main C++ program, the menu is attached to the window by calling the AssignMenu method, with the menu ID as the argument. The effect of this method is to assign the menu to the Menu attribute of the window's data structure, Attr. For Pascal programs, the LoadMenu function is used. The method of creating menus using Resource Workshop is described here and applies to both C++ and Pascal programs.

From within Resource Workshop, start the menu with Resource I New, selecting the MENU type. A new inner window is displayed, split into three sections (Figure 8.6):

- The left-hand side shows the properties for the currently selected menu name or menu item.

- The top part of the right-hand side shows how the menu will appear; clicking on an item here brings up the corresponding properties on the left.

- The third section shows an abbreviated form of the resource script for the menu.

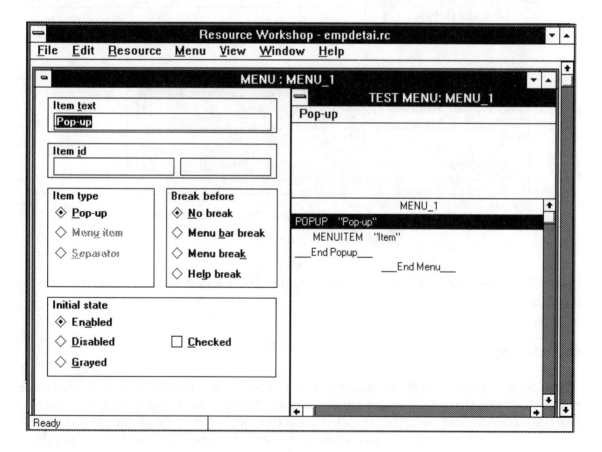

Figure 8.6 The menu editor

To create the new set of menus, the procedure is as follows:

1   First, add a standard File Menu. Resource Workshop has standard menus for File, Edit and Help. Click on the 'End Popup' line in the script window and then select Menu | New File Pop-up. An extensive File menu is added (Figure 8.7).

2   Repeat for New Edit Pop-up and New Help Pop-up.

3   Click on the dummy 'Pop-up' menu at the top of the script and remove it from the menu with Edit | Cut (SHIFT-DEL).

4   Insert the Employees menu by clicking on the 'End Popup' line above the Help menu and choosing Menu | New Pop-up. Edit the Item Text so that it becomes 'Employees'.

5   Move down to the MENUITEM line and edit 'Item' to become 'Enter Details...'.

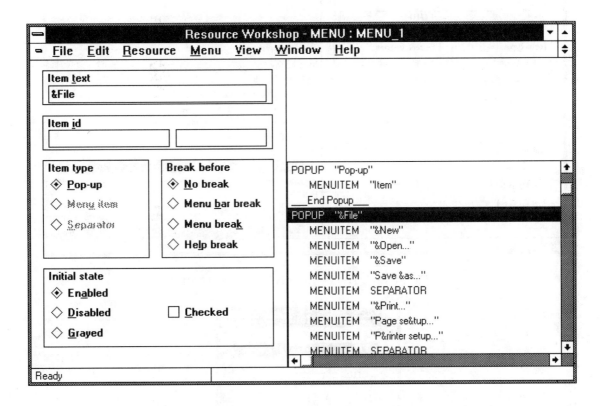

Figure 8.7 Inserting a File menu

The new menu system is shown in Figure 8.8. You can test the menus by clicking on the names in the top right section of the screen.

Finally, you should give each new menu item an Item ID, consisting of 'CM_' plus the menu and item names: for example, CM_FILEOPEN, CM_EMPLOYEESENTERDETAILS. (There is no need to do this for the standard menus, which are already catered for.)

Save the details with File | Save Project and close the Menu Designer window. The resource file window now shows the current contents of the file (Figure 8.9). Any of these items can be edited by double-clicking on them.

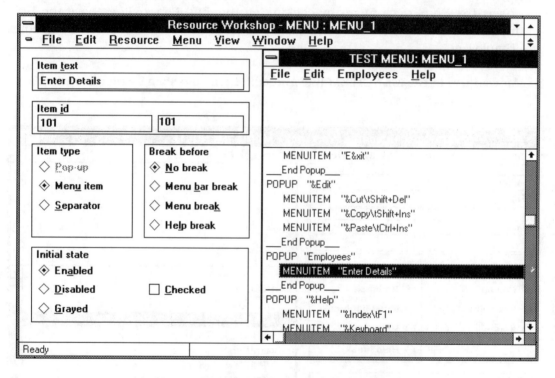

Figure 8.8 The completed menu system

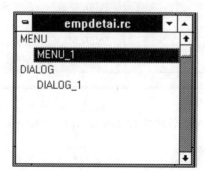

Figure 8.9 The updated resource list

Visual Basic

Visual Basic has an approach that is similar in some respects to that of App Studio. The form to which the menu is to be attached must be the active form; click on the form to make it so. (In the example, this is the main form, EmployeeDetails.)

Then select Window | Menu Design (or press CTRL-M) to load the Menu Designer. The top half of the window shows the menu properties, with the menu structure in the lower half.

Enter the menu name in the caption box at the top of the window, then give it a unique ID in the Name box. The other properties set the menu item's attributes. To enter an item for the menu, click on Next and then on the right-arrow button; this indents the item, indicating that it is part of the menu whose name is above.

After filling out one menu, click on Next and the left-arrow button to start the next menu. Then continue as before.

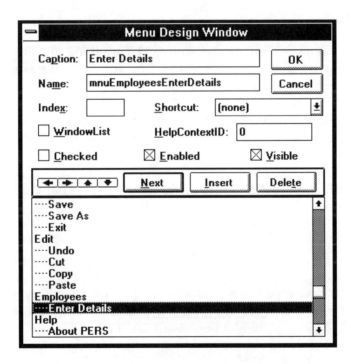

Figure 8.10 Visual Basic Menu Design Window

When the menu system is complete (Figure 8.10), the buttons in the middle of the Design Window can be used to tidy it up:

- The left-arrow button removes one level of indent, making a menu item into a menu; the right-arrow button increases the indent level, making a menu name into a menu item.

- The up-arrow button moves a menu component up the structure; the down-arrow button moves it down.

- The Next button highlights the next menu component.

- The Insert button inserts a new menu name or menu item.

- The Delete button deletes the highlighted name.

Clicking on OK saves the changes and attaches the menu system to the form. You can test the menus by clicking on them. Pressing CTRL-S saves the form with its menu.

MENU CAPTIONS

The captions for menu names and menu items can be anything you like. They can include spaces and may consist of one or more words. The size of each menu will be adjusted automatically to take the largest item in the menu.

There is a general convention that any menu item that leads to a dialogue box includes three dots at the end of the caption. This can be a helpful indication for the user that more information is needed.

If there are more menu names than will fit on the menu bar, the bar automatically spreads over to a second line.

SUB-MENUS

Any menu item can have a sub-menu attached, so that it effectively acts as if it were a menu name. Each item on this second-level menu may, in turn, have its own sub-menu, and so on. In all, you can usually reach about six levels of menu (menu name, main menu items and four levels of sub-menu).

However, sub-menus are confusing for the user and you should avoid having more than one level of sub-menu. Indeed, if possible, do not have any sub-menus at all. Sub-menus can often be replaced by dialogue boxes:

- Selecting a menu item can be simulated by clicking on one of a set of command buttons, or clicking on a radio button.

- Placing a check mark against a menu item is the same as clicking on a check box.

Development environments handle the creation of sub-menus in different ways:

- Sub-menus are created in the Microsoft Foundation Class Library by calling the CreatePopUpMenu method of the CMenu class. In App Studio, a sub-menu is attached by clicking on the check box for a menu item's Popup property.

- Menu resources for Borland's C++ allow sub-menus by adding further code to the resource file.

- Visual Basic provides the simplest method. An item is converted to a sub-menu item by clicking on the right-arrow button.

Note that not all top-level menu names have to have menu items attached to them. A menu name can result in action being taken directly, rather than leading to a drop-down menu.

ACCESS KEYS

Access keys are allocated to menus in the same way as for controls. An ampersand (&) should be inserted in the caption of either a menu name or menu item, in front of the access key. The access letter will be underlined on the menu bar or menu. The user selects a menu by pressing ALT and then the letter; when a menu is displayed the user just presses the letter key for the option required.

For example, the Caption for the File menu is usually '&File' and for the Save As option is 'Save &As'. The user can select Save As by pressing ALT F A or by clicking on File and then pressing A. Similarly, if the Save option has a caption of '&Save' the option is selected by pressing ALT F S.

Make sure that you allocate a different access key for each menu on the menu bar, and different keys for the options in any particular drop-down menu or sub-menu. (The same access key can be used for two menu items if they are in different menus.)

ACCELERATORS (SHORTCUT KEYS)

An alternative to access keys for the user is the use of accelerators. An *accelerator key* removes the need to go through the menu system. Accelerator keys are also called *shortcut keys*. For example, the accelerator key combination CTRL-S is often allocated to the File | Save option. Pressing CTRL and S together has the same effect of clicking on File and Save (or pressing ALT F S). Menu options often have both an access key and an accelerator key.

Using Accelerator Keys

When assigning accelerator keys you should bear in mind the following points:

- Be consistent about the use of different types of keys; use all CTRL keys or all function keys but do not mix them.

- If you have an Edit menu, use CTRL-INS for Copy, SHIFT-DEL for Cut and SHIFT-INS for Paste. These are the standards, which the user will expect. Do not use INS or DEL for anything else.

- For all other menus, stick to letter keys and function keys; there is no need for other keys and these are difficult to remember for the user.

- Only supply accelerator keys for the most frequently used options; if you apply too many accelerators the user won't be able to remember them all and so won't use them.

You can also attach accelerator keys to IDs other than those of menus. However, this is not usually a good idea.

Visual C++

In App Studio, the accelerator key is allocated in the menu option's Properties window. The accelerator keys are defined in a separate resource, the *accelerator table*. Before an accelerator key can be used it must be defined in the menu resource and then added to the accelerator table. An *accelerator table* provides a link between a key and a menu item, so that pressing the key invokes the menu item.

The first stage is to add the accelerator to the caption in the menu resource. Edit the caption (or create it with a shortcut to start with) by adding '\t' and the text you want to appear. '\t' represents a tab character, so shifts the shortcut text to the right. For example, the caption for File|Save might be changed to:

```
&Save\tCtrl+S
```

On the menu, this will appear as:

```
&Save       Ctrl+S
```

Whether you use '^S', 'Ctrl-S', 'Ctrl+S' or any other representation is a matter of preference. It does not affect the way accelerator is used; this is determined by the accelerator table.

The next stage is to load the accelerator table, either with Resource|New or Resource|Open (depending on whether you are creating a new table or amending an existing table – the usual practice). Select the resource type of 'Accelerator' and then give a filename for the table or choose an existing resource file.

The accelerator table lists the menu IDs with their corresponding keys (Figure 8.11). New entries are made by typing a menu ID in the empty box at the bottom of the list.

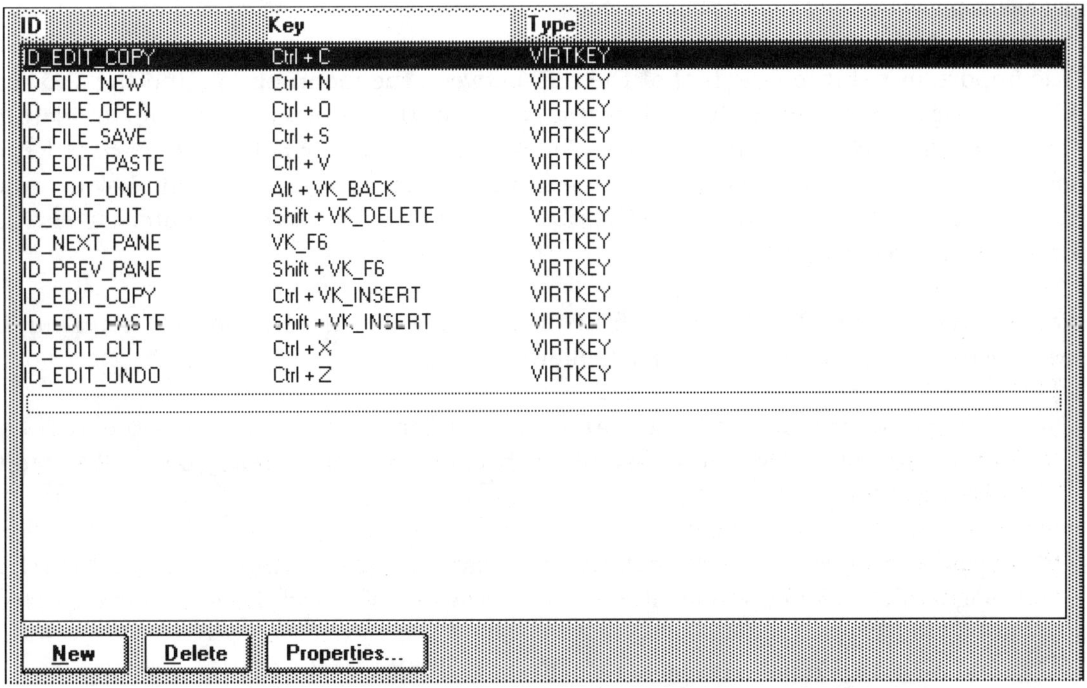

ID	Key	Type
ID_EDIT_COPY	Ctrl + C	VIRTKEY
ID_FILE_NEW	Ctrl + N	VIRTKEY
ID_FILE_OPEN	Ctrl + O	VIRTKEY
ID_FILE_SAVE	Ctrl + S	VIRTKEY
ID_EDIT_PASTE	Ctrl + V	VIRTKEY
ID_EDIT_UNDO	Alt + VK_BACK	VIRTKEY
ID_EDIT_CUT	Shift + VK_DELETE	VIRTKEY
ID_NEXT_PANE	VK_F6	VIRTKEY
ID_PREV_PANE	Shift + VK_F6	VIRTKEY
ID_EDIT_COPY	Ctrl + VK_INSERT	VIRTKEY
ID_EDIT_PASTE	Shift + VK_INSERT	VIRTKEY
ID_EDIT_CUT	Ctrl + X	VIRTKEY
ID_EDIT_UNDO	Ctrl + Z	VIRTKEY

New   Delete   Properties...

Figure 8.11 The accelerator table

The Properties window pops up and you can fill in the menu ID and the key. The key is either an ASCII key or a virtual key:

- An *ASCII key* is any standard key, usually a capital letter in the range A-Z, sometimes a number 0-9. Do not use other characters as accelerators; this is far too confusing for the user. The ASCII key is typed in either as a three-digit ASCII value or, more simply, as a single character (A-Z, 0-9).

- A *virtual key* is one of the special keys on the keyboard: INS, DEL, the function keys, CTRL, ALT, etc. The physical codes returned by these keys varies from one computer to another, so assigning a virtual key name rather than a key code means that you will always get the same result, whatever system the program is run on. Windows handles all the details of matching physical key codes with virtual key identifiers. Virtual keys are selected from the drop-down list.

Before entering the key select either the ASCII or VirtKey radio button.

Finally, you can add the CTRL, ALT or SHIFT modifiers (or a combination of them). For ASCII keys, you must have at least one modifier but you may have more: for example, CTRL-SHIFT-N. However, it is simpler for the user if you stick to just one modifier. For virtual keys, you do not have to have a modifier: for example, F9 and SHIFT-F9 are both acceptable.

The important point to note is that the link between the menu option and the shortcut key is made by the entry in the accelerator table, not the menu caption. If an accelerator key is assigned on the table it will be effective regardless of whether the correct key is given in the caption, or even if no key is mentioned in the caption at all. On the other hand, adding an accelerator key to the caption has no effect unless a matching entry is made in the accelerator table.

For example, in the IDR_MAINFRAME menu resource the new Employees menu can be given access keys and accelerators as follows:

1   Change the caption for the menu name to 'E&mployees'. This gives the menu an access key of ALT M. (Don't use ALT E because this has already been allocated to the Edit menu.)

2   Change the caption for the Enter Details option to '&Enter Details...\tCtrl+E' (Figure 8.12). The option will have an access key of E and there will be a shortcut of CTRL-E.

3   In the Accelerator list (also IDR_MAINFRAME), add an entry for ID_EMPLOYEES_ENTERDETAILS, consisting of the Key E and Modifier 'Ctrl', with a Type of 'VirtKey' (Figure 8.13).

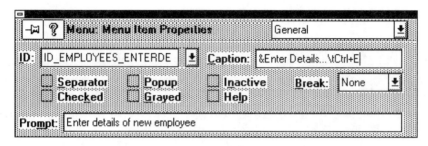

Figure 8.12 Assigning an access key

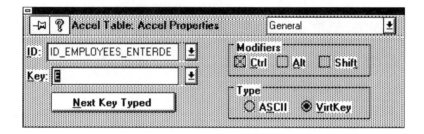

Figure 8.13 Adding an accelerator

The effect of these changes is that PERS.RC is updated to include the definition of the new menu (Figure 8.14). The following alterations are made:

- Instructions defining the new menu are included in the Menu section.

- The accelerator table entry for CTRL-E is inserted in the Accelerator section.

- The status-line prompt is defined by an addition to String Table section. (Note that the same identifier is used by Visual C++ to link the prompt to a menu option.)

The following line is added to RESOURCE.H:

```
#define ID_EMPLOYEES_ENTERDETAILS      32769
```

(Other ID values may also be changed.)

```
//////////////////////////////////////////////////////////////////////////
//
// Menu
//

...

    POPUP "E&mployees"
    BEGIN
        MENUITEM "&Enter Details...\tCtrl+E",    ID_EMPLOYEES_ENTERDETAILS
        , HELP
    END

...


//////////////////////////////////////////////////////////////////////////
//
// Accelerator
//

IDR_MAINFRAME ACCELERATORS PRELOAD MOVEABLE PURE
BEGIN
    "C",            ID_EDIT_COPY,            VIRTKEY,CONTROL, NOINVERT
    "E",            ID_EMPLOYEES_ENTERDETAILS,VIRTKEY,CONTROL, NOINVERT
    "N",            ID_FILE_NEW,             VIRTKEY,CONTROL, NOINVERT
    ...
END


//////////////////////////////////////////////////////////////////////////
//
// String Table
//

...


STRINGTABLE DISCARDABLE
BEGIN
    ID_EMPLOYEES_ENTERDETAILS "Enter details of new employees"
END

//////////////////////////////////////////////////////////////////////////
```

Figure 8.14 Changes to PERS.RC

ObjectWindows

Borland C++ and Pascal With Objects operate in a similar fashion to Visual C++. An accelerator table is set up, with entries in the same format as described above. The accelerator is added to the caption with the same '\t' tab character as Visual C++ and the link completed by making a corresponding entry in the accelerator table.

The default menus – File, Edit and Help – already have access keys and accelerators, so it is only the Employees menu that must be updated by inserting '&' and '\t' characters in the Item Text. It is also worth adding an accelerator of CTRL-S for the File | Save option.

The accelerator table is created with Resource | New, specifying a type of **ACCELERATORS**. The item IDs can be entered, with an accelerator key in each case (Figure 8.15). The easiest way of creating the correct key code is to use Accelerator | Key Value.

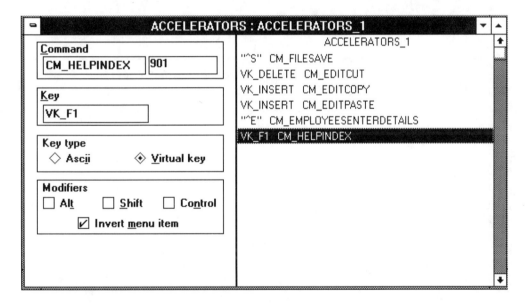

Figure 8.15 Assigning accelerators

It is advisable to take the #define statements out to a separate header or include file and then include that file in both the RC file and the source file.

The EMPDETAI.H file for C++ is shown in Figure 8.16 and the additional entries for EMPDETAI.RC are shown in Figure 8.17.

The files are similar for Pascal. The include file is called EMPDETAI.INC (Figure 8.18) and the first line of EMPDETAI.RC is:

```
#include "empdetai.inc"
```

```
#define CM_FILEOPEN            102
#define CM_FILESAVE            103
#define CM_FILENEW             101
#define CM_FILESAVEAS          104
#define CM_FILEPRINT           105
#define CM_FILEPAGESETUP       106
#define CM_FILEPRINTERSETUP    107
#define CM_FILEEXIT            108
#define CM_EDITCUT             201
#define CM_EDITCOPY            202
#define CM_EDITPASTE           203
#define CM_EMPLOYEESENTERDETAILS 301
#define CM_HELPINDEX           901
#define CM_HELPKEYBOARD        902
#define CM_HELPCOMMANDS        903
#define CM_HELPPROCEDURES      904
#define CM_HELPUSINGHELP       905
#define CM_HELPABOUT           999
```

Figure 8.16 Constant definitions in EMPDETAI.H

```
#include "empdetai.h"

MENU_1 MENU
BEGIN
    POPUP "&File"
    BEGIN
        MENUITEM "&New", CM_FILENEW
        MENUITEM "&Open...", CM_FILEOPEN
        MENUITEM "&Save\tCtrl+S", CM_FILESAVE
        MENUITEM "Save &as...", CM_FILESAVEAS
        MENUITEM SEPARATOR
        MENUITEM "&Print...", CM_FILEPRINT
        MENUITEM "Page se&tup...", CM_FILEPAGESETUP
        MENUITEM "P&rinter setup...", CM_FILEPRINTERSETUP
        MENUITEM SEPARATOR
        MENUITEM "E&xit", CM_FILEEXIT
    END

    POPUP "&Edit"
    BEGIN
        MENUITEM "&Cut\tShift+Del", CM_EDITCUT
        MENUITEM "&Copy\tShift+Ins", CM_EDITCOPY
        MENUITEM "&Paste\tCtrl+Ins", CM_EDITPASTE
    END
```

Figure 8.17 Additions to EMPDETAI.RC (continues)

```
    POPUP "E&mployees"
    BEGIN
        MENUITEM "&Enter Details...\tCtrl+E", CM_EMPLOYEESENTERDETAILS
    END

    POPUP "&Help"
    BEGIN
        MENUITEM "&Index\tF1", CM_HELPINDEX
        MENUITEM "&Keyboard", CM_HELPKEYBOARD
        MENUITEM "&Commands", CM_HELPCOMMANDS
        MENUITEM "&Procedures", CM_HELPPROCEDURES
        MENUITEM "&Using help", CM_HELPUSINGHELP
        MENUITEM SEPARATOR
        MENUITEM "&About...", CM_HELPABOUT
    END

END

ACCELERATORS_1 ACCELERATORS
BEGIN
  "^S", CM_FILESAVE
  VK_DELETE, CM_EDITCUT, VIRTKEY, SHIFT
  VK_INSERT, CM_EDITCOPY, VIRTKEY, SHIFT
  VK_INSERT, CM_EDITPASTE, VIRTKEY, CONTROL
  "^E", CM_EMPLOYEESENTERDETAILS
  VK_F1, CM_HELPINDEX, VIRTKEY
END
```

Figure 8.17 (continued) Additions to EMPDETAI.RC

```
const
    cm_FileNew                  =    101;
    cm_FileSave                 =    103;
    cm_FileOpen                 =    102;
    cm_FileSaveAs               =    104;
    cm_FilePrint                =    105;
    cm_FileExit                 =    108;
    cm_FileSetup                =    106;
    cm_FilePrinterSetup         =    107;
    cm_EditCut                  =    201;
    cm_EditCopy                 =    202;
    cm_EditPaste                =    203;
    cm_EmployeesEmployeeDetails =    101;
    cm_HelpIndex                =    901;
    cm_HelpKeyboard             =    902;
    cm_HelpCommands             =    903;
    cm_HelpProcedures           =    904;
    cm_HelpUsingHelp            =    905;
    cm_HelpAbout                =    999;
```

Figure 8.18 Pascal include file, EMPDETAI.INC

Visual Basic

Again, Visual Basic simplifies matters by handling the accelerator table for you. In the Menu Design Window, click on the menu item and then on the Shortcut drop-down arrow. A list of possible shortcut keys is displayed. Visual Basic limits this list to the following:

- CTRL plus a letter key

- SHIFT plus a letter key

- A function key

This should be enough for most applications. Click on the required key and the rest will be done for you.

CHECK MARKS

Any menu option can have a *check mark* (a tick) placed against it. The check can be put on when the menu is created, or toggled during the course of the program. Usually, the check mark is toggled on or off when the user clicks the option (rather like a check box). Alternatively, turning on the check mark for one option may turn off all the others on the menu or on part of the menu (like a set of radio buttons). If other menu options are affected, then the check marks must be changed in the menu items' procedures.

Check marks are used by Windows itself in a number of situations. Figure 8.19 shows the Window menu from Visual C++. Check marks indicate whether or not the toolbar and status bar are visible; these check marks are set independently of each other, and any combination can be turned on. The bottom part of the menu lists the open windows;

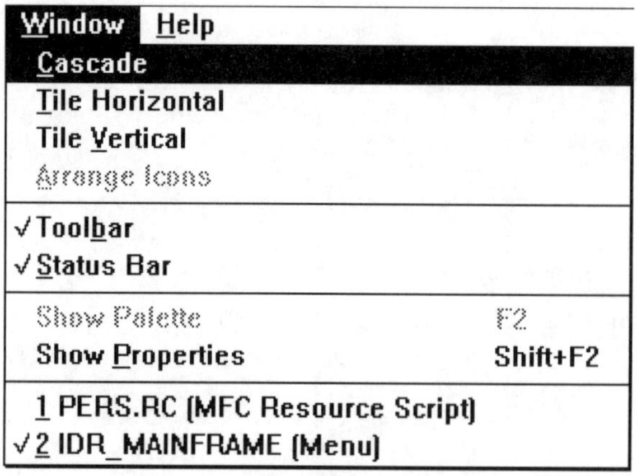

```
 Window   Help
   Cascade
   Tile Horizontal
   Tile Vertical
   Arrange Icons
 √ Toolbar
 √ Status Bar
   Show Palette              F2
   Show Properties           Shift+F2
   1 PERS.RC (MFC Resource Script)
 √ 2 IDR_MAINFRAME (Menu)
```

Figure 8.19 Menu with check marks, grey items & separators

here, the check mark identifies the current window and only one item may be checked at a time.

For the Microsoft Foundation Class Library, the CMenu class has a set of flags as part of its data, one of which determines whether a menu item is checked or unchecked when the object is created. The CheckMenuItem method is used within a program to turn the check marks on or off.

App Studio and Visual Basic both have Checked attributes in the Properties window. If this attribute is selected, the menu item will have a tick against it when the program is run. The check marks can be turned on or off within a procedure.

ObjectWindows allows similar flags to be set when the menu items are created and to be changed during the running of the program.

GREYED AND DISABLED ITEMS

In a similar way to the addition of check marks, a menu item can be 'greyed out', indicating that it is not currently available. This is done by displaying the menu item in a lighter colour (see Figure 8.19 above, where Arrange Icon and Show Palette are greyed out). Typically, when no data has been entered the File | Save option will be greyed out, as there is nothing to save.

The CMenu class for Visual C++ allows you to set three states:

- *Enabled*: option is available and not greyed out

- *Grayed*: option is not available and shown greyed

- *Disabled*: option is not available but shown in normal colour

The state is set when the menu is created and may be changed by a procedure.

App Studio and Visual Basic both have Enabled properties which, by default, are set on. In these environments, the menu items are set to Grayed when Enabled is turned off; there is no Disabled state directly available.

Borland menus have similar flags to those of CMenu.

SEPARATOR BARS

Sometimes it is useful to be able to subdivide menus so that related functions are grouped together. This is done by inserting separator bars in the menu. The *separator bar* is a dummy entry in the menu that appears as a thin line dividing entries. The bar takes up the same amount of space as a normal entry. It performs no other function; if the user clicks the separator bar there should be no effect at all. The separator bar is implemented as follows:

- The CMenu class has a Separator flag, along with the Checked, Greyed and other flags. In App Studio this is translated as a Separator box in the Properties window; clicking on this box converts the item into a separator bar.

- Borland's C++ window class has a similar flag, which must be set from within the Menu Editor. (There are examples in the default File menu.)

- For Visual Basic, a menu item is converted into a separator bar by putting a single dash (-) as the Caption.

In all these cases, each separator bar should be given a unique ID.

Where possible, separator bars should be avoided; often the need for separator bars is overcome by splitting a menu into two or by taking options out to a pop-up dialogue box. Sometimes, however, you have to have a large number of items in a menu and a separator bar then helps to make the menu less confusing. Always make sure that the separator bar provides a division that is logical and will make sense to the user.

Figure 8.19 above demonstrates the use of three separator bars to split the Window menu into four sections.

ATTACHING THE MENU

For the menu to be effective, it must be attached to the main window. For Visual C++ and Visual Basic, the menus are attached automatically. Borland C++ and Pascal require you to insert the code yourself.

Borland C++

For Borland C++, this is done by including an AssignMenu call in the TPersWindow constructor. The EMPDETAI.H header file must also be declared. EMPDETAI.RC must be added to the project file.

When the program is recompiled and run the menu will be effective (Figure 8.20), though as yet none of the options do anything. The revised program is shown in Figure 8.21.

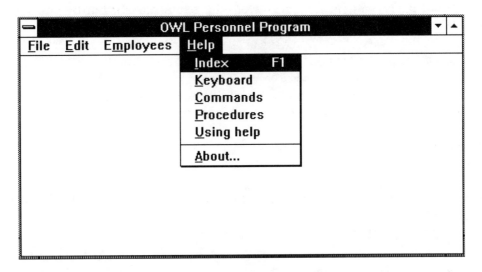

Figure 8.20 Menu attached to ObjectWindows program

```
// PERS2 ObjectWindows program

#include <owl.h>
#include "empdetai.h"

class TPersApp : public TApplication
{
public:
  TPersApp(LPSTR AName, HINSTANCE hInstance, HINSTANCE hPrevInstance,
    LPSTR lpCmdLine, int nCmdShow)
    : TApplication(AName, hInstance, hPrevInstance, lpCmdLine, nCmdShow) {};
  virtual void InitMainWindow();
};

_CLASSDEF(TMyWindow)
class TPersWindow : public TWindow
{
public:
//Revised declaration
  TPersWindow(PTWindowsObject AParent, LPSTR ATitle);
};

//Insert the constructor and assign the menu
TPersWindow::TPersWindow(PTWindowsObject AParent, LPSTR ATitle)
  : TWindow(AParent, ATitle)
{
  AssignMenu("MENU_1");
}

void TPersApp::InitMainWindow()
{
  MainWindow = new TPersWindow(NULL, Name);
}

int PASCAL WinMain(HINSTANCE hInstance, HINSTANCE hPrevInstance,
  LPSTR lpCmdLine, int nCmdShow)
{
  TPersApp PersApp("OWL Personnel Program", hInstance, hPrevInstance,
              lpCmdLine, nCmdShow);
  PersApp.Run();
  return PersApp.Status;
}
```

Figure 8.21 Revised PERS2.CPP

Borland Pascal

For Borland Pascal a number of changes must be made for the menu resource (and the dialogue box) to be used:

- The resource file must be saved in its binary (.RES) format (Figure 8.22).

- The $R directive must be included in the source file, specifying the .RES resource file.

- The $I directive must be used to specify the .INC include file.

- The Init method for the new class, TPersWindow, must be declared within the Type declaration and then defined.

- The LoadMenu function must be called from TPersWindow.Init, specifying the menu resource and putting the result in Attr.Menu.

The updated program is shown in Figure 8.23.

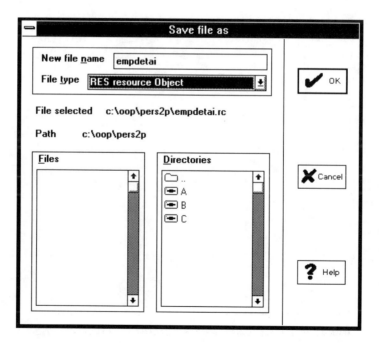

Figure 8.22 Saving the resource file in RES format

```
{**************************************************}
{                                                  }
{   ObjectWindows Minimal Program                  }
{                                                  }
{**************************************************}

program pers2p;

uses WinTypes, WinProcs, OWindows;

{$R EMPDETAI.RES}

{$I EMPDETAI.INC}

type
  PPersWindow = ^TPersWIndow;
  TPersWindow = object(TWindow)
    { Declare constructor }
    constructor Init(AParent: PWindowsObject; ATitle: PChar);
    { Message handlers will be declared here }
  end;
  TPersApp = object(TApplication)
    procedure InitMainWindow; virtual;
  end;

{ Define constructor for window }
constructor TPersWindow.Init(AParent: PWindowsObject; ATitle: PChar);
begin
  inherited Init(AParent, ATitle);
  Attr.Menu := LoadMenu(HInstance, 'MENU_1');
end;

procedure TPersApp.InitMainWindow;
begin
  MainWindow := New(PPersWindow, Init(nil, 'Pascal Personnel Program'));
end;

var
  PersApp: TPersApp;

begin
  PersApp.Init('Pers2p');
  PersApp.Run;
  PersApp.Done;
end.
```

Figure 8.23 Updated Pascal program, PERS2P.PAS

9 | Responding to Events

By now, the appearance of the finished application should have been determined. The program consists of a main window, child windows and dialogue boxes. The windows probably have menu bars, with full menu system set up, and the dialogue boxes should be filled with a full variety of controls. The program can be run and the windows and menu will appear on screen as expected. As yet, however, they don't do anything other than respond in the standard ways. The main window can be resized, minimised and maximised; the menus can be made to drop down; and the program can be terminated by double-clicking on the control-menu box. Other than these 'intuitive' responses, built into the classes from which the objects are created, there is no effective response to the user's actions.

This chapter looks at the ways in which the objects can be made to respond to the events that may occur: displaying a dialogue box when a menu option is selected or performing a calculation when a button is clicked, for example.

EVENTS

Windows programs are *event-driven*. That is, the order of execution of the program's procedures is determined by externally-generated actions, rather than by the program code itself. With traditional programming methods the user is offered a fixed list of options, available at any time, and the program waits until some action is taken, then reacts to it.

Every action that the program might have to respond to is called an *event*. Events are not only created by the user; they may also be generated by the computer or be simulated by a call from another procedure. Typical events include:

- The mouse being dragged or a button being clicked

- A window being moved or resized

- An object getting or losing the focus, being created or being destroyed

- A processor clock tick

A program can simulate an event by a procedure for one object simply calling one of the event-handling functions of another object.

Note that the same event can be generated by more than one user action. For instance, the Click event for a command button is generated by the following actions:

- Clicking on the button

- Tabbing to the button and pressing the spacebar

- Pressing the access key for the button

- Pressing ENTER for the Default button

All of these actions result in Windows sending the same message to the application.

MESSAGES

When any event occurs, Windows responds by sending a *message* to the application. These messages are sent to the Run function of the CWinApp object, where they are added to the *message queue*. The Run function consists of a loop that takes the next message from the queue and passes it to the appropriate object for handling. The Run loop continues until the application is closed down.

The message is passed to the most suitable object, usually the main window. Depending on the type of message, this object will either deal with the message itself or pass it on to some other object, such as a child window or a control. In this way, a command chain is built up.

For each object, the programmer needs to create a separate function to handle each message for which some special action is required. These functions are called *message handlers*; they are also referred to as *message-handler member functions* or *message response functions*.

You do not need to create a message handler for every possible event – only for those where there is something to be done. If there is no message handler for a particular event, then the system checks further along the chain or deals with the message at a higher level. Remember that all controls are also windows (derived from class CWnd for Visual C++ or TWindow for ObjectWindows), which in turn are derived from CCmdTarget, the *command-target class*, or TWindowsObject. (A *command target* is an object that may have a handler for a message.) Therefore, if an object does not have a message handler for a particular message, the default handler from a class higher up the hierarchy will be used.

TYPES OF MESSAGE

Messages are actually constants, representing an integer value. When an event occurs, Windows determines the constant that corresponds to the event and passes it to the application as a message (using one of two functions: SendMessage and PostMessage). Other messages are passed between procedures. Thus there are messages such as BN_CLICKED (indicating a command button click event), WM_QUIT (a request to end an application), WM_LBUTTONDOWN (the left mouse button has been pressed down) and LB_INSERTSTRING (an instruction to insert a string in a list box).

There are about 200 messages, which fall into four broad categories: Windows messages, control notifications, command messages and control messages. You can also define your own messages.

Windows Messages

Windows messages are sent to the application by Windows itself. These are the messages that are generated as a result of some user action or some activity in the computer. For example:

- WM_LBUTTONDOWN indicates that the user has pressed the left button. The parameters that are passed with the message indicate what other key (CTRL or SHIFT) or button (middle or right) is being pressed at the same time and the current co-ordinates of the pointer. WM_LBUTTONUP is sent when the button is released. WM_MOUSEMOVE indicates movement of the mouse. These three messages can be used together to detect dragging of the pointer.

- WM_SIZE indicates that the window size has been changed. The parameters give the type of change (minimised, maximised, resizing) and the new size of the window.

- WM_TIMER is sent when the time limit for a timer has been reached.

Windows messages include most of those that begin WM_, the main exception being WM_COMMAND (see below).

Control-Notification Messages

Control-notification messages are sent by controls and child windows to their parent windows when some event occurs that may require a reaction from the parent window.

These messages are sent as WM_COMMAND messages, with one of the parameters identifying the control and another giving the *notification code*. This code identifies the type of event. For example:

- LBN_SETFOCUS indicates that a list box has received the focus.

- EN_VSCROLL occurs when the user clicks the vertical scroll bar of a text box (edit control).

- CBN_DROPDOWN indicates that the list in a combo box is about to drop down.

The notification messages all have 'N' immediately before the underscore character in the message name.

Note that the BN_CLICKED message, which indicates that a button has been clicked, is treated as a command message (see below). BN_CLICKED is activated for command buttons, radio buttons and check boxes.

Command Messages

Command messages are notification messages sent by user-interface objects: menus, accelerator keys and toolbar buttons. These messages are also sent as parameters in WM_COMMAND messages, the particular message being identified by 'ID_' plus the object name (for example, ID_FILE_OPEN).

Whereas Windows messages and control-notification messages are handled by the receiving window, these messages are sent along the command chain described earlier.

Control Messages

Control messages are sent by an application to a control. These messages are used to change the state of a control or check the current state. For example:

- LB_ADDSTRING adds a string to a list box; LB_GETCOUNT returns the number of strings in the list box.

- EM_LINESCROLL scrolls the contents of a text box by a specified number of lines; EM_GETLINECOUNT returns the number of lines of text in the box.

- CB_SHOWDROPDOWN hides or shows the list for a combo box; CB_FINDSTRING finds the first item in a combo box that starts with a specified string.

These messages are sent from within the application program using the Windows SendMessage function.

MESSAGE PARAMETERS

Most message functions require four parameters:

- The handle of the window sending the message or the control ID

- The message identifier

- A word parameter, wParam

- A double-word parameter, lParam

The first two parameters make sure that the message is sent to the correct handler function. The function can then make use of wParam and lParam. wParam is a word parameter and (very rarely) is split into two separate bytes, WP.Hi and WP.Lo. lParam is a double-word (long) parameter that is frequently split into its high and low word components, LP.Hi and LP.Lo.

For example, the value of the wParam parameter for WM_LBUTTONDOWN tells you which other keys or buttons are currently being pressed. The lParam parameter contains the co-ordinates of the pointer when the button is pressed: LP.Hi for the Y co-ordinate, LP.Lo for the X co-ordinate. For LB_ADDSTRING, wParam is not used; lParam points to the string to be added.

MESSAGE MAPS

The classes that can handle messages are derived from CCmdTarget for Visual C++ or TWindowsObject for ObjectWindows. These classes have a *message map*, which provides the link between messages and message handlers.

Any messages that are not handled by a derived class are dealt with by the DefWindowProc function.

CODE FOR MESSAGE HANDLERS

When a message handler has been declared and the blank definition set up, it is simply a matter of filling in the relevant code. The actual code that is used will depend on the language being used but the statements that may appear in a handler will fall into the following general categories:

- Standard code statements

- Calls to Windows functions and class methods

- Changes or requests to object properties

The standard code statements are those you would find in any traditional C, Pascal or BASIC program. The function calls and property changes require a little explanation.

Function Calls

A procedure can call Windows functions directly and it can also call the member functions for any of the classes.

Windows Functions
You can call any of the Windows API functions (of which there are about 600) directly in the code for Visual C++ and ObjectWindows programs; such direct calls are not permitted in Visual Basic (without the functions being explicitly declared first). The Windows API functions are listed in the reference manuals for both Visual C++ and ObjectWindows. For example, GetCursorPos returns the current co-ordinates of the pointer and Empty-Clipboard clears the clipboard. In fact, although you can program at this level, there is seldom any need to do so. The classes provided by the class libraries have functions to do most of the things you are likely to need.

Class Member Functions
Most of the function calls will refer to the public functions for the classes that are being used. Each object is an instance of a class and that class has a number of public functions (or methods) that are available throughout the application. For example, in Visual C++ the CListBox class has functions such as AddString for adding a new string to the list and GetCurSel to return the index number of the currently selected string. The methods used are used by calling the function for a particular instance of the class. For example:

```
TDialog::Cancel(Msg);
List1 -> AddString("Item 1");
```

In the first case, the Cancel method for TDialog is called; in the second case, List1 is a pointer to an object of the TListBox class and the AddString method is invoked for that object.

Remember that each class inherits the functions of its base class. If a function is not redefined by the class, it can be called for any object for that class.

The Visual C++ *Class Library Reference* lists the classes of the Microsoft Foundation Class Library, along with their functions.

ObjectWindows has similar sets of functions. For example, its TListBox class has functions AddString to add a new string and GetSelIndex to return the index of the selected string.

In both cases – Visual C++ and ObjectWindows – the public methods call Windows API functions and send messages. For instance, AddString calls the Windows SendMessage function, specifying the LB_ADDSTRING message. In this way, the public methods save you having to deal with Windows functions and messages directly.

Visual Basic provides similar facilities, through by a mixture of methods and properties. The methods are used in the format:

```
form.object.method arguments
```

The *form* can be omitted if the object is in the current form and the *object* can be omitted if the *method* is for the current object. Note that the *arguments* are not placed in brackets. For instance, there is an AddItem method to add a string to a list box. However, the index of the currently selected item is found by inspecting the ListIndex property.

Object Properties

The implementation of each object is determined by a set of properties: for instance, for a command button, the width and height, caption and so on. These properties can be inspected or changed from within a program.

In Visual C++, some properties are set by the Create function and others by additional functions. Other functions are used to retrieve or change the current properties for an object.

ObjectWindows is similar, but the properties are set initially by the constructor function. Other functions retrieve or change the current properties.

Visual Basic has long lists of properties, which are set directly when the object is defined at design time. While the program is running, most of these properties can be retrieved or changed by simple statements (in which the properties act like normal variables). The properties take the form *form.object.property*. For example, Form1.List1.ListIndex returns the number of the currently selected item in a list box.

RESPONDING TO MESSAGES

Now that the theory of messages in Windows has been covered, the practical aspects of implementing message handling can be considered. In the cases of Visual C++ and Visual Basic, most of the hard wok is done for you. ObjectWindows requires more work from the programmer but provides direct access to all the C++ code.

ADDING SOME CODE

When the dialogue box is complete, you can add the code to make the box into an effective part of the application:

1   The dialogue box must be linked in to the rest of the application.

2   Variables need to be set up for the controls.

3   Code must be added for each message that is to be handled.

Each of these steps is considered here.

LINKING TO A MENU ITEM

The first stage is to link the dialogue box to a menu item. Code must be attached to the Employees | Enter Details menu option so that it calls up the dialogue box.

Visual C++

For Visual C++, this is done by adding a message handler to the application class, CPersApp. There is already one message handler for this class, which displays the 'About' dialogue box. The new handler is best added through ClassWizard, as follows:

1   Load ClassWizard (press CTRL-W), select the CPersApp class and click on the ID_EMPLOYEES_ENTERDETAILS object ID. Two possible messages are shown (Figure 9.1), COMMAND and UPDATECOMMAND_UI. The Member Functions box shows the existing handler, OnAppAbout.

2   The COMMAND message is the one that handles menu selections. Click on this message and then on Add Function.

3   ClassWizard suggests the new function should be OnEmployeesEnterdetails. Click on OK. A template for the new handler is added to PERS.CPP by ClassWizard.

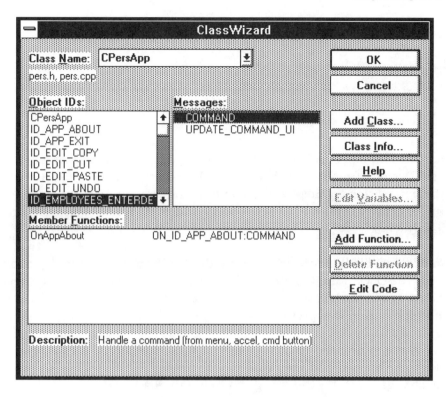

Figure 9.1 Member functions

4   Click on Edit Code to add some real code to the handler. The code will be similar to that for OnAppAbout, which is immediately above the new handler in the file (Figure 9.2).

5   Add the new code and save the changes (CTRL-S).

```
<2> C:\OOP\PERS\PERS.CPP
void CPersApp::OnAppAbout()
{
    CAboutDlg aboutDlg;
    aboutDlg.DoModal();
}

///////////////////////////////////////////////////////////
// CPersApp commands

void CPersApp::OnEmployeesEnterdetails()
{
    // TODO: Add your command handler code here
}
```

Figure 9.2 Message handler code

The code to load the dialogue box is as follows:

```
void CPersApp::OnEmployeesEnterdetails()
{
    EmpDetails DetailsDlg;
    DetailsDlg.DoModal();
}
```

This code creates an object called DetailsDlg for the EmpDetails class of dialogue boxes, then calls the DoModal function for that object. DoModal is a member function of CDialog, which is the parent class of EmpDetails. The function loads a modal dialogue box – one that ties up all activity until it is closed – and handles all interaction between the user and the dialogue box.

The OK and Cancel buttons are handled by the OnOK and OnCancel functions in the CDialog class. The OnOK function checks that all entries are valid; OnCancel restores the original values. When the box is closed, a value of either IDOK or IDCANCEL is returned, to indicate which button was pressed.

In this case, there is no need to change any of these functions. All we need is for the dialogue box to be opened and then closed. The revised PERS.H file is shown in Figure 9.3 and the changes to PERS.CPP are given in Figure 9.4.

```
// pers.h : main header file for the PERS application
//

#ifndef __AFXWIN_H__
    #error include 'stdafx.h' before including this file for PCH
#endif

#include "resource.h"           // main symbols


/////////////////////////////////////////////////////////////////////////////
// CPersApp:
// See pers.cpp for the implementation of this class
//

class CPersApp : public CWinApp
{
public:
    CPersApp();

// Overrides
    virtual BOOL InitInstance();
```

Figure 9.3 Revised PERS.H header file (continues)

```
// Implementation

   //{{AFX_MSG(CPersApp)
   afx_msg void OnAppAbout();
   afx_msg void OnEmployeesEnterdetails();
   //}}AFX_MSG
   DECLARE_MESSAGE_MAP()
};



////////////////////////////////////////////////////////////////////////////
```

Figure 9.3 (continued) Revised PERS.H header file

```
// pers.cpp : changed sections only
//

#include "stdafx.h"
#include "pers.h"

#include "mainfrm.h"
#include "persdoc.h"
#include "persview.h"
#include "empdetai.h"

/////?//////////////////////////////////////////////////////////////////////
// CPersApp

BEGIN_MESSAGE_MAP(CPersApp, CWinApp)
   //{{AFX_MSG_MAP(CPersApp)
   ON_COMMAND(ID_APP_ABOUT, OnAppAbout)
   ON_COMMAND(ID_EMPLOYEES_ENTERDETAILS, OnEmployeesEnterdetails)
   //}}AFX_MSG_MAP
   // Standard file based document commands
   ON_COMMAND(ID_FILE_NEW, CWinApp::OnFileNew)
   ON_COMMAND(ID_FILE_OPEN, CWinApp::OnFileOpen)
END_MESSAGE_MAP()

////////////////////////////////////////////////////////////////////////////
// CPersApp commands

void CPersApp::OnEmployeesEnterdetails()
{
   EmpDetails DetailsDlg;
   DetailsDlg.DoModal();
}
```

Figure 9.4 Changes to PERS.CPP to include message handler

Borland C++

For ObjectWindows, the link between the message and the message handler is made by giving the handler function a *dispatch index.* The equivalent of the Visual C++ message map is a *dynamic dispatch virtual table* (DDVT). This table is used by the compiler to match a handler to a message.

The dispatch index is allocated to the handler when the handler is declared. The index consists of the message code added to an ObjectWindows constant, WM_FIRST. The index is put in square brackets after an '=' sign.

By convention, the name of the handler function is created by taking the underscores out of the message name and converting to a mixture of upper and lower case. Therefore the declaration of the message handler for a left mouse button press is as follows:

```
virtual void WMLButtonDown(RTMessage Msg) = [WM_FIRST + WM_LBUTTONDOWN];
```

Msg is a variable of type RTMessage, which is a reference to a TMessage structure. This structure contains all the parameters that are passed along with the message.

The handler is defined in the main source file and is called a *message response member function.*

Similarly, handlers can be set up for the events that are generated when a menu option is clicked. For example, the handler to call the dialogue box will be declared in the TPersWindow definition as follows:

```
virtual void CMEmployeesEnterDetails(RTMessage Msg)
  = [CM_FIRST + CM_EMPLOYEESENTERDETAILS]
```

Note that, for menus, the base constant is CM_FIRST. The name of the function is fixed by convention only but the menu ID *must* match the ID given in the resource file.

The function is defined as follows:

```
void TPersWindow::CMEmployeesEnterDetails(RT Message)
{
  PTDialog DetailsDlg;
  DetailsDlg = new TDialog(this, "DIALOG_1");
  GetApplication()->ExecDialog(DetailsDlg);
}
```

The new dialogue box is created by specifying the DIALOG_1 identifier and the modal dialogue box is then put on screen by the ExecDialog function. The effect is that clicking on Employees | Enter Details brings up the dialogue box. (The dialogue box could be made modeless by using MakeWindow instead of ExecDialog.)

Visual Basic

Visual Basic operates on a similar basis to Visual C++. For each object, a number of events are catered for. The code for any object/event combination is entered in the Procedure window (Figure 9.5).

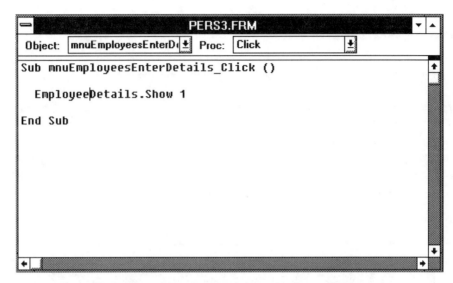

Figure 9.5 Visual Basic procedure to show dialogue box

The Procedure window is invoked in the following ways:

* Click on the View Code button in the Project Window.

* Double-click on a control or on a blank area of a form.

The Procedure window has boxes at the top for choosing the object and procedure. All objects created so far (forms and controls) and listed in the Object box. Having chosen one, the Proc box lists all the procedures that can be created for the object. These procedures correspond to the messages that may be received (i.e. the events that may occur).

When the object and procedure have been selected, the procedure itself can be entered in the main part of the window. The procedure name takes the form *Object_Proc*.

For example, to activate the EnterDetails form, the object is the menu item mnuEmployeesEnterDetails and the event is Click. Therefore the procedure is mnuEmployeesEnterDetails_Click. The code to bring up the second form is:

```
EmployeeDetails.Show 1
```

The Show method displays a form and triggers the Load event for the EmployeeDetails form; this event can be used for any initialisation that is needed for the form. The value 1 indicates that the dialogue box is to be modal (omit it for a modeless box).

The procedures for any form are saved when the form is saved.

CREATING MESSAGE HANDLERS

The next task is to set up message handlers for particular events.

Visual C++

When creating programs in Visual C++, message-handling is dealt with by ClassWizard. This utility can be invoked from either Visual Workbench or App Studio. The ClassWizard window lists the objects for the application (Figure 9.6).

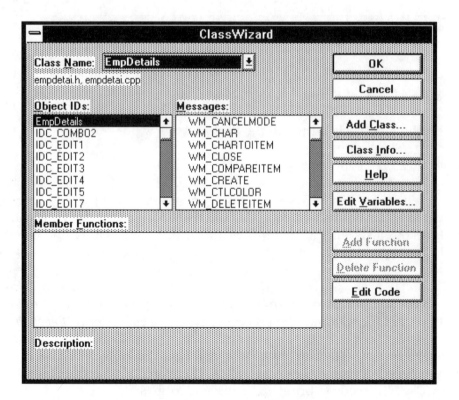

Figure 9.6 Main ClassWizard window

Adding Variables

Visual C++ has features called Dialog Data Exchange (DDX) and Dialog Data Validation (DDV). DDX allows you to set initial values for variables or access the values associated with controls. DDV applies data validation to the variables.

You will need variables for any controls where you want to access the data. To create control variables in Visual C++:

1   In the ClassWizard window, click on Edit Variables.

2   In the Edit Member Variable window, click on the control ID for which the variable is to be added and then on Add Variable.

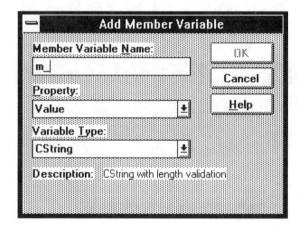

Figure 9.7 Adding a new member variable

3   The Add Member Variable box is displayed (Figure 9.7). Fill in the variable name, property and variable type. For instance, to define an integer variable to hold the Employee Number, the name can be m_intEmpNo, the property is Value and the variable type integer (Figure 9.8). Click on OK.

4   The Edit Member Variables window shows the new variable and allows you to enter validation details: for an integer, minimum and maximum values (Figure 9.9).

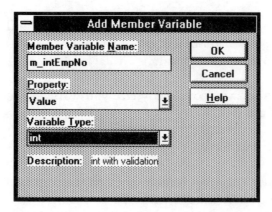

Figure 9.8 Defining an integer member variable

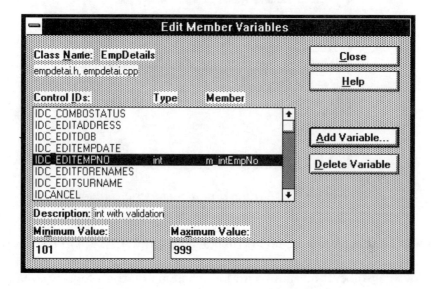

Figure 9.9 Integer variable validation

You can add variables at any time. The names should follow these conventions:

- The name starts with 'm_' (to indicate a member variable, supplied automatically).

- There should be an abbreviation to indicate the type of variable: for values, this is 'int', 'str', etc.; for controls, this is the control type, such as 'btn' for buttons or 'edit' for text boxes.

- The last part of the name should match the control name.

Variables fall into two main categores:

- *Value variables* take the value of the control: the text of a text box, the status of a radio button (0 off, 1 on), etc.

- *Control variables* allow you to refer to the control itself.

Validation can only be applied to value variables.

The validation for string variables consists of a test on the maximum number of characters; for instance, you may create a variable for the Surname text box, calling it m_strSurname, and limiting it to 25 characters.

You can have one variable of each type for a control. For instance, for the Employee Number, you can define a control variable called m_editEmpNo. All variables will be listed in the Edit Member Variables list (Figure 9.10).

When you have finished adding variables, click on Close.

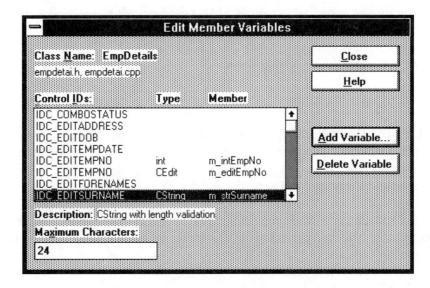

Figure 9.10 String variable length validation

Creating Message Handlers

You will need to create a message handler for any control and message that is to have a special effect. It is here that you actually have to start adding your own code.

For example, suppose that you want Employee Number 999 to be reserved for special use. The value must be checked each time the user changes the contents of the text box.

There are two alternative messages that could be used:

- EN_CHANGE is generated every time any change is made to the box (a new character being added or an existing character deleted).

- EN_KILLFOCUS is generated when the user tries to move out of the box.

At first glance, EN_CHANGE seems the obvious candidate. However, it soon becomes clear that this is impractical, since invalid values may arise while the user is editing the box. EN_CHANGE is suitable only when you want to restrict the characters a user may type: for instance, to stop the user typing alphabetic characters in a numeric entry box.

Therefore, the message to use is EN_KILLFOCUS. A handler must be provided for this message for the IDC_EDITEMPNO object.

In App Studio, the procedure is as follows:

1   Activate ClassWizard (press CTRL-W).

2   Click on the Class Name (EmpDetails), Object ID (IDC_EDITEMPNO) and message (EN_KILLFOCUS).

3   Click on Add Function.

4   You are asked for a function name (Figure 9.11). The system suggests a name consisting of 'On', the main part of the message and the object ID (e.g. OnKillfocus-Editempno). This should be satisfactory, so click on OK.

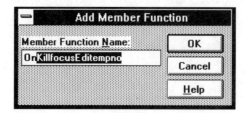

Figure 9.11 Adding a new member function

5   The new function is added to the list in the bottom half of the window. ClassWizard then performs the following actions:

- An entry is written in the message map.

- A declaration of the handler function is added to the class header (.H) file.

- An empty function is included in the source code (.CPP) file.

The new function is added to the 'Member Function' box. Initially, the function does nothing and consists of just a function template. By clicking on the Edit Code button, the actual code for the function can be inserted.

To insert some code for the function, click on Edit Code. The EMPDETAI.CPP file is displayed, with an empty message handler set up (Figure 9.12).

```
<2> C:\OOP\PERS\EMPDETAI.CPP*

void EmpDetails::OnKillfocusEditempno()
{
    // TODO: Add your control notification handler code here


}
```

Figure 9.12 Template for message handler

The comment can be replaced by the handler code, as follows:

```
void EmpDetails::OnKillfocusEditempno()
{
    UpdateData(TRUE);
    if(m_intEmpNo == 999)
      {
        m_strSurname = "Reserved Record";
        UpdateData(FALSE);
      }
}
```

The files will now be as shown in Figures 9.13 and 9.14.

```
// empdetai.h : header file
//

////////////////////////////////////////////////////////////////////////
// EmpDetails dialog

class EmpDetails : public CDialog
{
// Construction
public:
   EmpDetails(CWnd* pParent = NULL);   // standard constructor

// Dialog Data
   //{{AFX_DATA(EmpDetails)
   enum { IDD = IDD_DIALOG1 };
   CEdit m_editEmpNo;
   int          m_intEmpNo;
   CString      m_strSurname;
   //}}AFX_DATA

// Implementation
protected:
   virtual void DoDataExchange(CDataExchange* pDX);     // DDX/DDV support

   // Generated message map functions
   //{{AFX_MSG(EmpDetails)
   afx_msg void OnKillfocusEditempno();
   //}}AFX_MSG
   DECLARE_MESSAGE_MAP()
};
```

Figure 9.13 EMPDETAI.H with message handler declarations

```
// empdetai.cpp : implementation file
//

#include "stdafx.h"
#include "pers.h"
#include "empdetai.h"

#ifdef _DEBUG
#undef THIS_FILE
static char BASED_CODE THIS_FILE[] = __FILE__;
#endif
```

Figure 9.14 EMPDETAI.CPP with message handlers (continues)

```
//////////////////////////////////////////////////////////////////////////
// EmpDetails dialog

EmpDetails::EmpDetails(CWnd* pParent /*=NULL*/)
   : CDialog(EmpDetails::IDD, pParent)
{
   //{{AFX_DATA_INIT(EmpDetails)
   m_intEmpNo = 0;
   m_strSurname = "";
   //}}AFX_DATA_INIT
}

void EmpDetails::DoDataExchange(CDataExchange* pDX)
{
   CDialog::DoDataExchange(pDX);
   //{{AFX_DATA_MAP(EmpDetails)
   DDX_Control(pDX, IDC_EDITEMPNO, m_editEmpNo);
   DDX_Text(pDX, IDC_EDITEMPNO, m_intEmpNo);
   DDV_MinMaxInt(pDX, m_intEmpNo, 101, 999);
   DDX_Text(pDX, IDC_EDITSURNAME, m_strSurname);
   DDV_MaxChars(pDX, m_strSurname, 24);
   //}}AFX_DATA_MAP
}

BEGIN_MESSAGE_MAP(EmpDetails, CDialog)
   //{{AFX_MSG_MAP(EmpDetails)
   ON_EN_KILLFOCUS(IDC_EDITEMPNO, OnKillfocusEditempno)
   //}}AFX_MSG_MAP
END_MESSAGE_MAP()

//////////////////////////////////////////////////////////////////////////
// EmpDetails message handlers

void EmpDetails::OnKillfocusEditempno()
{
   UpdateData(TRUE);
   if(m_intEmpNo == 999)
     {
       m_strSurname = "Reserved Record";
       UpdateData(FALSE);
     }
}
```

Figure 9.14 (continued) EMPDETAI.CPP with message handlers

The effect of the UpdateData function is to transfer values between the fields of the dialogue box controls and the corresponding control variables. The parameter for the function should be one of the following:

- TRUE updates the control variables with the current values of the display fields.

- FALSE updates the display with the values of the control variables.

The first time UpdateData is called in the message handler, m_intEmpNo is updated with the value that has been entered. If the value is 999, m_strSurname is given the new text string and the values are transferred back to the dialogue box display fields.

Borland C++

In the example program, the following tasks must be completed:

- File the Marital Status combo box with a list of suitable values.

- Check the Employee Number box for valid values and, for a value of 999, put 'Reserved Record' in the Surname field when this value is entered.

- Close the dialogue box when OK or Cancel is clicked.

The first stage is to assign identifiers to the boxes that are to be referenced: ID_EDITEMPNO, ID_EDITSURNAME, ID_MARITALSTATUS, IDOK and IDCANCEL for example. (If you use IDOK and IDCANCEL for the buttons, they will be handled automatically.) Make sure that a different numeric ID value is associated with each control on the dialogue box.

Values can be assigned to dialogue fields with the function SendDlgItemMsg. For example, the instruction to add a string to the combo box is as follows:

```
SendDlgItemMsg(ID_MARITALSTATUS, CB_ADDSTRING, 0, (LONG)"Single");
```

The first parameter specifies the control identifier, the second is the message to be sent to the control. The last two parameters are the wParam and lParam values required by the message (in this case, constant 0 and the text to be added).

Although instructions can be passed on in this way, there is a more convenient method of setting up communication between the program and the dialogue box, as described below. The updated program is shown in Figure 9.15.

```
// PERS2 ObjectWindows program

#include <owl.h>
#include <dialog.h>
#include <edit.h>
#include <combobox.h>
#include "stdlib.h"
#include "empdetai.h"

class EmpDialog : public TDialog
{
public:
  PTEdit EditEmpNo;
  PTEdit EditSurname;
  PTComboBox MaritalStatus;
  EmpDialog(PTWindowsObject AParent, LPSTR name);
  virtual void Ok(RTMessage Msg);
  virtual void Cancel(RTMessage Msg);
  virtual void HandleEmpNoMsg(RTMessage Msg)
    = [ID_FIRST + ID_EDITEMPNO];
  virtual void HandleMarStatMsg(RTMessage Msg)
    = [ID_FIRST + ID_MARITALSTATUS];
  virtual void SetUpStatus();
};


class TPersApp : public TApplication
{
public:
  TPersApp(LPSTR AName, HINSTANCE hInstance, HINSTANCE hPrevInstance,
    LPSTR lpCmdLine, int nCmdShow)
    : TApplication(AName, hInstance, hPrevInstance, lpCmdLine, nCmdShow) {};
  virtual void InitMainWindow();
};


_CLASSDEF(TPersWindow)
class TPersWindow : public TWindow
{
public:
  TPersWindow(PTWindowsObject AParent, LPSTR ATitle);
  virtual void CMEmployeesEnterDetails(RTMessage Msg)
    = [CM_FIRST + CM_EMPLOYEESENTERDETAILS];
};

EmpDialog::EmpDialog(PTWindowsObject AParent, LPSTR name)
                :TDialog(AParent, name)
{
  EditEmpNo = new TEdit(this, ID_EDITEMPNO, 10);
  EditSurname = new TEdit(this, ID_EDITSURNAME, 30);
  MaritalStatus = new TComboBox(this, ID_MARITALSTATUS, 20);
}
```

Figure 9.15 Message handling in Borland C++ (continues)

```
void EmpDialog::Ok(RTMessage Msg)
{
  //Insert special instructions for this dialogue box here
  TDialog::Ok(Msg);
}

void EmpDialog::Cancel(RTMessage Msg)
{
  //Insert special instructions for this dialogue box here
  TDialog::Cancel(Msg);
}

void EmpDialog::HandleEmpNoMsg(RTMessage Msg)
{
  char EmpNo[10];
  long EmpNoVal;

  if ( Msg.LP.Hi == EN_KILLFOCUS )
  {
    EditEmpNo -> GetLine(EmpNo, 10, 0);
    EmpNoVal = atoi(EmpNo);

    if ( EmpNoVal < 100 || EmpNoVal > 999 )
    {
      EditEmpNo -> Clear();
    }

    if ( EmpNoVal == 999 )
    {
      EditSurname -> SetText("Reserved Record");
    }
  }
}

void EmpDialog::HandleMarStatMsg(RTMessage Msg)
{
  if ( Msg.LP.Hi == CBN_DROPDOWN )
  {
    SetUpStatus();
  }
}

void EmpDialog::SetUpStatus()
{
  MaritalStatus -> ClearList();
  MaritalStatus -> AddString("Single");
  MaritalStatus -> AddString("Married");
  MaritalStatus -> AddString("Widowed");
  MaritalStatus -> AddString("Divorced");
  MaritalStatus -> AddString("Separated");
  MaritalStatus -> AddString("Unknown");
}
```

Figure 9.15 (continued) Message handling (continues)

```
TPersWindow::TPersWindow(PTWindowsObject AParent, LPSTR ATitle)
  : TWindow(AParent, ATitle)
{
  AssignMenu("MENU_1");
}

void TPersWindow::CMEmployeesEnterDetails(RTMessage)
{
  GetApplication()->ExecDialog(new EmpDialog(this, "DIALOG_1"));
}

void TPersApp::InitMainWindow()
{
  MainWindow = new TPersWindow(NULL, Name);
}

int PASCAL WinMain(HINSTANCE hInstance, HINSTANCE hPrevInstance,
  LPSTR lpCmdLine, int nCmdShow)
{
  TPersApp PersApp("OWL Personnel Program", hInstance, hPrevInstance,
              lpCmdLine, nCmdShow);
  PersApp.Run();
  return PersApp.Status;
}
```

Figure 9.15 (continued) Message handling in Borland C++

Setting Up Dialogue Objects

The controls on the dialogue box are *control interface elements*, rather than objects, and are defined in the resource file. Communication with these elements is set up by creating objects to correspond to the controls.

Header files must be included for the types of control that are to be used. For example:

```
#include <edit.h>
#include <combobox.h>
```

The standard library is also needed, so that the atoi function can be used to convert a string to an integer value:

```
#include <stdlib.h>
```

Pointers to the control objects must be defined in the EmpDialog class declaration:

```
PTEdit EditEmpNo;
PTEdit EditSurname;
PTComboBox MaritalStatus;
```

The methods that are to be used must also be declared:

- A SetUpStatus method is needed to fill the combo box list.

- Two methods are needed to handle notification messages from the Employee Number text box and the combo box: HandleEmpNoMsg and HandleMarStatMsg.

- OK and Cancel methods will override the TDialog functions of the same name.

In the EmpDialog constructor, three objects must be created to correspond to control elements. The statements are in the form:

```
EditEmpNo = new TEdit(this, ID_EDITEMPNO, 10)
```

The this pointer points to the current dialogue box, the second parameter identifies the control and the final identifier gives the maximum text length.

Finally, the new methods can be defined.

Filling the Combo Box
The list for the combo box is filled by intercepting any messages from the combo box. These are automatically passed to the HandleMarStatMsg procedure, which was declared earlier and given a dispatch index of [ID_FIRST + ID_MARITALSTATUS]. The incoming notification message is identified by looking at the high word of the lParam parameter in the Msg variable (i.e. Msg.LP.Hi). If this message is CBN_DROPDOWN, indicating that the list is about to drop down, the SetUpStatus method is called. This method starts by clearing any existing values in the list and then adding a series of new items. The ClearList and AddString functions that are called are defined in TListBox, which is the base class for TComboBox.

An alternative approach is to fill the list when the dialogue box is displayed (this is demonstrated in the Visual Basic example).

Checking the Employee Number
The checks on the EmployeeNumber are dealt with by HandleEmpNoMsg. This function only has an effect if the EN_KILLFOCUS notification method is received, indicating that the text box is about to lose the focus. The GetLine function is used to retrieve the current contents of the text box, putting the text in the variable EmpNo; GetLine is defined in TStatic, the base class for TEdit.

The incoming text is converted to the numeric variable, EmpNoVal, using the atoi function. This value is then tested. If it is outside the range 100-999, the text box is cleared; if it has a value of 999 precisely, the text 'Reserved Record' is put into the surname box, using the function SetText (also defined in TStatic).

Closing the Dialogue Box

Methods for closing the dialogue box already exist and are defined in DIALOG.CPP. These methods are effective if the identifiers for the OK and Cancel boxes are IDOK and IDCANCEL repectively. To add your own code for tidying up the data before the box closes, redefine the OK and Cancel methods, making sure you end with a call to the original TDialog methods.

Visual Basic

Change the Name of the Employee Number text box to txtEmpNo and that of the Surname box to txtSurname. Similarly, change the Name of the OK button to btnOK and that of the Cancel button to btnCancel, and the combo box name to cboMStatus.

Visual Basic uses the same Procedure window for control-based events as for dialogue boxes. A procedure is created for an event by selecting the object in the Object box and then choosing an event from the list in the Proc box. The Proc box lists only those events that are appropriate for the selected object.

When the dialogue box is first displayed, a Load event occurs for the form. This is a good time to fill the combo box. The procedures attached to the Load event should contain statements in the form:

```
cboMStatus.AddItem "Single"
```

The AddItem method for combo boxes adds a text string to the bottom of the existing list. The full procedure is shown in Figure 9.16.

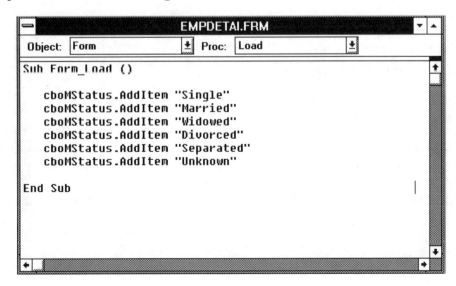

Figure 9.16 Filling the combo box list in Visual Basic

The procedure for validating the Employee Number entry when the box loses the focus is shown in Figure 9.17. If the entry is outside the allowed range, the computer beeps, the entry is cleared and the user is forced to re-enter. For a value of 999 the text 'Reserved Record' is placed in the Surname field.

Figure 9.18 shows the code for the Click event for the OK button (activated by a button click or pressing ENTER). As it stands, it simply removes the window from the screen,

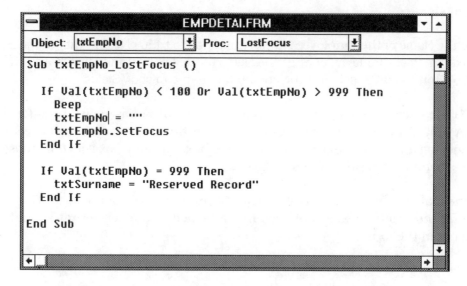

Figure 9.17 Validating Employee Number in Visual Basic

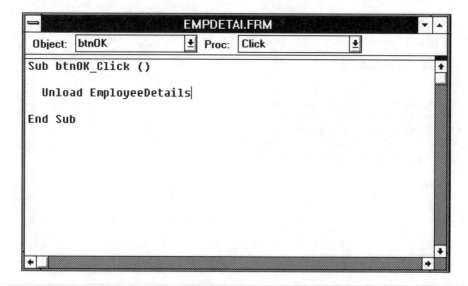

Figure 9.18 Procedure for handling OK button

restoring the focus to the main window. In a real application, code would also be needed to save the data. A similar procedure for btnCancel_Click unloads the window and abandons any data changes.

TESTING THE PROGRAM

The program is now ready to test. Rebuild the .EXE file and then run it. You will notice the following:

- The dialogue box is displayed when you click on Employees|Enter Details (or when you press ALT E E or CTRL-E).

- Entering a value outside the range 100-999 for the Employee Number leads to an error message or the box being cleared.

- Entering a value of 999 results in the text 'Reserved Record' being inserted in the Surname box.

- Clicking on OK or Cancel closes the dialogue box.

Following the same general principles, other message handlers can be added to create a useful program, performing checks on the data and saving the changes to file.

10 | Graphics Operations

Most Windows applications depend on the use of controls to perform the tasks that are required of the program. However, there are occasions when you want to write text or graphics directly to a window, without using controls. This chapter looks at the facilities provided by Windows for direct graphics operations.

GRAPHICS DEVICE INTERFACE

The graphics operations are a set of Windows functions that make up the Windows *Graphics Device Interface* (GDI). This is a subset of the full Windows API, and the GDI functions will be found mixed in with the other API functions in the reference books.

The GDI functions are used for the following tasks:

- Creating and deleting device contexts (described below)

- Changing the co-ordinate system

- Changing the graphics-drawing area

- Creating, selecting and changing pens and brushes

- Drawing points, lines and shapes

- Changing colours and palettes

- Creating and selecting fonts

- Writing text to the window

Each of these groups is described below.

DEVICE CONTEXTS

A *device context* (DC) represents the 'logical' drawing area of a window and provides the link between the application and the device driver. A device context can apply to the screen, the printer or any other output device. Borland use the term *display context* when referring to screen output.

When writing graphics directly to the screen with Visual C++ or ObjectWindows, you must follow these three steps:

1   Access a device context, using the GetDC Windows function. Windows allocates a device context for the window whose handle was specified in the GetDC call and returns a handle to the device context. This handle is referenced in all other GDI function calls.

2   Write the graphics to the device context. The commands are processed and passed to the device driver, which interprets them in a form suitable for the output device. This means that all the graphics instructions are device-independent and the application should always operate in the same way, regardless of the output device.

3   Release the device context, using the ReleaseDC function. This is essential, as Windows only has a limited number of device contexts available.

This whole process means that you do not have to worry about the physical characteristics of the devices that will eventually have to deal with your instructions. For example, if you want to draw a line from the top left-hand corner of the window to the centre, using a specified colour, you need only specify the logical co-ordinates of the line ends and the colour. (The logical co-ordinates assume that the window is of a certain size, regardless of its actual size in pixels.) Windows communicates with the device driver to determine the actual screen pixels that need to be coloured in and changes the colour that is closest to that required. So it doesn't matter how many pixels there are on the screen, how many colours are available or where on the screen the user has moved the window to; you can set up complex graphics output and always know that the end result is the best possible for the device being used.

The most important point to remember is that the device context must always be released as soon as the graphics are complete. Windows has only five device contexts available, so if they are not released they will be quickly used up and the system will hang. Always keep the GetDc and ReleaseDc functions tightly packed in the same procedure, with the graphics statements, so that there is no danger of some other procedure being invoked before the device context is freed.

Note that the Microsoft Foundation Class Library has a CDC class for handling device contexts.

When using Visual Basic, the device contexts are handled automatically. You only need give the graphics statements; the system gets and releases device contexts for you.

Device Context Defaults

When a device context is supplied by Windows, it comes with a set of default attributes, which includes the following:

- White background

- Thin, black pen and white brush

- Default palette

- Co-ordinates based on pixels, with origin in top-left corner

- Entire window (below title bar) as drawing area

- System font

The GDI functions are used to override these defaults.

THE CO-ORDINATE SYSTEM

When drawing points or lines on a window, or adding text, you must specify the location of the point, the ends of each line or the position at which the text is to begin. This is done by specifying a pair of (X,Y) co-ordinates. By default, the X co-ordinate determines the distance across the screen, from left to right; the Y co-ordinate gives the distance down the screen, from the top. The *origin* – position (0,0) – is at the top left-hand corner of the device context.

All graphics are written to the device context using *logical units*. These are then converted by Windows to *physical units* according to the co-ordinate system being used. For example, a horizontal line of 100 units long in the logical co-ordinate space will have a physical length of 1 inch if the co-ordinate system maps each logical unit to 0.01 inches. If the mapping is 1 unit to 0.1 millimetres, the line will be 10mm long. Windows makes the conversion of logical units to physical units, and the information contained in the screen's device driver is then used to work out the number of pixels for a line of this physical size.

Windows allows you to change the co-ordinate system, using the SetMapMode function. One of the function's parameters determines the *mapping mode*, which gives the relationship between a logical unit and a physical unit, and decides whether the Y-axis starts at the top and extends downwards or works from the bottom up. The mapping modes are as follows:

Mode	Physical unit	Y-axis direction
MM_TEXT	Pixel	Downwards
MM_HIENGLISH	0.001 inch	Upwards
MM_LOENGLISH	0.01 inch	Upwards
MM_TWIPS	$1/1440$ inch	Upwards
MM_HIMETRIC	0.01mm	Upwards
MM_LOMETRIC	0.1mm	Upwards
MM_ISOTROPIC	User-defined	User-defined
MM_ANISOTROPIC	User-defined	User-defined

For the MM_ANISOTROPIC mode, the physical relationship is set independently for the Y-axis and X-axis; for all other modes, a logical unit results in the same physical unit both horizontally and vertically. For the MM_TEXT mode, a pixel vertically results in a longer unit than one horizontally. This is because pixels are usually taller than they are wide (a ratio of about 4:3). Therefore, a 'square' of 100 units x 100 units will result in a square on the screen for any mode apart from MM_TEXT and MM_ANISOTROPIC; for MM_TEXT you will get a tall rectangle, for MM_ANISOTROPIC the end result will depend on the units that have been set.

When converting non-pixel units to pixels, the system applies a scale factor so that lines with the same number of units horizontally and vertically appear the same length. The GetDeviceCaps function is used to return the number of pixels per inch horizontally and vertically; the same function also returns a number of other device characteristics.

The default co-ordinate system for Visual C++ and ObjectWindows is MM_TEXT. Because of the difficulties arising from rectangular pixels and varying numbers of pixels for different screen types, it is better to select a new system with SetMapMode.

For Visual Basic, the default system is MM_TWIPS. This is changed with the ScaleMode property for forms and picture boxes.

CLIPPING REGION

The area of the window that is available for graphics operations is called the *clipping region*. By default, the clipping region is the whole of the window's *client area*: that is, everything inside the window borders and below the title bar (and menu bar, if there is one).

Any graphics written to points outside the clipping region will be ignored and will not be visible on the screen. This means that if the user resizes a window the graphics within it will be clipped. If you write some graphics that have co-ordinates which are outside the current clipping region, they will not be drawn; there will be no error message.

Note that a change to the position or size of a window does not affect the origin. This will always stay in the same place (top left or bottom left corner), regardless of how the window is resized. Graphics are always clipped to the right, and at the top or bottom of the window (depending on the mapping mode).

There are a number of Windows GDI functions for clipping regions, of which the most useful are as follows:

- SelectClipRgn selects a new clipping region within the window's client area.

- OffsetClipRgn moves the clipping region to a new position (useful for allowing the user to drag a graphic partly off the window).

- ExcludeClipRect takes a rectangle out of the clipping region.

Note that you cannot change the clipping region in a Visual Basic application except by direct calls to the Windows functions.

PENS AND BRUSHES

By default, the device context has a *pen* that draws black lines which are one pixel wide. This pen is used whenever you draw a line or simple shape on the drawing surface.

There are three standard pens – black, white and null – which can be selected with the GetStockObject function.

A new pen can be defined with the CreatePen function. The arguments to this function dcfinc thc following:

- The style

- The width (in logical units)

- The colour

The style can be solid, dash, dot, dash-dot, dash-dot-dot, null (draws nothing) or inside-frame (where the line is drawn inside the boundary of graphics such as rectangles, rather than being drawn centred on the specified co-ordinates).

The CreatPen function returns a handle to the pen. The pen cannot be used until it is assigned to the device context with SelectObject. When you have finished with the pen, it must be released from the device context with DeleteObject.

In a similar way, you can use a *brush*. This is the tool that is used to fill areas with solid colours and patterns. By default, the brush is white. Using GetStockObject you can select five different brushes giving solid colours: black, white, and dark, medium and light grey.

A new brush can be created with several functions:

- CreateSolidBrush creates a brush with a specified solid colour.

- CreateHatchBrush creates a brush with one of six hatch patterns (consisting of horizontal, vertical and diagonal lines).

- CreatePatternBrush creates a brush with a pattern made up by repeating a specified bitmap.

- CreateDIBPatternBrush creates a brush from a device-independent bitmap (DIB).

- CreateBrushIndirect creates a brush from a data structure pointed to by the function's parameter.

As for the pen, the new brush must be made available to the device context with SelectObject and released with DeleteObject.

For Visual Basic, there is no need to select pens and brushes in this way; all this is handled by the properties of the tools being used to draw.

POINTS, LINES AND SHAPES

You do not usually want to paint individual points on the screen. If you do, then the best method for C++ is to draw a very short line. For Visual Basic, points are added with the PSet method, which takes the form:

```
PSet (x, y), colour
```

This puts a point at the position given by the co-ordinates (x, y), in the *colour* specified. If no colour is given, the current colour is used.

Lines

The first stage in drawing a line is to move the current drawing point to the start of the line. This is done with the MoveTo Windows function. The line is then drawn with LineTo, which specifies the end of the line. Note that the line that is drawn starts at the current drawing position and ends one pixel short of the line end; the end point specified is not included. The end of the line becomes the current drawing position, so another LineTo instruction draws a line that starts at the end of the first line.

The line is drawn using the current pen, so if you want a line of a different colour or thickness, you must first create a new pen.

Figure 10.1 shows the relevant sections of C++ code to allow you to draw a line on the surface of a window by dragging the mouse. The sample program is called GRAPH. When the left mouse button is pressed the current mouse pointer position is stored in the variable StartPoint (of type point). The mouse can then be moved and, when the button is released, a line is drawn from the start point to the current pointer position. The default pen is used. The effect of this code is shown in Figure 10.2.

For Visual Basic, the Line instruction handles the MoveTo and LineTo functions and also deals with the creation of a suitable pen. The syntax of the instruction is:

```
object.Line (x1, y1) - (x2, y2), colour, box
```

If *object* is omitted, the instruction draws on the current form or picture box. The two sets of co-ordinates give the start and end of the line in absolute units. If 'step' is placed in front of (x1, y1), the co-ordinates of the start of the line are relative to the current drawing position; similarly 'step' in front of (x2, y2) specifies an end position relative to the start.

If *colour* is omitted, the current pen colour is used; *box* can take values of 'B' or 'BF' for drawing rectangles, or be omitted for drawing lines.

```
// Definitions needed for message handling functions

   CDC*       hDC;
   CPoint     StartPoint;

// Function when left button is pressed
// - current position of mouse pointer is saved in POINT variable StartPoint

void CGraphView::OnLButtonDown(UINT nFlags, CPoint point)
{
   StartPoint = point;
   CView::OnLButtonDown(nFlags, point);
}

// Function when left button is released
// - drawing position is moved to StartPoint and then line is drawn to
//   current mouse pointer position

void CGraphView::OnLButtonUp(UINT nFlags, CPoint point)
{
   hDC = GetDC();
   hDC - MoveTo(StartPoint);
   hDC - LineTo(point);
   ReleaseDC(hDC);

   CView::OnLButtonUp(nFlags, point);
}
```

Figure 10.1 C++ code for line drawing

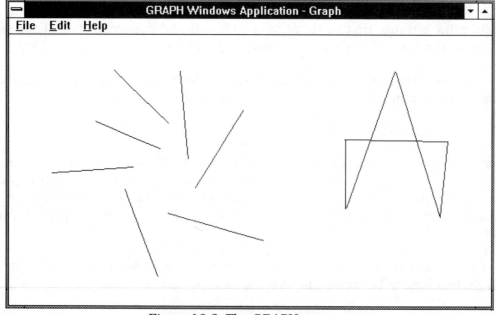

Figure 10.2 The GRAPH program

The width of the line and the style (dots, dashes or solid) are given by the DrawWidth and DrawStyle properties for the form or picture box. The DrawMode property determines whether the line colour is the same throughout or whether it varies according to the background colour; for instance, the line may be set to be the inverse of the background colour, so that it always shows up on any background.

Note that Visual Basic also has a Line control in the tools palette, which adds a line as an object.

Shapes

There are a number of Windows API functions which produce a variety of shapes:

- Rectangle draws a rectangle while RoundRect draws a rectangle with rounded corners (a rounded box).

- Ellipse draws an ellipse inside a specified rectangle; make the rectangle a square to draw a circle.

- Arc draws a portion of an ellipse (or circle), Chord draws a slice off the side of an ellipse and Pie draws a wedge from an ellipse (an arc with lines drawn from its ends to the centre of the ellipse).

- Polygon draws an irregular polygon (a series of points joined by lines, with the last point joined to the first); PolyPolygon draws a series of polygons.

In all cases apart from Polygon and PolyPolygon, the shape is defined by a *bounding rectangle*. This is the rectangle within which the shape is drawn. Two pairs of co-ordinates must be specified: the top left-hand corner and the bottom right-hand corner. As for lines, the second pair of co-ordinates give the point adjacent to the final point. That is, if the co-ordinates are $(x1, y1)$ and $(x2, y2)$ the rectangle runs from $(x1, y1)$ to $(x2 - 1, y2 - 1)$.

All of these shapes are drawn with the current pen and then (apart from Arc) filled in with the current brush.

Visual Basic allows you to create the shapes either with instructions in the code or as objects selected from the toolbox. Rectangles are drawn with the Line instruction, adding 'B' to create a hollow rectangle or 'BF' for a filled box (as described above). Ellipses are drawn with the Circle instruction, whose syntax is:

```
Circle (x, y), radius, colour, start, end, ratio
```

The ellipse has a centre specified by (x, y), with the given horizontal *radius* and *colour*. The *start* and *end* parameters are needed only for drawing an arc; these are angles in radians, measured anticlockwise, with 0° being 'due East'. The *ratio* determines whether the shape in a circle or an ellipse:

- If omitted, the shape is a circle; the vertical radius is set to the number of pixels needed to make a near-perfect circle (bearing in mind that pixels are tall and thin, so fewer pixels are needed vertically than horizontally).

- If the *ratio* is 1, the result is a tall, thin ellipse.

- If the *ratio* is greater than 1, the height is fixed but the width reduces (the ellipse becomes thinner).

- If the *ratio* is less than 1, the width is fixed but the height get less (the ellipse gets closer to a circle and then, after passing a certain point, becomes short and wide).

Other shapes are drawn by combining lines and arcs.

COLOURS AND PALETTES

When creating a pen or brush, you must specify the colour that is to be used. This is done by giving one of three values:

- An RGB value

- An index to a palette

- A palette-relative RGB value

Although most monitors these days can produce hundreds of thousands of colours, there is usually a limit to the number of colours that can be used on the screen at any one time: for example, a VGA monitor can display up to 262,000 different colours but only 256 at a time.

All colours are made up of differing amounts of three colour components: red, green and blue. Each pixel has these three components, and each component can be set to a different intensity independently of the others.

When an RGB value is to be used, this is given as a double-word value. The low-order byte represents the red contribution to the colour, the second byte is the green and the third byte is the blue; the fourth (high-order) byte is always 0 for RGB values. For example, the hex value &H00FF0000 represents dark blue (the blue byte is at its maximum value; &H00800080 produces violet (red and blue, each at half intensity).

Palettes

A *palette* is a selection of colours used in a display. The colours in the palette are given an index number to identify them; for example, if the palette has 256 colours, these are numbered 0 to 255. Associated with each index is the RGB value that defines the colour actually used. For instance, the first three colours in the palette may be black, pure red and pure green; then palette colour 0 represents &H00000000, colour 1 is &H000000FF and colour 2 is &H0000FF00.

Most devices have a *system palette*, which holds the colours they are currently using for the display. Initially, the palette is empty but as each new colour is requested by Windows or an application, it is added to the palette as follows:

- If a colour is requested that has not yet been used, it is added in the first available slot.

- If a requested colour has been used before, the device already has a palette index number for it; there is no change to the contents of the palette.

- When the palette is full, the system substitutes the closest match it can find in the palette for any new colour that is requested.

The system palette identifies the colours used throughout the system, in all applications. If there is a limit of 256 colours for the display, and these are used up by an application, then any other application is restricted to these colours.

Logical Palettes

Instead of using RGB colours in every function call, it is usually easier to define your own *logical palette*. The palette is created by calling CreatePalette, one of its parameters pointing to a data structure that contains a list of the palette's colours. The palette is attached to the device context by the SelectPalette function. The colours in the logical palette are added to the system palette using the same rules as for RGB colours. Each time you select a colour from the logical palette, this is added to the system palette.

The colours in the palette are identified in function calls by giving a double-word value that consists of 1 in the high-order byte and the palette index number in the bottom two bytes. For example, a request for palette colour 3 is given by &H01000003 and colour 20 is &H01000014. The 1 in the high-order byte identifies these values as palette indexes rather than RGB colours.

There are several advantages to using palettes:

- It is easier to be consistent in using the same colours for similar purposes when you do not have to keep track of complicated RGB values.

- Using the same palette for more than one application gives a consistent appearance to the applications.

- Changing the colours used by an application requires only that the palette data structure be changed; the actual function calls in the program do not have to be changed at all.

Visual Basic does not allow the direct use of palettes but provides an RGB function, with the syntax RGB(*red, green, blue*), which returns an RGB value.

TEXT AND FONTS

Text is written to the device context using the Windows TextOut function. The parameters specify:

- The device context

- The co-ordinates of the top left-hand corner of the rectangle containing the first character

- A pointer to the text string

- The length of the string

The text is written in the current font. The current drawing position is not updated by this function. Other SetText functions allow you to change the alignment, justification and inter-character spacing of the text.

The GDI has files that define a number of fonts. Any of these can be selected with the CreateFont function, which allows you to choose a named font and specify characteristics such as the height, width, orientation and weight of characters. This function does not allow you to create a completely new font; it just lets you decide how an existing font is to be used.

Visual Basic uses the Print method to display text. The syntax is similar to the traditional BASIC Print instruction. Ending the instruction with a semi-colon results in the next Print instruction continuing on the same line, a comma moves the print position to the next tab stop; otherwise, the print position moves to the start of the next line.

The properties of the window or picture box being used for the output determine the start position as a pair of character co-ordinates (CurrentX and CurrentY), the height of each line (TextHeight) and the font (FontName, FontSize, FontBold, etc.)

PICTURE BOXES

Visual Basic has a special *picture box* control. This is added to the screen as a rectangle and can be used for displaying a bitmap, icon or metafile. The picture box can also accept the graphics commands described in this chapter. This provides a means of creating graphics within a confined space. Picture boxes have similar properties to forms, so any instruction that would draw graphics or text on a form can also be used on a picture box. The instruction should be prefixed by the picture box ID.

METAFILES

Any graphic image is created either from a bitmap (where the image is stored on a pixel-by-pixel basis) or from a series of GDI instructions (such as those to draw lines and shapes or write text to the screen). When GDI functions are used, these can be stored away for later use. A *metafile* is a special-format file that stores a sequence of GDI function calls. Rather than executing the instructions directly, they are added to the metafile. The metafile is then *played* and the instructions are executed to create the graphics. Metafiles can be created in memory or stored on disk.

Creating a Metafile

The first stage is always to use CreateMetaFile to create a special type of device context. The function returns a handle to the device context, which is used in all other metafile functions. You must not use a normal device context when creating metafiles. The parameters to the function specify either a pointer to the filename in which the instructions are to be stored or, if the metafile is to be held in memory, NULL.

The GDI functions to create the graphics image are then given. Not all GDI functions can be used; in particular, you must not use those that retrieve information (the Get... functions) or those relating to bitmaps. Within the metafile you should define the pens and brushes you need; otherwise, the current pen and brush will be used and the future appearance of the graphic image will depend on the pen and brush in use when the metafile is called.

When the image has been defined, close the metafile with CloseMetaFile. This function returns a handle to the metafile and, for disk files, saves the file on disk. (Note that you can also create a disk file from a memory file using CopyMetaFile.)

Replaying a Metafile

To play a metafile – that is, to execute the GDI instructions it contains – call the PlayMetaFile function, specifying the handle returned by CloseMetaFile. For disk files, first call the GetMetaFile function, specifying a pointer to the filename. This function returns the handle, for use in PlayMetaFile.

When the metafile is no longer needed, DeleteMetaFile releases the memory it was using; this function has no effect on the disk file.

The advantage of using disk metafiles is that the same instructions can be used over and over again, in many applications. The graphic image can be changed by altering the contents of the metafile or substituting a completely new metafile; no changes at all are required to the applications that use the metafile.

11 | The Clipboard

The Windows clipboard is a means of transferring data between applications. The clipboard is based on the common data formats and operating environments of all Windows applications and uses this built-in uniformity to provide programmers with a standard method for allowing users to transfer data. This chapter shows that access to the clipboard can be incorporated in an application with very little effort.

CLIPBOARD FEATURES

The clipboard is an area of memory used for the temporary storage of data. There is only one clipboard for any Windows session but it is available to all applications that have implemented clipboard routines. The clipboard can hold different types of data:

- Text: either standard text or DDE link data

- Graphics: bitmaps, device-independent bitmaps, metafiles or colour palettes

When data is stored in the clipboard, the format must be specified. Each clipboard format is identified by a number, which is represented by a standard symbolic constant, as follows:

Format	Number	Constant
Text	1	CF_TEXT
Bitmap file (.BMP)	2	CF_BITMAP
Metafile (.WMF)	3	CF_METAFILE
Device-independent bitmap (.DIB)	8	CF_DIB
Colour palette	9	CF_PALETTE
DDE information	&HBF00	CF_LINK

These are the standards that you are most likely to encounter but Windows does recognise other predefined formats. You can also use the RegisterClipboardFormat function to create new formats.

The clipboard can hold only one item of data at a time for any format but there may be data from more than one format. For example, the clipboard can hold a paragraph of text and a bitmap image simultaneously but cannot hold two independent text strings.

Every time a new piece of data is copied to the clipboard, the new data replaces any existing data in the same format.

Since the clipboard is a universal feature, available to all Windows application in the current session, it can be used for transferring text between applications. The text is stored in a standard format, so any application you create will be able to read the clipboard text, no matter where it was copied from; similarly, any text written to the clipboard by your application can be inserted by any other application with clipboard access.

For those objects where the user can enter text – primarily text boxes (edit controls) and combo boxes – there are usually three options available, generally from an Edit menu:

- Cut, to copy the highlighted text to the clipboard and delete it from the control

- Copy, to copy the highlighted text to the clipboard, leaving the original intact

- Paste, to insert the clipboard text at the cursor position

There is often also an Undo menu option to cancel the last Edit action, and sometimes a Redo option to cancel out the effects of Undo (i.e. restore the last Edit action). Some applications have a Delete or Clear option, which deletes the current selection without copying to the clipboard.

These options usually have accelerator keys, for which there are two main standards:

Option	Microsoft	Borland
Cut	CTRL-X	SHIFT-DEL
Copy	CTRL-C	CTRL-INS
Paste	CTRL-V	SHIFT-INS
Delete	DEL	CTRL-DEL
Undo	CTRL-Z	ALT-BACKSPACE

Most Microsoft products use the first standard.

CLIPBOARD MESSAGES AND FUNCTIONS

The Windows API has several messages for implementing the clipboard features:

- WM_CUT deletes the highlighted text in a text box or combo box, and stores it in the clipboard.

- WM_CLEAR deletes the text but has no effect on the clipboard.

- WM_COPY copies the text to the clipboard, leaving the original text unchanged.

- WM_PASTE inserts the text from the clipboard at the current text cursor position.

- WM_UNDO cancels the previous cut, clear or paste action, re-inserting the deleted text or deleting any inserted text (applies to text boxes only).

Note that WM_UNDO cancels only the last clipboard command. There is also an EM_UNDO message specifically for text boxes; EM_CANUNDO returns a non-zero value if the last operation can be undone. The last change to the text is stored in an *undo buffer*. If you want to prevent the user from cancelling a clipboard action, send the EM_EMPTYUN-DOBUFFER message, which clears the buffer.

Windows has a number of functions for handling the clipboard, including:

- OpenCliboard, which opens the clipboard for data transfer (in the same way as opening a file)

- SetClipboardData, which identifies data to be added to the clipboard

- GetClipboardData, which retrieves data

- EmptyClipboard, which clears the clipboard of its current contents

Other functions provide more complex clipboard tasks.

These messages and functions are automatically handled by the relevant classes in both the Microsoft Foundation Class Library and ObjectWindows.

Visual C++

For the Microsoft Library:

- The CEdit and CComboBox classes have methods called Cut, Clear, Copy and Paste.

- The CEdit class has an Undo function; there is also a CanUndo function, which returns a non-zero value if the last operation can be undone, and EmptyUndoBuffer, which clears the undo buffer.

- Command IDs are defined for the standard Edit menu options: ID_EDIT_CUT, ID_EDIT_COPY and ID_EDIT_PASTE. The handlers for these commands are installed automatically if an Edit menu is created with these command IDs.

- Other command IDs, such as ID_EDIT_UNDO and ID_EDIT_REDO, are recognised but no handler is implemented for them.

Therefore most of the hard work is done for you. The skeleton application created by AppWizard automatically adds a standard Edit menu. Note that the text boxes and message handlers recognise both standard sets of shortcut keys.

ObjectWindows

ObjectWindows has a similar approach:

- The TEdit class has methods called Cut, Copy and Paste. There are also two functions for deleting text: DeleteSelection to delete the selected text and Clear to delete *all* text.

- TEdit has Undo and CanUndo functions but no built-in function for clearing the undo buffer.

- The TComboBox class has a Clear function to delete all text but no clipboard functions.

- TEdit has six functions that automatically implement the clipboard functions: CMEditClear, CMEditCopy, CMEditCut, CMEditDelete, CMEditPaste and CMEditUndo. In any text box, any of the shortcut keys listed earlier will be effective, without any extra code required. Both sets of standards are implemented (Microsoft and Borland).

For these functions to be effective when called from a menu, the menu IDs *must* be called CM_EDITCLEAR, CM_EDITCOPY, etc. The menu options will then be handled automatically; there is no need to set up special handlers. Resource Workshop allows you to add a standard Edit menu.

Visual Basic

Visual Basic text boxes have the usual clipboard functionality built in. You can mark a piece of text and then use any of the standard shortcut keys (both sets are recognised). However, if you add an Edit menu and give the menu options the standard accelerators, these will not be effective until you add the necessary code. This allows you to vary the way in which the shortcut keys behave.

Visual Basic does not have functions built-in for the standard Edit menu options but they are easily implemented. All instructions refer to a Clipboard object, which has the following methods:

- Clear empties the clipboard.

- GetFormat returns a non-zero value if the clipboard contains data in the format specified.

- SetText copies text or DDE information to the clipboard, GetText retrieves text.

- SetData copies a bitmap, metafile or colour palette to the clipboard, GetData retrieves such data.

The Edit menu options are implemented by combining these methods with the following text box or combo box properties:

- SelText returns the currently-selected text.

- SelLength returns the number of characters selected (0 if no characters are selected).

- SelStart identifies the start of the selected text or the position of the text cursor if no text is selected.

These properties can also be set from within a program. Figures 11.1 to 11.3 show how the standard Edit options can be implemented.

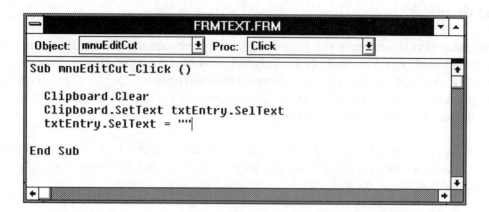

Figure 11.1 File | Cut option

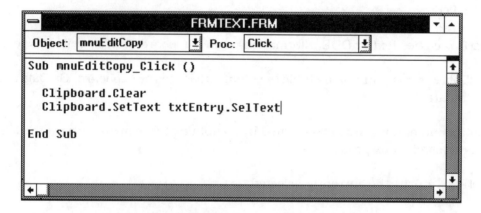

Figure 11.2 File | Copy option

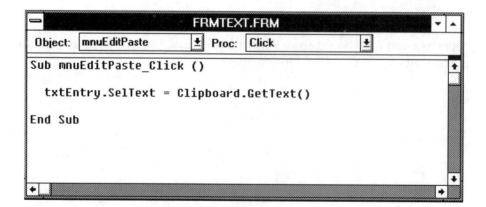

Figure 11.3 File | Paste option

THE CLIPBOARD VIEWER

Windows includes a *clipboard viewer*, which displays the current contents of the clipboard – both text and data. The clipboard viewer is available to the user at any time, and can also be used to change the contents of the clipboard.

The clipboard viewer will show either text or graphics, as illustrated in Figures 11.4 and 11.5.

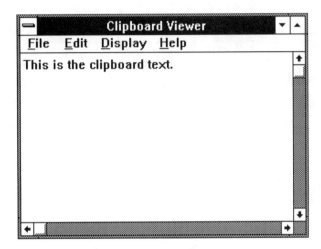

Figure 11.4 Clipboard Viewer after text copy

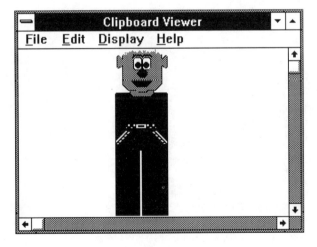

Figure 11.5 Clipboard Viewer after bitmap copy

12 Bitmaps, Icons and Cursors

Graphics images are an important feature of most Windows applications. Apart from their use for displaying pictures or providing a background to a window, these images are used in many other ways: on the faces of toolbar buttons, as icons when windows are minimised, and as mouse pointers and text cursors. Other uses for bitmaps include drop-down menu items and images for the Help program.

This chapter describes the way in which these images are created and stored, and how they can be used in Windows applications.

BITMAPS

A *bitmap* is a representation of a graphics image in which each pixel of the displayed or printed image is represented by one or more *bits* of data. All computer data, whether stored on disk, in memory or in some other form, is stored as a string of bits, each of which can represent a value of 0 or 1. Bits are combined for convenience; for instance, a group of eight bits forms a byte, the standard unit of computer data.

Chapter 10 described metafiles, which are one way of storing graphics data. A metafile is a sequence of instructions for forming an image. This reduces the amount of space needed to store the image; for instance, the instruction to draw a line takes up the same amount of space, no matter how long the line is. The disadvantage is that the images must be of a type that can be broken down into simple drawing instructions; metafiles are not suitable for drawing pictures, where each pixel may be coloured independently of the rest. This is where bitmaps are useful: each pixel in the image is mapped directly to one or more bits in the bitmap.

The number of bits per pixel depends on the number of colours available on the output device. Typically, a bitmap has 1, 4 or 8 bits per pixel.

- A monochrome bitmap, representing a black-and-white image, needs only one bit per pixel: 0 represents black, 1 is white.

- A 16-colour display requires 4 bits per pixel (2^4=16).

- A 256-colour VGA display requires 8 bits (one byte) per pixel.

For convenience, a byte should represent a whole number of pixels.

When the bitmap is created, the pixels are translated into the appropriate number of bits. The pixel data is encoded using the logical palette. For example, if a pixel is colour 5 from a 16-colour palette, it will be represented by 0101 in the bitmap.

All pixels are encoded in the bitmap, so that redrawing the image becomes a matter of decoding each bit or group of bits in the same one-to-one manner. All bitmaps, whether in memory or on disk, have some header information at the beginning. The structure of a bitmap header is defined by the BITMAP data structure, which appears in WINDOWS.H. (It is well worth inspecting WINDOWS.H, as this contains a large variety of predefined data structures and constant definitions for all aspects of Windows programming.)

Bitmaps are usually stored on disk files with a .BMP extension. Bitmap files are also used for icons and cursors, with extensions of .ICO and .CUR respectively. Bitmaps can be created in a number of ways:

- Using Windows Paintbrush or some similar painting program

- Within a programming environment, such as App Studio's bitmap editor

- By capturing a Windows screen with the PrtSc key

A PrtSc screen dump is held in the clipboard as a bitmap image, which can then be saved to disk using the clipboard viewer or copied into a program such as Paintbrush.

USING BITMAPS

Bitmaps are used in a Windows program by adding them to the application's resource file. When the bitmap has been defined as a resource, it can be loaded into memory using the LoadBitmap function. The bitmap is then assigned to a device context using Select-Object. However, a bitmap can only be selected for a *memory device context*. A memory device context is a representation in memory of another output device context. When an image has been built in memory, it can then be transferred to the output device. The BitBlt function transfers the contents of one device context to another. (Memory device contexts can be useful in other situations; an image can be built up in memory and then transferred to the output device when it is complete. This hides the drawing actions from the user. This method is also useful when the same image needs to be used more than once: for example, when creating patterns.)

Visual C++

The App Studio utility, supplied with Visual C++, includes a comprehensive graphics editor. This allows you to edit any bitmap that has been included in the resource file. After opening the resource file, choose one of the following commands:

- Resource | New to create a new bitmap in the resource file

- Resource | Import to import an existing bitmap file to the resource file

- Resource | Type to edit an existing bitmap in the resource file

In each case, you must choose between .BMP bitmaps, icons and cursors. Any bitmap can also be stored as a separate file (for use in other applications) using Resource | Export.

The App Studio graphics editor has all the features you would expect to find in a paint-type program: tools for drawing lines and shapes, options for cutting, copying and moving sections of the bitmap, colour palettes, and so on. Therefore, you can create your bitmaps here just as easily as in Paintbrush or any other similar program.

Note that the Microsoft Foundation Class Library has a CBitmap object, derived from CGdiObject, which has functions for handling the bitmap directly, should you need to do so.

The graphics editor is illustrated below.

Borland C++ and Pascal

Resource Workshop has a similar graphics editor, with the same sort of facilities. This is described in more detail below (see *Icons*).

Visual Basic

Visual Basic has a *picture box control* in its toolbox, represented by a cactus (the same icon as is used by App Studio to represent a bitmap resource). The picture box is added in the same way as any other control. The surface of the box can then be drawn on directly, using the standard methods, such as Pset, Line and Circle. Alternatively, its Picture property can be set to the name of a disk file for a bitmap (.BMP or .DIB), icon or metafile. The bitmap will be loaded when the program is run.

The picture can be changed while the program is running with the LoadPicture method; any changed graphics (e.g. drawings made by the user) can be saved with SavePicture.

There is also an *image control*, represented by mountains, which is similar to the picture box; it can be redrawn more quickly but has more limited properties and methods.

DEVICE-INDEPENDENT BITMAPS

Bitmaps are a reasonable way of representing graphic images but there are disadvantages associated with them:

- Bitmap files are large: a 16-colour bitmap 100 pixels square takes up a 50 Kb file.

- Bitmaps redrawn on devices with a different resolution or different colours will not look the same as the original: the bitmap will be squashed up or stretched, and the proportional change in size may not be the same both horizontally and vertically.

- If a different colour palette is being used, the bitmap will end up with completely different colours.

The first problem – that of bitmap file size – can be overcome by the use of some form of file compression technique. The other problems relate to the fact that the format of the bitmap is dependent on the device for which it was originally created. For this reason, the traditional bitmap files are sometimes referred to as *device-dependent bitmaps* (DDBs).

In an attempt to overcome these disadvantages, Microsoft introduced a new format of bitmap file with Windows 3.0. This is the *device-independent bitmap* (DIB). The header information is more complex than that of the DDB and there is also a data structure for defining the colour palette that is to be used.

However, although this sounds like a great step forward, Windows itself does not make it easy for you to use DIBs. In order to maintain compatibility with applications written for earlier versions of Windows, the LoadBitmap function automatically converts any DIB file into DDB format, losing the extra colour palette information along the way. If you want to make really good use of the new format you will have to devise your own routines for extracting the colour data and creating a suitable palette before displaying the image. The SetDIBitsToDevice and StretchDIBits functions copy a DIB from a memory device context to the output device.

ICONS

An *icon* is a small bitmap that represents a minimised window. Usually icons are 32 pixels square. Some standard icons are supplied with programming environments but it is easy enough to create and use your own icons. (Note that the term 'icon' is sometimes used to refer to other small images in applications, such as toolbar buttons and bitmap menu items.)

In the normal course of events, an icon is associated with a window class in the WinMain function. This icon then becomes the *class icon*. Whenever an icon is about to be redrawn on the screen – for example, when a window is being minimised – Windows sends a WM_PAINTICON message. The class icon is then drawn.

The LoadIcon function loads an icon and associates it with this particular instance of the application. All windows created with the same window class will have the same icon.

It is possible to specify that there should be no icon for the class, as follows:

```
wndclass.hIcon = NULL;
```

When a window of this class is minimised, it will be represented by a blank bitmap. The program can then draw any graphics it likes on this bitmap. (Remember that a minimised window is still a window, so still has a client area that can be drawn on.) This approach is used by utilities such as clocks, which draw a clockface on the blank icon and update it with each new WM_PAINTICON message.

Note that you can also use LoadIcon at other times within a program to load other standard icons: IDI_ASTERISK, IDI_EXCLAMATION, IDI_HAND and IDI_QUESTION, the icons used in message boxes.

Visual C++

App Studio lets you create and edit icons with the graphics editor in much the same way as any other bitmap. However, different icons may be required for EGA/VGA, CGA and monochrome screens. The editor lets you create all three types of icon, and your application will then load the relevant one for the display that is in use.

The limits on the icons are as follows:

Display	Width x Height	Colours
EGA/VGA	32x32	16
CGA	32x16	2
Monochrome	32x32	2

Icons are saved in the resource file but can be exported (or imported) like any other bitmap.

For example, to create a new icon for an application, the procedure is as follows:

1   Select Resource|New from the App Studio menu. From the list of resource types, choose Icon (Figure 12.1).

2   The Icon Editor is displayed (Figure 12.2). This consists of two windows: one to hold the icon, the other containing a toolbox of standard painting tools, shapes and colours.

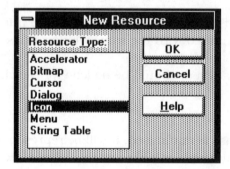

Figure 12.1 Selecting a new icon resource

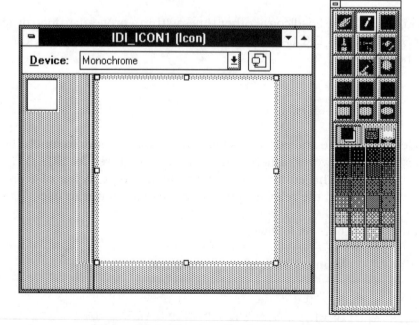

Figure 12.2 The App Studio icon editor

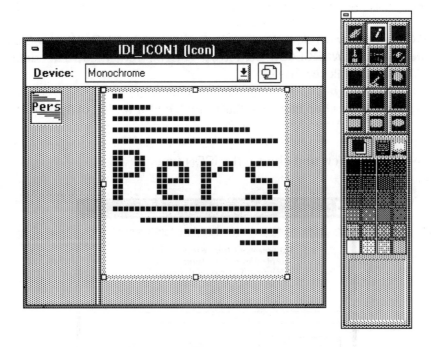

Figure 12.3 Creating a new icon with App Studio

3   Fill in the large square in the icon window, either by painting on it directly or by pasting in a graphic from the clipboard. As the icon is developed, an actual-size representation of it appears on the left of the window (Figure 12.3).

4   Save the changes to the resource file.

The new icon is stored in a new file (e.g. RES\ICON1.ICO). The icon is implemented by an amendment to the .RC file; for example:

```
IDI_ICON1   ICON   DISCARDABLE   "RES\\ICON1.ICO"
```

If you change the program item properties in Program Manager the new icon can be selected (Figure 12.4).

Personnel

Figure 12.4 The new icon

Borland C++

For Borland C++, the new window class must be registered with GetWindowClass, in which the hIcon field of the WNDCLASS structure can be redefined. The default icon is IDI_APPLICATION, a blank rectangle.

Borland's Resource Workshop has a similar bitmap editor to that of App Studio. To create a new icon:

1   Select Resource | New and choose the ICON type.

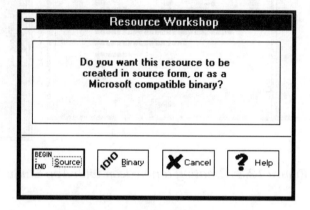

Figure 12.5 Selecting the icon format

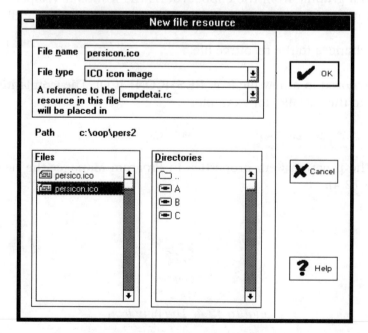

Figure 12.6 Naming the icon file

2 Choose between saving the file in source format or as a Microsoft-compatible binary file (Figure 12.5).

3 Give the icon file a name (Figure 12.6).

4 Choose the size of icon to work with (Figure 12.7).

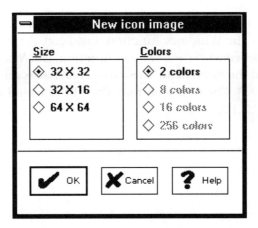

Figure 12.7 Selecting the icon size

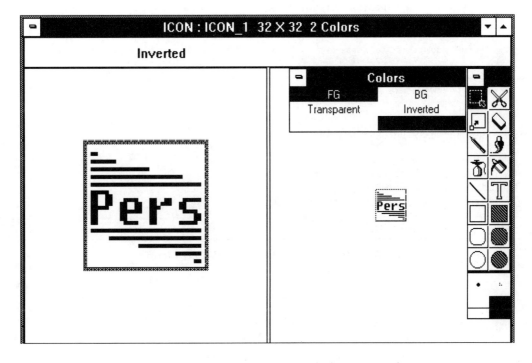

Figure 12.8 The Resource Workshop icon editor

5   The icon editor is displayed, with similar facilities to those of App Studio. The icon can be created bit-by-bit, an actual size representation being shown on the right (Figure 12.8).

The new icon appears in the resource file in the following form:

```
ICON_1 ICON "persicon.ico"
```

The handle of the icon used by a window when it is minimised is held in the hIcon field. This is given a value by the Windows function, LoadIcon. A new Window class must be defined and can be retrieved with the TWindow function, GetWindowClass. The new cursor can then be assigned to the hIcon field. The extra code necessary to load a new cursor is illlustrated in Figure 12.9. The new icon may then be selected in the Program Manager Properties box (Figure 12.10).

```
class TPersWindow : public TWindow
{
public:
  TPersWindow(PTWindowsObject AParent, LPSTR ATitle);
  //Declare two new override functions
  LPSTR TPersWindow::GetClassName();
  virtual void TPersWindow::GetWindowClass(WNDCLASS& AWndClass);
  virtual void CMEmployeesEnterDetails(RTMessage Msg)
    = [CM_FIRST + CM_EMPLOYEESENTERDETAILS];
};


LPSTR TPersWindow::GetClassName()
{
  //Define new window class
  return "TPersWindow";
}


void TPersWindow::GetWindowClass(WNDCLASS& AWndClass)
{
  //Get handle to window class
  TWindow::GetWindowClass(AWndClass);
  //Assign new icon to window class
  AWndClass.hIcon = LoadIcon(NULL, "PERSICON");
}
```

Figure 12.9 C++ code for loading an icon

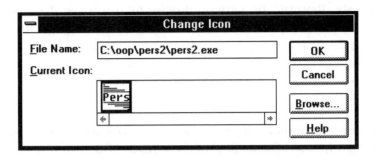

Figure 12.10 Applying the new icon

Visual Basic

A Visual Basic form gets its icon from the Icon property. This is either set at design time or changed while a program is running. If no icon is specified the default icon – a blank box with folded corner – is used.

When loading the icon at run-time, use the LoadPicture method. Using this function with no argument – i.e. LoadPicture() – results in a blank icon being displayed, on which ordinary graphics can be drawn (for example, a clock face or constantly-changing image).

Any icon file with .ICO format can be used, including those created with App Studio. Visual Basic also supplies an Icon Library in the ICONS subdirectory.

You can also specify the icon that will be used when an object is being dragged. In this case the icon is a replacement for the mouse pointer. The icon is defined by the DragIcon property and may be a reference to a form's icon, another DragIcon icon or a LoadPicture() function, specifying a .ICO bitmap file.

CURSORS

It is important to make a distinction between the two types of cursor that may appear on a Window screen:

- The *mouse cursor* (or *mouse pointer*) is a graphic image that mimics the physical movement of the mouse.

- The *text cursor* (or *caret*) indicates the current insertion point in a text box or combo box.

In each case, there is only one cursor active at any one time for the whole Windows session; if you click on a text box, the caret appears there but disappears from its previous location. (Obviously, it would be very confusing for the user if more than one were displayed.) The mouse pointer and caret may both be visible at the same time (and frequently are).

Mouse Pointer

The mouse pointer is a bitmap, of the same size as the icon. In the same way as the application icon, the mouse hCursor field of the WNDCLASS structure is assigned a value with LoadCursor. By default, the pointer is IDC_ARROW, the standard pointer in a rectangle.

If no pointer is defined (by setting hCursor to NULL), Windows expects the application to define the pointer type each time the pointer is moved over a window. In this case, the program should respond to the WM_MOUSEMOVE message by calling SetCursor. The function requires a handle to a cursor; the handle must have been returned by LoadCursor. When the pointer moves out of the window, Windows restores the original cursor.

The mouse pointer can be shown or hidden with the ShowCursor function. If you hide the pointer, make sure it is restored when the pointer is moved out of the window or when some other application takes control. (In general, it is not a good idea to hide the cursor.)

The current position of the pointer can be obtained with GetCursorPos; the position can be changed with SetCursorPos. More usefully, the cursor can be confined to a specific rectangle with ClipCursor; however, make sure you give the user a way of getting out of the rectangle!

Mouse pointers are created in App Studio and Resource Workshop in a similar way to icons. The main difference is that for a pointer you must also define a *hot spot*. This is the part of the bitmap that defines the current position of the pointer. For example, for the standard pointer the hot spot is the top left-hand corner (at the tip of the arrow).

Caret

The text cursor, or caret, can take several forms:

- A vertical bar or character underline

- A solid or grey block (with the character inverted)

- A bitmap (the size of a single character)

Whatever form the caret takes, it automatically flashes at the current text insertion point.

In general, the Windows default (a vertical line) is fine for most purposes. To override this, you must respond to the WM_SETFOCUS message with CreateCaret, followed by ShowCaret. You can choose a new position with SetCaretPos or temporarily remove the caret with HideCaret. When the focus moves away from the text box (resulting in the WM_KILLFOCUS message), the caret must be removed with DestroyCaret. If the new caret is to be a bitmap, the bitmap must be loaded into memory with LoadBitmap.

BITMAPS ON TOOLBARS

When you display a toolbar in a window, as an object derived from the MFCL CToolBar class for example, this has a single bitmap that includes all the images on the bar. The toolbar is divided into a number of *tiles*, all of the same size, each of which has the image for one button. The default size of each tile is 16 pixels wide by 15 pixels high.

When creating or editing a toolbar you should note the following points:

- For each button on the toolbar, the same image is used to create all the different states that the button can adopt: for instance, the greyed-out state when a button is not available is achieved by making alternate pixels white.

- Because of the way in which Windows varies the images to create different effects, it is better to use a bitmap that uses only black and white pixels. To add shading use grey, but avoid colours.

Toolbar bitmaps can be edited in App Studio.

BITMAPS ON MENUS

You can use bitmaps in place of text items on drop-down menus. For the Microsoft Foundation Class Library bitmaps are loaded with the SetMenuItemBitmaps function of the CMenu class.

13 | Disk File Access

Most applications require access to disk files in one way or another – programs that neither read data from disk nor allow new data to be saved are few and far between, and usually fairly pointless. The actual opening and closing of files, and saving of data, is handled by the standard instructions in each of the languages. However, Windows also has its own file-handling functions.

In addition, the user must be able to choose or enter a filename when opening or saving a file. The IDE gives the programmer varying degress of help in setting up these standard tasks.

FILE OPERATIONS

All file operations must ultimately be carried out by the MS-DOS *interrupts*, a set of low-level routines that form part of the operating system.

Before a file can be used, it must be *opened*. This operation prepares a file – whether new or existing – so that it can receive data, or data can be read from it. A transfer buffer is reserved in memory and the file is allocated a *file handle*. This handle is used in all subsequent operations to identify the handle.

Once opened, the file is available for reading and writing data. To the operating system any file is just a string or data bytes, with no particular structure. The structure must be imposed on the file by the applications. Essentially, files fall into two broad categories:

- *Sequential files* are strings of individual bytes (e.g. text files), for which there are usually only three operations available: read from the beginning, rewrite from the beginning or add new data to the end.

- *Random access files* are divided into *records*, each of a fixed length, and any record can be read or written, or new records can be added at the end.

These actions are achieved by low-level operations for moving to a particular byte, reading a byte, writing a byte and appending a byte to the end of the file.

When the file access is complete, the file must be *closed*. This releases the file handle and associated memory for another file. The maximum number of files that can be open at any one time is given by the FILES value in CONFIG.SYS.

These operations are performed in C++ with the functions of FSTREAM.H. Visual Basic uses the standard OPEN, INPUT, PRINT, WRITE and CLOSE instructions.

As an alternative, you can use the Windows functions instead; this is the equivalent of calling the MS-DOS interrupts from within a high-level language. The Windows functions are:

OpenFile	Opens, create or deletes a file
_lopen	Opens an existing file
_lcreat	Create a new file
_llseek	Moves to a new position in the file
lread	Reads data
lwrite	Writes data
lclose	Closes a file

Normally, OpenFile should be used in preference to the other functions. The functions beginning with an underscore character existed in Windows 2 but were undocumented, and became official functions in Windows 3. Note that there are _hread and _hwrite functions for reading or writing more than 64K of data at a time.

Usually, it should be possible to avoid the Windows file functions.

SELECTING A FILE

Before you can read data or create a new file you need a filename and a location where the file can be found (drive and directory path). For existing files, the user must be able to choose from a list; for new files the user must be able to enter a new name (or possibly overwrite an existing file). If filenames are typed in, the program must check that the name is valid; any directory specified must already exist.

In non-Windows programs, these operations take quite a bit of processing. The windows IDEs do most of the work for you.

Windows Functions

Even if you don't use one of the IDEs, Windows itself gets you most of the way there. The DlgDirList function fills a list box in a dialogue box with the filename corresponding to a file specification (such as '*.TXT' or 'C:\WORD*.DOC'). Any standard DOS file specification can be given and you can use the DOS wildcards. The list will also include [..] to indicate the parent directory and may show the name of subdirectories and the drive names (e.g. [-a-] for drive A).

The arguments to the function include the following:

- The handle of the dialogue box

- A pointer to the DOS file specification string

- The list box ID

- The ID of a label control where the path name can be shown

- The attributes of the file to be shown

The attributes allow you to decide whether the list should include files such as system and hidden files, but also determine whether subdirectories and drives are included.

The DlgDirSelect function retrieves the filename of the currently selected file. There are similar functions for use with combo boxes, DlgDirListComboBox and DlgDirSelectComboBox.

Visual C++

The Microsoft Foundation Class Library has a CFile class for handling data transfer to and from files and a CFileDialog class which is specially set up to handle Open and Save As operations. The CListBox class has a Dir function that adds a list of files to the list box. The DlgDirList function of CWnd provides the full implementation of the DlgDirList function.

For applications created by AppWizard, a standard File menu is set up automatically, with handlers already in place for File | New and File | Open.

ObjectWindows

ObjectWindows also provides a ready-made solution for the standard Open and Save As options. The TFileDialog class provides dialogue boxes for both of these. One of the parameters for the constructor to this object must be either SD_FILEOPEN or SD_FILESAVE, depending on which option has been selected.

The dialogue box includes a text box for entering the file specification, a label showing the current path, lists of files and directories (including drives), and OK and Cancel buttons. All processing is handled automatically while the dialogue box is on-screen. If the OK button is pressed, the selected filename is returned.

The resource definitions for the two types of dialogue box are held in FILEDIAL.DLG.

Visual Basic

Visual Basic adds a degree of simplification by removing some of your choices. Three distinct controls are presented:

- File-list boxes

- Directory-list boxes

- Drive-list boxes

You cannot mix the three different types of entry in a single box. However, these three classes, derived from simple list boxes, have been set up for you and adding them to the dialogue box is very simple.

The initial attributes of the controls determine their initial settings. By default, they will show the current drive and directory but these can be changed. The relevant attributes are as follows:

- The drive-list box has a Drive property, containing the selected drive (e.g. c:).

- The directory-list box has a Path property, containing the full directory path, including drive (e.g. c:\ or c:\oop, the final backslash only being required for the root directory).

- The file-list box has three properties: a Path property (as for directories), a Pattern property for the file specification (e.g. *.txt) and a Filename property for the current-ly-selected file (without directory parth).

It should also be noted that the file-list box has Archive, Hidden, ReadOnly, System and Normal properties for reducing the lists to files with certain properties. By default, Archive and Normal properties are set to True, the others are False. ('Normal' files are those for which none of the attributes is set.)

The properties for all three types of control should be kep in step, both when the dialogue box is initialised and when selections are made by the user. The advantage of Visual Basic's modular approach is that once you have set up one Open or Save As form, it can be used time and again in other applications.

Figures 13.1 and 13.2 show a simple text editor program, consisting of two windows. The corresponding procedures are shown in Figures 13.3 to 13.5.

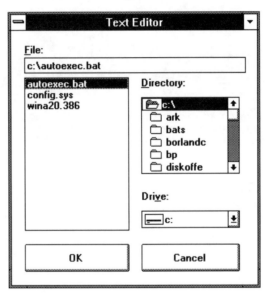

Figure 13.1 Text editor file selection window

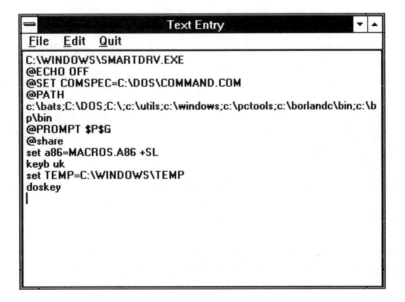

Figure 13.2 Text editing window

```
Sub Form_Load ()

  ' Procedure to load main form - sets up Filename box
  ' txtFile is Filename box, Dir1 is directory box

   txtFile.Text = Dir1.Path

End Sub

Sub Drive1_Change ()

  ' Drive1 is drive box

   Dir1.Path = Drive1.Drive
   txtFile.Text = Dir1.Path

End Sub

Sub Dir1_Change ()

   File1.Path = Dir1.Path
   txtFile.Text = Dir1.Path

End Sub

Sub File1_Click ()

  ' New path has been selected
  ' Add \ to path if not already there

   txtFile.Text = File1.Path
   If Right$(txtFile.Text, 1)  "\" Then
     txtFile.Text = txtFile.Text + "\"
   End If

  ' File specification = path + filename
   txtFile.Text = txtFile.Text + File1.FileName

End Sub

Sub cmdOK_Click ()

  ' OK button has been clicked
  ' Call LoadFile procedure to load existing text
   LoadFile

   frmText.Show
   frmText.Enabled = 1

End Sub
```

Figure 13.3 Procedures for file selection window

```
Sub Form_Resize ()

  ' User has changed size of window
  ' Change text box txtEntry so that it still fits in window frmText
  txtEntry.Height = frmText.Height - 400
  txtEntry.Width = frmText.Width - 120

End Sub

Sub mnuFileNew_Click ()

  ' File|New option: clear text box
  txtEntry = ""

End Sub

Sub mnuFileSave_Click ()

  ' File|Save option: call SaveFile procedure
  SaveFile

End Sub

Sub mnuEditCut_Click ()

  ' Standard Edit|Cut option
  Clipboard.Clear
  Clipboard.SetText txtEntry.SelText
  txtEntry.SelText = ""

End Sub

Sub mnuEditCopy_Click ()

  ' Standard Edit|Copy option
  Clipboard.Clear
  Clipboard.SetText txtEntry.SelText

End Sub

Sub mnuEditPaste_Click ()

  ' Standard Edit|Paste option
  txtEntry.SelText = Clipboard.GetText()

End Sub

Sub mnuQuit_Click ()

  ' Quit option: remove form from screen - forces Unload event
  Unload frmText

End Sub
```

Figure 13.4 Procedures for text entry window (continues)

```
Sub Form_Unload (Cancel As Integer)

  ' Remove window from screen - check to see if text should be saved

  Dim Message As String, Title As String
  Dim Answer As Integer

  Message = "Click on Yes to save the changes"
  Title = "Save the Data?"
  Answer = MsgBox(Message, 51, Title)

  If Answer = 6 Then
    ' Yes button clicked - call SaveFile procedure
    SaveFile
  End If

  If Answer = 2 Then
    ' No button pressed
    Cancel = -1
  End If

End Sub
```

Figure 13.4 (continued) Procedures for text entry window

```
' General procedures, available to routines in all forms

Sub LoadFile ()

  Dim FiletoLoad As String, OneLine As String
  Dim LineNo As Integer

  'Load file using the name typed in the Filename box
  'in the Main window

  FiletoLoad = frmMain.txtFile.Text
  LineNo = 0

  Open FiletoLoad For Input As #2

  Do While Not EOF(2)

    LineNo = LineNo + 1

    If LineNo  1 Then
      ' Add CR/LF to existing text
      frmText.txtEntry.Text = frmText.txtEntry.Text + Chr$(13) + Chr$(10)
    End If

    ' Read next line of text
    Line Input #2, OneLine
    ' Add to existing text
    frmText.txtEntry.Text = frmText.txtEntry.Text + OneLine

  Loop

  Close #2

End Sub

Sub SaveFile ()

  'Save file using the name typed in the Filename box
  'in the Main window

  Dim FileToSave As String

  FileToSave = frmMain.txtFile.Text

  Open FileToSave For Output As #1
  Print #1, frmText.txtEntry.Text
  Close #1

End Sub
```

Figure 13.5 Global procedures for text editor application

INITIALISATION FILES

Each time you leave Windows, the current settings are stored in WIN.INI (unless this has been disabled by the Windows I Save Settings option being turned off). In addition, WIN.INI holds much other information relating to the operation of Windows and other applications.

Windows provides functions that allow an application to add to this WIN.INI file or access its contents. (Unfortunately, there are no functions for reducing the size of WIN.INI, so the file usually gets full of settings that have been long redundant.) The initialisation file consists of sections that have the following form:

```
[section]
entry1 = value1
entry2 = value2
. . .
```

The GetProfileString function returns the string *value* for any given *section* and *entry*. Similarly, GetProfileInt returns an integer *value*.

WriteProfileString sets the *value* for a given *section* and *entry*. If either the *section* or *entry* within section do not exist, they are created. If an *entry* exists, its existing value is overwritten. So you can set up new sections within WIN.INI and extend any section. In all cases, the case of the *section* and *entry* is not important.

In a similar way, you may want to set up an initialisation file for a particular application. This can be used to hold the user's settings (such as the last file used or the settings of menu options). The file has the same format as WIN.INI. Normally, the file is given a .INI extension and, unless you specify otherwise in the Windows functions, should reside in the Windows subdirectory (e.g. C:\WINDOWS). These application-specific initialisation files are updated with the GetPrivateProfileString, GetPrivateProfileInt and WritePrivateProfile-String functions. These work in the same way as their WIN.INI counterparts but require as a parameter the name of the initialisation file (including full path where necessary).

14 | The Help System

One of the standard features that users expect to find on any Windows application is a help system in the standard format. Outside Windows, implementing help systems is a tedious and troublesome task and, as a result, is seldom accomplished satisfactorily. Windows provides a standard help system that is relatively simple to implement and can be used to provide the user with a comprehensive, context-sensitive, on-screen guide to the operation of an application. In addition, the user will almost certainly know how to use the help system already without extra tuition. Whatever you may think about the effectiveness of the Windows help system, these facts make the incorporation of the system a necessity for most serious applications.

USING THE HELP SYSTEM

From the user's point of view, the first few attempts to use the help system are likely to be fraught with difficulties. The help system tends to be so comprehensive that is not easy to use. However, once it has been mastered, the user can be satisfied that the help provided for every other Windows application will work in the same way.

As a general rule, the Help menu on the menu bar contains the following options:

- Contents, which provides a list of subject from which the user can choose

- Search For Help On, which gives an index of topics

- How To Use Help, which offers help on using the help system

- About Application, which usually leads to an information dialogue box

The Contents option is the usual entry point to the help system. This results in a list of help subjects, in logical order (Figure 14.1). Clicking on one of these brings up help on a particular topic. Various other options are then available, including the ability to move on to other topics. Confusingly (and incorrectly) the contents list is often referred to as the *index*.

Search For Help On is a more direct way of bringing up help on a particular topic. A full list of help items is presented in the top part of the window, in alphabetical order (Figure 14.2). This is equivalent to a real index. An item is selected is one of the several ways:

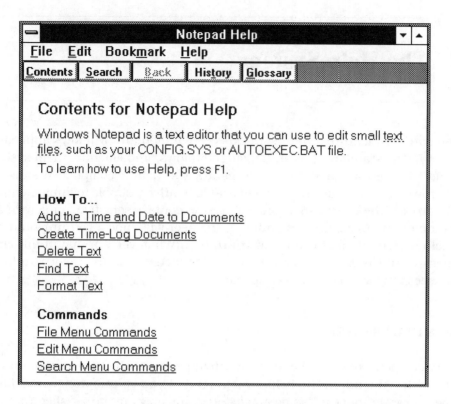

Figure 14.1 Help Contents

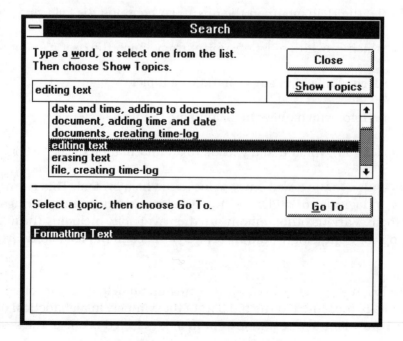

Figure 14.2 The Help Search option

- Typing the first few letters takes you to the first item that matches.

- Double-clicking an item selects it.

- Clicking on an item and then on Show Topics also selects it.

When an item is selected, the corresponding topic is displayed at in the bottom part of the window. Note that the list at the top is not a list of topics, merely of items that lead to topics. For example, 'Saving files' and 'Files, saving' may both lead to an option called 'Save Files'.

When the user clicks on the topic, the help for that topic is displayed.

The How To Use Help option loads the help program but with help about itself (Figure 14.3). It may seem perverse to use the help system to show the user how to use the help system but the user should be able to work out what is going on by trial and error.

The final option on the menu, About..., generally leads to a simple dialogue box giving a few itmes of information about the application, such as copyright details. This option is really nothing to do with the help system, but this is the traditional place to put it.

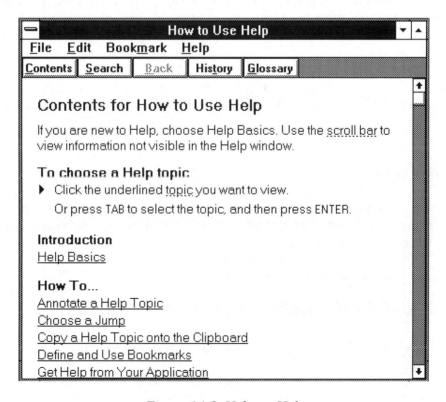

Figure 14.3 Help on Help

Glossary Entries and Hypertext Jumps

Each help *topic* consists of an independent chunk of text giving help on that topic. Two special features are provided within the text to take the user further.

A word or phase may be displayed in a different colour (or have a dotted underline on monochrome screens). This is a *glossary entry*. Clicking on the text at this point results in a pop-up box appearing, containing a definition of the marked text. Clicking again clears the box.

Similarly, a word or phrase may be displayed in another colour (or underlined on monochrome screens). This is the location of a *hypertext jump*. If the user clicks here, the system will display text for a new topic relating to the marked text. As for the Search option, the marked text may not be precisely the same as the topic name; the topic name is hidden in the text at that point. ('Hypertext' is a rather grand term for text that has built-in links, allowing the user to jump from one point to another.)

As a general rule, help files should be constructed so that the user can go to any topic from the Contents page. That is, the Contents list will lead to a number of topics; each of these may lead to other topics, which in turn may go on to further topics, and so on. It should be possible to reach every topic in this way. Of course, it may be that a topic can be reached by more than one route, or even that a series of topics may lead back to the beginning again. This doesn't matter, as long as the help system appears easily accessible to the user.

One of the most common ways of making a help topic lead to other topics is to have a 'See Also' paragraph at the end of the topic, where the phrases that follow are hypertext jumps.

Help Window Buttons

The Help window has a set of buttons above the help text. This window is the same whether the program was run with the Contents or Search options. These buttons and their effects are as follows:

* Contents takes you straight to the contents list.

* Search leads to the search list.

* Back takes you back to the last help topic you were looking out.

* History lists all the topics that have been inspected in the current session and lets you choose one again.

- Glossary lists all the glossary terms (those that result in a pop-up box being displayed) and lets you view any glossary entry.

The first two buttons have an identical effect to the corresponding Help menu options. Back and History allow you to review previous help, and Glossary is useful if you don't understand the application's jargon.

Help Menus

The Help program also has a fairly standard set of menus, which are as follows:

- The File menu has a Print Topic option to print the help information currently being viewed; Print Setup allows you to change the printer set-up; Exit closes down the Help program.

- The Edit menu has a Copy option to copy the current help topic text to the clipboard; the user can then paste this into another Windows application. There is also an Annotate option, which allows the user to add extra notes to the supplied text.

- The Bookmark menu lets you mark topics that have been viewed so that you can return to the later.

- The Help menu provides another entry point for How To Use Help, allows you to always have the help window on the top of the display, and has the inevitable About Help option.

There will be some variations in the menu, depending on the way in which the help file was created.

CREATING A HELP DOCUMENT

There is no need to create your own help program; this is already done for you. The WINHELP.EXE program, supplied with Windows, operates as described above. All you have to do is create the help file (containing the help text) and then link it into your application.

The Help Document

The first stage is to create a *help document*, which will contain all the help text plus a set of codes by which Windows can organise the text. The easiest way to create the document is by using Microsoft Word or Word For Windows. Not surprisingly perhaps, Microsoft have devised a system that makes use of a set of features which are available in its word processor: single- and double-underlining, hidden text, footnotes and the ability to create RTF files. You can use another word processor, providing it has these features, but it is generally easier to stick to Word.

Part of a help document is shown in Figure 14.4. In the illustration, the footnote entries are shown on separate lines. Hidden text is represented by [square brackets] and {braces}. The list of footnotes is given in Figure 14.5.

The main text of the document should be organised so that it starts with the contents list and then continues with each individual help topic; the topics are separated by page breaks. (In the illustration, page breaks are represented by [page].) The topics should be in some logical order; this is not essential but it helps when tracking down problems later. As a general rule, the document ends with the glossary entries, again separated by page breaks.

Context Labels

Each help topic is identified by a *context label*. This label is usually included on the first line of the text, with the main title. The context label must be entered as a footnote, specifying # as the Footnote Reference Mark. The restrictions on the label are as follows:

- Only letters, numbers, full stops and underscores are allowed – no spaces

- Maximum 255 characters

- No difference between capitals and lower-case letters

- Must be unique in the document

Every topic should have a context label.

```
Toto Help Contents

Using Toto:
    About Toto[H_About_Toto]
    Creating Data Regions[H_Creating_Regions]
    Using Sets[H_Name_Sets]
    Data Information[H_Data_Info]
    Search Database[H_Database]

Toto Menu Options:
    New Data Region[H_New_Data]
    New Set[H_New_Set]
    Save Worksheet[H_Save_Worksheet]
    Close Toto[H_Close_Toto]

[page]
# H_About_Toto
$ About Toto
K About Toto
+ Toto_General:10
About Toto

Toto provides a new way of storing data, using an Excel worksheet. The data is
stored in a data region{H_Region} and is defined by the labels around the edge of
the region (the context{H_Context}), rather than by the physical position of the
data.

When a data region has been defined, you can change the context and a different
set of data is displayed. (See Creating Data Regions[H_Creating_Regions].)

Information on each data item, and its origin, is displayed by double-clicking on
the cell. (See Data Source[H_Data_Source])

[page]
# H_Creating_Regions
$ Creating Data Regions
K Data Regions; Creating Data Regions
+ Toto_General:20
Creating Data Regions

A data region{H_Region} acts like a window onto a Toto database{H_Database}. Any
part of an existing Excel worksheet can be used as the basis of a data region.
The region consists of a rectangular block of data, with headings for each row
and column, and additional labels in other cells. The labels can be taken from
anywhere on the worksheet.

The data region can be redefined at any time.

[page]
# H_Name_Sets]
$ Using Sets
K+ Sets;Using Sets
+ Toto_General:30
```

Figure 14.4 Part of a help document (continues)

Using Sets

Toto allows you to create sets of names which may be used in <u>Set Regions</u>**[H_Set_Region]**: for instance, a set of month names or a set of towns.

<u>Whole Set Regions</u>**[H_Whole_Sets]**.

Whole sets, or subsets can be used in row or columns headings; for example, the column headings along the top of the <u>data region</u>**{H_Region}** may be the set of month names, while the row headings to the left of the region could be the set of towns.

<u>Choose from Set Regions</u>**[H_Choosing_Sets]**

Single cells, or (exceptionally) ranges, may be used to select from a set. Such cells would then either directly be included in the <u>context</u>**{H_Context}** for one or more data regions, or be used to derive other context cells to affect the data in the region.

Sets Regions are created using the <u>New Set</u>**[H_New_Set]** window.

[page]
H_Data_Info
$ Data Information
K+ Data Information
+ Toto_General:40
Data Information

The data information window is displayed when the user double-clicks on a data cell within a <u>data region</u>**{H_Region}**.

Pressing Esc closes the window.

[page]
H_Database
$ Search Database
K Search Database
+ Toto_General:50
Search Database

The Search Database Window is accessed from the <u>Data Information</u>**{H_Data_Info}** window and is used to list all data items for a selection of names. The names are listed, one name per line.

Click on Select to view the <u>Data Audit</u>**{H_Data_Audit}** window or click on Cancel to return to the worksheet.

...

[page]
H_Context
The context is a group of labels that uniquely identifies an item of data. Usually the context consists of a new heading, a column heading, and one or more

Figure 14.4 (continued) Part of help document (continues)

additional labels. There may, however, be more than one set of column headings or
row headings, and these do not have to align to the data region to which they
apply.

Context regions are marked in yellow using the default <u>colouring</u>{H_Colours}.

...

Figure 14.4 (continued) Part of a help document

```
# H_About_Toto
$ About Toto
K About Toto
+ Toto_General:10
# H_Creating_Regions
$ Creating Data Regions
K Data Regions; Creating Data Regions
+ Toto_General:20
# H_Name_Sets
$ Using Sets
K Sets;Using Sets
+ Toto_General:30
# H_Data_Info
$ Data Information
K Data Information
+ Toto_General:40
# H_Search_Database
$ Search Database
K Search Database
+ Toto_General:50
# H_New_Set
$ New Sets
K Sets;New Sets
+ Toto_General:60
# H_Choosing_Sets
$ Choosing Sets
K Sets;Choosing Sets
+ Toto_General:70
# H_Whole_Sets
$ Whole Sets
K Sets;Whole Sets
+ Toto_General:80
# H_Set_Region
$ Set Regions
K Sets;Set Region
+ Toto_General:90
...
# H_Context
...
```

Figure 14.5 Footnotes for help document

Hypertext Jumps and Glossary Entries

When the user clicks on a hypertext jump phrase, the relevant help topic is displayed. This is achieved as follows:

- The text to be highlighted is marked with a double underline.

- Immediately following this must be the context label marked as hidden text.

Any item of text can be highlighted but the context label must precisely match that of a help topic. The same topic can be called from several places in the document.

The use of hypertext jumps is essential on the Contents page and useful for 'See Also' sections.

In a similar way, glossary entries are identified by a single underline, again followed by the context label in hiddent text. When the user clicks on the highlighted text, the specified topic pops up and remains on-screen as long as the mouse button is pressed.

In Figure 14.4 the hidden text following hypertext jumps is shown in [square brackets] and that for glossary entries is in {braces}. (In the actual help document there would be no distinction between the two types, the difference being marked by the underlining.)

Titles and Bookmarks

Associated with each main topic there will usually be a *title string*.

As for context lables, the title strings are included as footnotes, usually on the first line of the topic, identified by the $ reference mark. Titles can include any printable (ANSI) characters and may be up to 128 characters long. There is no need to attach titles to glossary entries.

Titles are used as follows:

- As bookmarks: when the user retrieves a bookmark it is the title string that is shown

- In the History List: only topics with footnote titles are included

- In the bottom half of the Search window

The bookmarks and history lists are handled automatically by the system.

Searching for Key Words

When the user clicks on the Search button or chooses the Search option from the Help menu a list of *key words* is displayed in the top half of the Search window. These key words are identified in the text or footnotes with a K reference mark. There should always be a title footnote on the same line as any key word.

When the user clicks on a key word in the Search menu, the corresponding title is displayed in the bottom half of the window. Clicking on the title brings up the help topic.

- There can be more than one key word in the K footnote, separated by semi-colons. All the key words are included in the search list but lead to the same title string.

- The same key word can be used more than once. Clicking on the key word in the search list results in all corresponding titles being listed.

In general, there will be a keyword for every title, apart from the Contents title.

Other Footnotes

Two other types of footnote can be used:

- The + footnote is used for *browsing sequences.*

- The * footnote indicates a *buildtag.*

The browsing sequence determines the order in which the topics will be displayed when the user clicks on one of the Browse buttons. The footnote consists of the sequence name (following the same rules as context labels), a colon and a sequence number. This number determines the browsing order.

Note that the numbers are compared character by character, rather than numerically; for instance, 20 is considered to be less than 3. Therefore all numbers should be padded with leading zeros to make tham all the same length.

The numbers do not have to be consecutive; indeed, it is better to leave a gap so that new topics can be inserted without having to re-arrange all the other browse numbers. By using different sequence names, you can create more than one browse sequence.

The buildtags let you compile parts of a help file, based on some condition (see below).

Graphics

Graphics images can be included in help documents. If the document is being prepared in Word, the bitmap image is incorporated in the usual way; if another word processor is being used, a special instruction must be inserted in the text. This will have one of the following forms:

{bml *file*}   Image is on the left, and text may be displayed on the right

{bmc *file*}   Image is centred, with text flowing round it

{bmr *file*}   Image is on the right, with text to the left

The full filename must be given, including the .BMP extension.

Saving the Document

The finished document must be saved as an RTF (rich text format) file. Microsoft Word allows files in this format to be both read and written.

COMPILING THE HELP FILE

The help document is compiled into a *help file* with the HC31.EXE help compiler (for Windows 3.1) or equivalent. The compiler needs a project file, which tells it how the document is to be interpretted. The project file must have a .HPJ extension and will create a help file with a .HLP extension.

The project file is an ASCII file, with the same format as a .INI file. There may be up to six sections, each of which sets a number of paramters. An example help project file is shown in Figure 14.6.

[OPTIONS]

This section of the file provides general information for the compiler. The parameters that may be included are:

TITLE   A string to appear of the help window title bar, to which will be added 'Help-' and the help filename

ROOT   The location of all files needed by the help compiler

INDEX   The context label for the Contents topic, if this is not the first topic in the file

```
[OPTIONS]
TITLE=TOTO - Excel Help
COPYRIGHT=Copyright Ambit Research Ltd. London. 1993
COMPRESS= TRUE

[FILES]
TOTOHELP.RTF

[MAP]
#include :\totodoc\totohelp.h
```

Figure 14.6 Help project file

COMPRESS   Determines whether or not the help file is compressed (FALSE by default)

WARNING   Controls debug information: values 1, 2 or 3, with 1 being the minimum amount

FORCEFONT   Forces all text to use a specified font, regardless of what is used in the original document

MAPFONTSIZE   Converts one or more fonts sizes to a specified font size

MULTIKEY   Allows the creation of additional key word lists, using letters other than K

BUILD   Specifies one or more buildtags to be used in the creation of the help file

The [OPTIONS] section is not required but it is usual to at least give a title for the help window.

[MAP]
This section allows you to provide context-sensitive help. Each topic in the help document should have been given a context label. This label is used for jumping around the help file but can also be used to specify the first topic in the help file to be displayed, usually when the function key F1 is pressed.

Each context label must be mapped to a unique number. (Making this the same as the browse sequence number makes life easier.) The WinHelp function that loads the help program can have the context number given as a parameter, in which case the relevant help topic is displayed.

[FILES]

This is the only required section of the project file and lists the documents to be compiled. (A help file can be compiled from more than one document.) The files are assumed to be in the same directory as the project file, unless a different directory is specified with the ROOT parameter or the filename here includes a directory path.

[BITMAPS]

All bitmap files that have been included in the document as part of a {bml}, {bmc} or {bmr} instruction must be listed in this section. As for the [FILES] section, the directory is set by the ROOT parameter or is specified with the name; otherwise the directory containing the project file is assumed.

[ALIAS]

The [ALIAS] section allows you to replace one context label with another. This saves having to change the footnotes in the document but can lead to confusion and is best avoided.

[BUILDTAGS]

This section allows for conditional compilation of the help file. If this facility is used, each topic in the help document must be given a buildtag, using the * footnotes. A topic can have more than one buildtag.

For instance, suppose that there are to be two versions of an application, Standard and Enhanced; then the same help document can be used to create a different help file for each. The following footnotes could be used with any topic:

*Standard   Help for Standard version only

*Enhanced   Help for Enhanced version only

*Standard; Enhanced   Help for both versions

All the buildtags must be listed in the [BUILDTAGS] section of the project file. The BUILD parameter in the [OPTIONS] section specifies which buildtags are to be used, and therefore which sections are to be included in the compiled help file. Buildtags can be combined in the BUILD value using the following operators:

I	Or
&	And
~	Not

Brackets can also be used.

Compilation

The help file is compiled with the help compiler, HC31.EXE, which is invoked from the DOS prompt as follows:

```
HC31 file
```

The project file should be specified, *not* the help document file. For example:

```
HC31 TOTOHELP.HPJ
```

The result is a file with a .HLP extension (e.g. PERSHELP.HLP). This file can be read by WINHELP.EXE.

THE WINHELP FUNCTION

The help program is invoked with the WinHelp function. The arguments to the function are the window's handle, a pointer to the help file name, a help command and a data value. When the function is called, WINHELP.EXE is executed (unless it is already running), and loads the help file specified.

The help command can be any of following:

HELP_INDEX	Displays the contents list
HELP_SETINDEX	Chooses a contents list if there are more than one; the data value identifies the context number associated with the list
HELP_CONTEXT	Displays a particular help topic; the data identifies a context number
HELP_KEY	Displays a particular help topic; the data is a key string
HELP_MULTIKEY	Display a topic based on an alternate key table, as specified by the MULTIKEY option in the help project file
HELP_QUIT	Closes down the help system for the current application
HELP_HELPONHELP	Activates the help system with its own internal help file

Therefore you will need to include calls to the WinHelp function for each of the options in the Help menu. The function can also be invoked at other places in the program, where context-sensitive help is required. As a general rule, help is invoked when the F1 key is pressed; specifying a context number results in the corresponding help topic being displayed.

For example, to call the help window from the Help I Index option requires the following function declaration in a Borland C++ program:

```
virtual void CMHelpIndex(RTMessage Msg) = [CM_FIRST + CM_HELPINDEX];
```

The help window could be invoked as follows:

```
void TTotoWindow::CMHelpIndex(RTMessage)
{
  WinHelp(HWindow, "totohelp.hlp". HELP_INDEX, NULL);
}
```

The principle is the same for any other programming language.

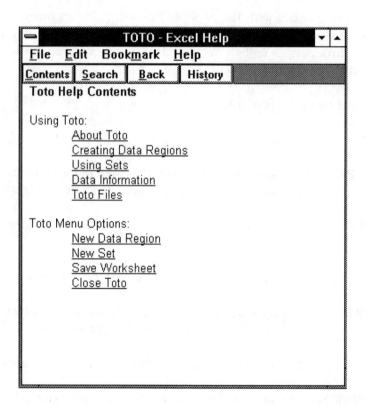

Figure 14.7 Sample Help Contents

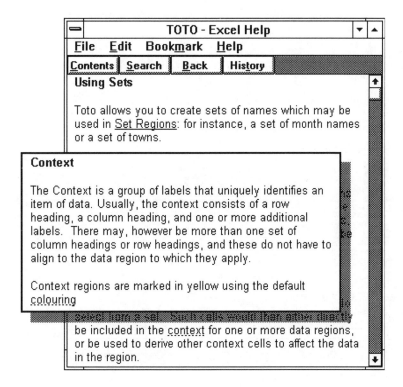

Figure 14.8 Sample help glossary item

The call to a particular help item, based on a test of key presses, would take the following form:

```
case WM_KEYDOWN:
  if (wParam == VK_F1)
    WinHclp(HWindow, "totohclp.hlp". HELP_KEY,
      (DWORD) (LPSTR) "Data Regions");
```

The effect of the help file in Figure 14.4 when called from the Help menu is shown in Figures 14.7 and 14.8.

15 Data Transfer

The Windows environment provides a high degree of compatibility between applications and, as a result, there are several ways of transferring data between applications. The clipboard has already been described; this is a method by which the user can move data from one application to another. However, it is also possible for the application to communicate with another Windows application and ensure that data is updated automatically. Two methods are described here: Dynamic Data Exchange (DDE) and Object Linking and Embedding (OLE).

DYNAMIC DATA EXCHANGE (DDE)

The DDE methods lets you create a link between your application and any other application with DDE capabilities. It is important to stress that *both* applications must be programmed for DDE. However, many of the most-commonly used applications have DDE built in: for example, Microsoft Excel, Word for Windows and Paintbrush.

The link between the applications is generally referred to as a *conversation*. Two applications take part in each conversation:

- The application receiving data is the *destination* or *client*.

- The application sending data is the *source* or *server*.

Each conversation needs three types of information:

- The *application* identifies the source program.

- The *topic* is the subject of the link (such as a filename).

- The *items* are the data items that are being transferred.

The application and topic are fixed for any conversation, but once the conversation has started many items of data may be transferred.

Initiating the Conversation

The DDE conversation is started by the destination sending the WM_DDE_INITIATE message via the SendMessage function. The parameters for this message include the application and topic names. SendMessage despatches the message to every application currently running.

- Those applications that do not have DDE capabilities ignore the message.

- Applications set up for DDE check the application name; if the name is not one for which they are prepared, again the message is ignored.

- If a DDE application receives a message giving the correct application name, then it responds by sending an acknowledgement.

The acknowledgement takes the form of a WM_DDE_ACK message, posted directly to the destination application. This message includes the window handle for the source application. The destination now knows which application it is talking to and has a window handle. Therefore all other messages can be sent directly to the source with the PostMessage function (which requires a window handle as parameter), rather than broadcasting them to the system as a whole.

Now that the conversation has been initiated, data can be transferrd. The way in which data is passed depends on the type of link that is used.

Hot Link

With a *hot link* data is passed from the source to the destination every time there is a change in the data. For instance, if a spreadsheet is linked into a database program, every time there is a change in the spreadsheet the database is updated immediately. This is also suitable for data received by a communications program via a modem, where the data is to be passed on to some other application.

To start a hot link, the destination sends a WM_DDE_ADVISE message to the source. The source responds by sending the data in a WM_DDE_DATA message every time there is a change in the relevant values. The destination may acknowledge this with WM_DDE_ACK (depending on the paramters set up in the link).

When the destination wants to end the conversation it sends a WM_DDE_TERMINATE message, and this is echoed back by the source.

Warm Link

Many applications have other work to do, apart from receiving DDE data, and are therefore unable to deal with incoming data all the time. In these cases, a *warm link* is more appropriate.

The main part of the conversation starts with a WM_DDE_ADVISE message, specifying a warm link. This time the source responds by sending a WM_DDE_DATA message, with a NULL value in place of the data, every time the data changes. If the destination is not ready, the message can be ignored; it will be sent again later. However, if the destination is able to receive data it sends a WM_DDE_REQUEST message. The source responds with another WM_DDE_DATA message, this time with a pointer to the data block. The destination may acknowledge the message with WM_DDE_ACK.

The conversation is again terminated with WM_DDE_TERMINATE.

Cold Link

The third type of link is the *cold link*. Here, the source does not send any data until asked; everything is initiated by the destination. When the destination is ready to update its data, it sends a WM_DDE_REQUEST message to the source. The source transmits the location of the data in a WM_DDE_DATA message and the destination confirms that the data has been received with WM_DDE_ACK.

This continues until the message is ended with WM_DDE_TERMINATE.

OBJECT LINKING AND EMBEDDING (OLE)

An alternative form of data transfer allows one application to be activated from within another program. With Object Linking and Embedding (OLE), an imported item of data is displayed. When the user double-clicks on the item, the application that created the data is activated. Typically, an OLE object will display a bitmap created with Paintbrush; double-clicking on the bitmap loads Paintbursh, with the bitmap ready for editing.

There are two types of OLE object, holding the data in different ways:

- *Linked data* is loaded from an external source when required. The same data can be displayed on many OLE objects; changing the source data results in all the OLE objects showing the changed data.

- *Embedded data* is held as part of the destination's data, so there can be only one copy of it. If the data orginated from an external file, then any change to that file will not affect the embedded data.

The choice of object type depends on the way in which the data is to be used.

DYNAMIC LINK LIBRARIES (DLLs)

All programmers eventually discover that most programs operate on similar principles and are required to perform the same tasks. Once a problem has been solved in one program, the code that provides the solution can be re-used in another program with the same requirements. Re-use of code in this way saves the programmer time, helps to ensure bug-free programs, and leads to applications that behave in the same way.

Over the years, programmers have also found that their re-usable segments of code may be useful to other programmers. This led to the creation of *libraries*, collections of functions and procedures that can be called from within an application and linked into the program when it is compiled.

C is a language that is heavily dependent on libraries. The language itself is very small and most of the functionality is contained in a set of standard libraries. To use any of these functions in these libraries, all you need do is #include the relevant library header file in the main header file and then call the functions. When the program is linked, the functions that are called by the main program are added into the final executable file. Only those functions that are needed are included, so there is a minimum of wasted code.

Windows programming takes this a stage further by the introduction of Dynamic Link Libraries (DLLs). The problem with Windows programs, as described in earlier chapters, is that they make use of may hundreds of external functions. If all these functions had to be included in the final executable file, the files would be huge (even more so than they are at present). The use of DLLs solves this problem.

A DLL is a library of compiled functions and procedures that may be called from within a Windows application, just like any other standard library. However, when the main application is compiled, the DLL functions are not added to the executable file. The DLL functions that are to be used must be declared in the main application, specifying the name of the DLL file so that Windows knows where to look for them. Then, when the function call is encountered at run-time, Windows executes the corresponding functions from the DLL.

This approach has a number of advantages:

- Executable files are kept as small as possible.

- The same DLL functions can be used by different programs at the same time.

- The functions in a DLL can be changed without changing or recompiling the applications that use them.

- Once a DLL has been debugged it can be used again and again without further work.

Windows relies heavily on DLLs. All the Windows functions are held in DLLs, and are therefore accessible to all programs. Creating your own DLLs is a fairly straightforward task. DLLs can also be attached to other people's applications; for intance, DLLs can be written to add options to Excel menus and interact with spreadsheet data.

The DLL does not have a WinMain function but it does require two other functions: LibMain and WEP.

- LibMain is called when the DLL is loaded into memory for the first time. This function calls UnlockData, which unlocks the DLL's data segment in memory. You may also add other initialisation code, for example code to allocate memory blocks.

- WEP is called by Windows immediately before the DLL is removed from memory. You can add other functions to de-allocate memory, for example.

Most of the work of creating DLLs is done for you, if you use one of the IDEs.

Visual Basic

Visual Basic does not allow you to create DLLs but you can access the functions contained in DLLs, including the Windows functions.

All procedures and functions that are to be used must be included in the [declarations] section of the form or module that is to make the calls. The declarations should take the following forms:

```
Declare Sub procname Lib DLLname (parameters)

Declare Function procname Lib DLLname (parameters)
```

Use Sub if no value is returned from the DLL; otherwise use Function. The declared procedures and functions can then be called from within the code in exactly the same way as any other procedure.

MULTIPLE DOCUMENT INTERFACE (MDI)

The examples considered so far have consisted of a main window with pop-up dialogue boxes and message boxes. This is fine when you know exactly what windows are needed, but sometimes you will want to allow the user to determine how many windows are needed. The *Multiple Document Interface* (MDI) is a method for a main window to contain an undefined number of other windows.

Many of the most common Windows applications use MDI:

- The Program Manager has icons and windows for many program groups, and more can be added by the user at any time.

- Microsoft's Excel allows the user to open several spreadsheet windows at the same time, so that data can be copied between them; similarly, Word for Windows allows for a number of open document windows.

- The SYSEDIT application (supplied with Windows) has windows for editing AUTOEXEC.BAT, CONFIG.SYS and WIN.INI.

- Visual C++, Borland's C++ and Visual Basic all make extensive use of MDI.

In an MDI application the window that is to contain the other windows is called the *frame window*. The smaller windows are *child windows*. (To avoid confusion with the parent windows and child windows described earlier – e.g. controls as child windows of a parent window – the child windows here will be referred to as *MDI child windows*.)

There are a number of important features in MDI applications:

- An MDI child window can be moved around within the frame window and can be resized, but cannot be moved out of the client area of the frame window.

- When an MDI child window is minimised, the icon is put *inside* the frame window, at the bottom (rather than at the bottom of the screen).

- When a child window is maximised, it fills the frame window and its title is added to that of the frame window.

- Any child window can be closed independently of the others but closing the frame window also closes al child windows; similarly, when the frame window is minimised it takes all the child windows with it.

In this way, an MDI system behaves just like a smaller version of a full Windows system. As a general rule, all child windows will be instances of the same class, so they will all look the same and behave in the same way. The usual reason for wanting to use MDI is so that you can allow the user to control the number of window objects that are created. This is achieved by attaching a piece of code to a menu option, or some other event handler, which creates the new object, usually slightly offset a little from the last one (resulting in cascading windows).

Note that you can only have one MDI frame window in an application.

MDI Windows Structure

The first stage in setting up an MDI system is to set up a frame window. You can then create an *MDI client window* from the MDIClient class. This window will be a child of the frame and its only task is to handle the client area of the frame window.

Finally, the MDI child windows are created as children of the MDI client window.

MDI Functions and Messages

Although you could set up an MDI system using all the standard Windows functions, there are a number of functions and messages specifically designed to make MDIs easier to set up.

The DefWindowProc function, which handles messages that have not been dealt with elsewhere, is replaced by two new functions: DefFrameProc and DefMDIChildProc.

The MDI messages put into effect the special MDI activities:

- WM_MDICREATE creates a new MDI child, WM_MDIDESTROY removes an MDI child window.

- WM_MDICASCADE arranges the MDI child windows as cascading windows, WM_MDITILE arranges them as tiles.

- WM_MDIMAXIMIZE maximises an MDI child, WM_MDIRESTORE restores an MDI child to its normal size and WM_MDIICONARRANGE tidies up any MDI child icons at the bottom of the frame window.

- WM_MDIACTIVATE transfers the focus to an MDI child and WM_MDINEXT passes the focus to the next MDI child in sequence; WM_MDIGETACTIVE tells you which MDI child currently has the focus.

- **WM_MDISETMENU** combines the menus of the MDI child window with the frame window.

Most of these activities are handled automatically for you if you use one of the IDEs to set up the system.

MDI Menus

Each MDI child window can have its own independent menu system, and the frame window may also have menus of its own. However, the MDI child menus are not shown in the MDI child window; instead, when an MDI child window gets the focus, its menus are combined with those of the frame window and shown along the frame window menu bar. When the frame window has the focus, of there are no child windows, only the frame window menus are shown.

A good example of this can be found in Microsoft Excel. When there are no spreadsheet or chart windows open, the main window has only two windows: File and Help. When a spreadsheet or chart window is opened, the menu system is expanded to show a number of new menus. The menus that are available depend on whether the active MDI child window contains a spreadsheet or chart.

In general, it is good practice to use the same menus for each MDI child, where possible, as this minimises confusion for the user. You should also include a Window menu, where all existing MDI child windows can be listed and selected by the user.

Visual C++

To include MDI windows in Visual C++ programs, specify the Multiple Document Interface option in AppWizard when the application is being set up. The skeleton application will then allow for MDI objects.

The main frame window is derived from CMDIFrameWnd and the child windows are derived from CMDIChildWnd. The document template is derived from CMultiDocTemplate.

ObjectWindows

In the ObjectWindows hierarchy a frame window must be derived from TMDIFrame. Within this window, in the client area, another window must be displayed, derived from MDIClient. MDI child windows can then be derived from TWindow in the usual way.

Visual Basic

To set up an MDI system in Visual Basic, the frame window must be created with File | New MDI Form. You cannot convert an ordinary form into an MDI form.

The MDI child windows are created as normal forms but then have their MDIChild property set to True. Any form – new or existing – can be made into an MDI child. There is only one MDI form, so all MDI child forms are automatically associated with it. To include a list of open MDI child windows in the Window menu, switch on the Window List check box in the Menu Designer. All other MDI processing is dealt with by Visual Basic.

Index